Education and Social Structure

Education and Social Structure

Edited by
Dr. S.K.PANNEER SELVAM
Assistant Professor, Department of Education
Bharathidasan University, TN
and
Mrs.R.DEVI
Assistant Professor,Merit College
of Education Ariyalur, Tamil Nadu

RANDOM PUBLICATIONS
NEW DELHI (INDIA)

Education and Social Structure

ISBN 978-93-5111-357-7

Published in 2014 in India by

RANDOM PUBLICATIONS

4376-A/4B, Gali Murari Lal, Ansari Road
New Delhi-110 002
Phone: +9111-43580356, 23289044
E-mail: randomexports@gmail.com; sales@randompublications.com; info@randompublications.com

Reprinted 2021

Type Setting by : Shah Computer Graphics, Delhi-110094
Digitally Printed at : Replika Press Pvt. Ltd.

Contents

1

The fast Changing of the Social order Through Higher Education

The fast changing technologies have put some special demands on the education and training sectors. The conventional education was successful in meeting the stable or slowly changing needs of the industry of the earlier times but fails to respond to the needs of the fast changing technologies which characterise the modern industry. Similarly the large retraining needs emanating from fast changing technologies is not addressed by the conventional educational systems. The huge gap in manpower requirements has thus created a need for alternate higher education systems. An academic-Industry partnership today is the key to fulfilling the needs of the nation and placing India on the global education map. The paper discusses the need for alternate education systems and a model to produce the multimedia professionals in the country through an academic – industry partnership. The model discusses technology based delivery model which increases the reach of education to produce the right kind of professionals in multimedia.

The changes in Science, Technology and Business that are taking place and the pace at which they are taking place have influenced the world profoundly. It has affected the way the societies behave and societies respond to the situations. Further the expectations of the people in general have changed. It has created demand for new kind of dynamic skills at various levels. These courses currently do not exist in the universities and the universities also are not normally geared to take up these fast-changing courses. The educational institutions are asked to be more responsive to the needs of the society, operate with much reduced budgets, and interface with industry and society. The needs of the society in fast changing world and the inaction from the educational system have left a huge gap. Necessarily, many smaller and not so well prepared systems have tried to fill the gap with varying degrees of success and at huge cost to the society.

Higher education and training, especially in the area of IT and multimedia has played a key role in the sustainable economic growth and human development of nations through enhancements in production, manufacturing, export and human development. The experience from the newly industrialised countries indicates that the economic growth is strongly linked to the investments, which in turn depends upon the level of cognitive and psychomotor skills possessed by the workforce at middle level of the technical and vocational education spectrum. With the introduction of high degree of automation and the entertainment industry growing at a fast pace , the role and demand for personnel in this area has expanded considerably and so the job profiles. The fast changing technologies have put some special demands on the education and training sectors. The school based education system was successful in meeting the stable or slowly changing needs of the industry of the earlier times. However this model fails to respond to the needs of the fast changing technologies and situations requiring rapid response, which characterise the modern industry. Similarly the large retraining needs emanating from fast changing technologies could not be responded by the conventional educational systems. The huge gap in manpower requirements has thus created a gap in the need for alternate systems.

Expectations from alternate educational systems

In order to cope with some of the issues discussed above, the future educational systems have to respond to the following needs:

- Increasing the reach of educational systems in a cost effective manner
- Providing continuing education for fast changing technologies – anywhere, anytime learning with synchronous and asynchronous learning.
- Providing education facilities for the non-formal, continuing education groups (covers school dropouts and the industrial workers) needs on-demand education characterised by 'learning anywhere-anytime-any aspect'.
- The convergence of school-based formal education programmes, continuing education programmes for the professionals from the industry and the distance education programmes for the dropouts, personnel from the industry, and others put considerable financial demands on the conventional education system.
- Shrinking educational budgets and the increasing number of students requires cost effective and innovative instructional systems are to be devised.

An IT based instructional system project

The currently available computer and communication technologies offer unprecedented access to information, greater degree of interaction between the teacher/instructional materials and the student, greater reach in terms of geographical access and educational access to the segments of society that did not get the benefit earlier. Internet has the potential to reach every corner of the country and provide quality multimedia based education, on-demand, in a cost-effective manner. This feature of Internet supplemented by the interactivity of the computer assisted learning can be effectively used to provide education to large target population. Internet based education system provides information in a flexible, powerful, non-linear and modular way using the hypermedia technologies that form the basis for naturalistic inquiry mode of learning. Using the computers and communication technologies, good quality instructional materials (Skinner 1968, Gagne, 1985) based on both conventional and hypermedia can be prepared, modified, and updated in a relatively easy and cost effective manner and distributed or transmitted instantaneously at very low cost. The inter-linking feature of the hypermedia provides a great opportunity to build flexible instructional materials and systems. The Internet based instructional systems support a variety of communication methods, which could be used to provide the much needed group interaction between the teacher and the student, amongst the students, between the teachers and the students. The fast changing technological environment has created a situation that the knowledge does not anymore exclusively reside within the four walls of the academic institutions. Internet provides excellent tools to access globally distributed knowledge, to collaborate in offering the instructional programmes by pooling the resources of institutes together, with each institute contributing their best. The Internet provides a variety of facilities and tools that are needed to build instructional systems but careful planning is needed to build the system using the facilities and tools.

The paper proposes a model that can lead the country to higher standards with the generation of people for the multimedia industry. The model is to establish a strong partnership between the university and animation industry to deliver an ideally designed curriculum with inputs from both the sectors through a blended educational delivery model in order to achieve the objectives stated above in the paper. The planning of curricular activities should be done in partnership to encompass all the aspects of teaching such as what subject matter is to be taught, what should be the depth of treatment, what instructional strategies are needed to communicate the knowledge, what instructional materials are to be used and what learning materials are to be provided, what assignments are to be given, what project work is to be done and how to evaluate the student regarding the attainment etc. The co-curricular activities include all the support activities needed such as group discussions, seminars, libraries, industrial or social project visits etc. A schematic of the IT based instructional project proposed is given below.

The proposed education system assures the users of the products of its system, i.e. the employers, about the proficiency or capabilities acquired by its students as a result of going through its educational programmes. For this it uses some form of testing and evaluation leading to certification. Often, the certification awarded by the educational institutions in the form of degrees, diplomas and

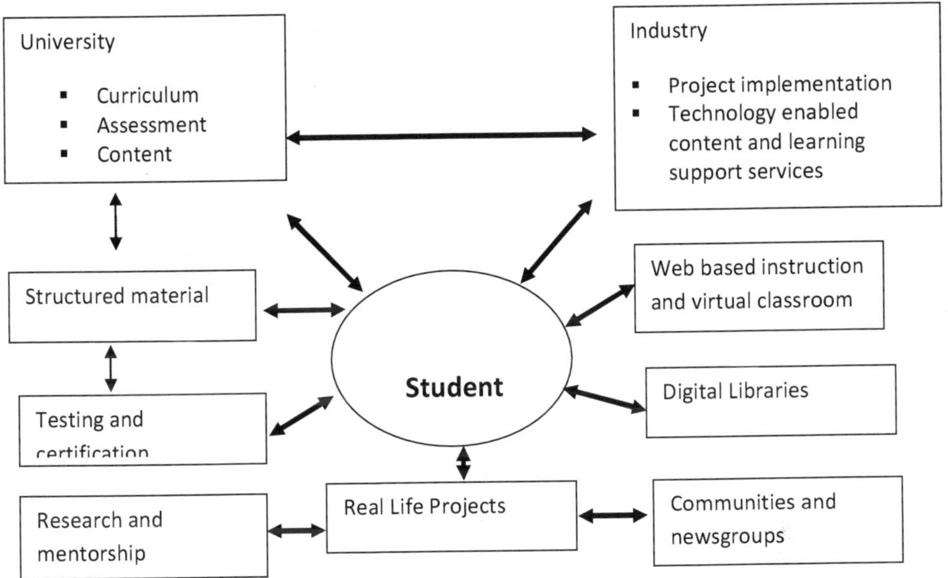

certificates is accepted by the society for various purposes and is taken as quality certification. The conventional university system assures the quality of its product by controlling the inputs, resources, process of instruction and the student evaluation. For this, it uses the teachers as a key resource of the system. The teachers make use of the knowledge of the domain, and that of the students, to guide the students through complex instructional processes and then evaluate them. Three important processes closely linked to each other have influenced the quality of education. They are:

a) integration of instructional objectives and instructional strategies (Bloom, 1956) to ensure congruence between these elements to ensure the development of desired competencies to the desired degree of proficiency;

b) spreading out the process of evaluation([Meena Kumari , 1998] through various activities over the whole period of learning to improve the reliability of the evaluation;

c) Focusing on the evaluation of learning process rather than simple competencies.

The model proposed above ensures all the factors are kept in mind to ensure the generation of the highest quality multimedia professionals.

Salient features of the proposed collaborative model

a) The enrolment will be provided through both online and through conventional modes.

b) The enrolled students are given an identity code. This identity code enables them to access the course on the Internet and also to undergo on-line evaluation.

c) The model facilitates learning through an ideal mix of class room and electronic mediation.

d) Access to courses may be improved by supplementary Intranets, multiple Internet servers and use of CDs

e) These Internet technology based systems can draw the information/ knowledge from multiple dispersed sources; multiple experts can be made available for interaction with students.

f) Authenticated base Instructional materials can be produced by a group whose members are located at different places

g) The system uses different types of learning supports and thus caters to the needs of professionals and regular students

h) All aspects of the systems can be monitored closely and necessary corrections applied

i) A team of course tutors help the students in their learning task The learning materials are presented to the enrolled trainees in the form of Web pages and the trainees' access these pages by presenting identity code issued to the trainees.

j) An on-line course tutor will attend to the difficulties of the individual students and provide guidance to them. The interaction between the course tutor and the student could be through email and chat room discussions. The student could raise his/her difficulties and teacher could clarify the problems using both these modes. The chat-room based group discussions will be held for two hours a week for each group of 10 students.

k) The trainees and the tutors could also collaborate, interact, and exchange information through newsgroups or list server forums.

Role of various organisations

The Industry could play a role in the following activities:

- Coordinate the IT based instructional project including the development of courseware, hosting of the courses, and enrolment, evaluation of the students.
- Collaborate with the educational institutions like colleges, universities, technological firms like Microsoft, IBM, etc., and other experts in pursuing its objectives.
- Host and run the courses developed by other organisations like teacher training colleges, universities etc.
- Define the format and standards of the instructional materials so that the development effort can go on in different organisations.
- Assist in providing real life internship and subsequent placements in the area of specialization.

The Universities could assist in:

- Development of curriculum, courses either independently or in collaboration and get them put on the web.
- Support the conduct of the courses by providing the affiliation/ recognition to the promoters, course tutors, conducting the end-of-course evaluation, and by organising the contact programme.
- Evaluation and certification in the form of diplomas and degree
- Incorporating higher education options in the curriculum to enable students to pursue education

As an alternate educational system, depends upon the interaction (Meena Kumari, 1999) and the evaluation that is built into the learning process. Keeping this in mind the evaluation system has been designed looking at the learning and certification needs at different stages of the learning process. The evaluation system has to respond to the challenge by using a wide range of test items as each type of test item has a specific role to play. The current technologies that are available for testing have adequate capability to support the learning process and are to be harnessed. The model allows close interaction between the teacher & student, beyond the boundary of the curriculum – interaction spreads into philosophies, research etc. The free, frequent and continuous dialogue in the content area between students & teachers results in quality education being delivered. The teaching focuses on the development of generic capabilities such as thinking, learning to learn, conducting research etc., than providing simple information. This partnership could steer the country into the world map in the area of higher education besides satisfying the national requirements of generating high quality multimedia professionals.

References

1. Bloom, B.S. (Ed.). (1956). Taxonomy of educational objectives. Handbook: Cognitive domain. New York: McKay
2. Gagne, R.M. (1985). The conditions of learning (4th ed.). New York: Holt, Rinehart and Winston.
3. Katre Dinesh (2005) : Multimedia education : Current Trends and Future Potential, Sampada Special Issue on Education, Maharatta Chamber of Commerce Industries and Agriculture, July 2005, pp 27-29
4. Meena Kumari (1998): "Instructional design practices" , CSI news letter
5. Meena Kumari et al. (1999): "Making technology based learning effective: a unique online learning architecture" Presented at the Common Wealth Learning conference in West Indies in Nov 99.
6. Nasscomm - Indian Animation Market – Fact sheet , 2003,2004
7. Piaget, J.(1952). Origins of intelligence in children. New York: International Universities Press.
8. Skinner, B.F. (1968). The technology of teaching. New York: Appleton-Century-Crofts.

2

Social Guidance Through Humanities Courses in Higher Education

Half of the students enrolled in higher education worldwide live in developing countries. Yet, in many developing countries, government and education leaders express serious concerns about the ability of their colleges and universities to effectively respond to the pressures posed by changing demographics, new communication technologies, shifts in national political environments, and the increasing interconnectedness of national economies. Now, there is a general acceptance of the fact that higher education is essential for the economic and social development of the nation. So, how do we accomplish the desired goal in the era of liberalization, privatization and globalization? We are witnessing gradually increase of population in general and fast growing number of students which has resulted into demand for propagation of higher education. With Huge diversity, and different levels of development, the nation's focus in higher education which is being concentrated on access and equity rather than quality. Professional social work practice is distinctive from other helping professions in its approach of assisting clients to function optimally within their environments. The person-in-environment approach is central to social work practice. Through this perspective, professional social workers are uniquely trained to help clients maximize the opportunity for change in themselves and or their situations. Social work-higher education system offers expanding and challenging opportunities for social work practice and innovation. The social work specialization emphasizes social work services in schools/colleges/universities as a process in school-community-student relations that focuses on planned system change, consultation, and interdisciplinary teaming by net working and establishing strong linkages with grassroots' and intermediary level development agencies. Social workers for practice in the various settings and includes knowledge and skills to address the most pressing needs of the society. How do we ensure participation of civil society in social work higher education and coping mechanism with the field realities and addressing sustainability questions?

Developments in Asia particularly in India have tremendous significance for the rest of the world. India has a rapidly expanding economy and is home to most of the world's population. It is a land of tremendous size and equally great diversity. At times India seems to be an economic and military threat to the West, while on other occasions it seems to be a valuable partner in the emerging global economy. The technological, political, and economic developments that have taken place in India are largely the result of Indian higher education.

Half of the students enrolled in higher education worldwide live in developing countries. Yet, in many developing countries, government and education leaders express serious concerns about the ability of their colleges and universities to effectively respond to the pressures posed by changing demographics, new communication technologies, shifts in national political environments, and the increasing interconnectedness of national economies. The critical issues with which higher education institutions in the developing world must grapple as they respond to these changing contexts: seeking a new balance in government-university relationships; coping with autonomy; managing expansion while preserving equity, raising quality, and controlling costs; addressing new pressures for accountability; supporting academic staff in new roles.

THE HIGHER EDUCATION SYSTEM IN INDIA

Addressing the graduates of the Allahabad University in 1947, Jawaharlal Nehru, the first Prime Minister of India, said: "A university stands for humanism, for tolerance, for reason, for the adventure of ideas and for the search for truth. It stands for the onward march of the human race toward higher objectives. Universities are places of ideals and idealism. If the universities discharge their duties adequately, then, it is well with the nation and the people." This statement effectively initiated the formulation of the essential purpose of university education in independent India. Universities in India have been the living storehouse of a long-cherished heritage - a heritage continually revitalized by the teachers and researchers by their contribution to and interaction with it.

It has constantly striven to build universities as places of culture and of learning open to all and, above all, reinforcing the theme of learning throughout life. Participating in and contributing to major debates concerning the direction and future of society is seen as a major task and a moral obligation as well, of the university system in outreach.

The first major step taken by the Ministry of Education after independence (1947) in higher education was to appoint a Commission on university education under the Chairmanship of Dr. S. Radhakrishnan to report on Indian university education. In its report, the Commission said: "Democracy depends for its very life on a high standard of general, vocational and professional education. Dissemination of learning, incessant search for new knowledge, unceasing effort to plumb the meaning of life, provision for professional education to satisfy the occupational needs of our society are the vital tasks of higher education." Now, there is a general acceptance of the fact that higher education is essential for the economic and social development of the nation. So, how do we accomplish the desired goal in the era of liberalization, privatization and globalization?

CONTEXTUAL REALITIES IN INDIA

We are witnessing gradually increase of population in general and fast growing number of students which has resulted into demand for propagation of higher education. With Huge diversity, and different levels of development, the nation's focus in higher education which is being concentrated on access and equity rather than quality. We are facing shortage of (skilled) human capital. We have question pertaining to quality of higher education in the context of globalization and quality of higher education in the context of marketable of education.

A SOCIAL WORK APPROACH

Professional social work practice is distinctive from other helping professions in its approach of assisting clients to function optimally within their environments. The person-in-environment approach is central to social work practice. Through this perspective, professional social workers are uniquely trained to help clients maximize the opportunity for change in themselves and/or their situations. The term client encompasses individuals, families, groups, organizations, and communities.

Social work is distinctive also for its professional values and ethics, appreciation for human diversity, emphasis on social and economic justice, understanding of social welfare policy and services, and strong foundation in field education. Its unique approach to problem solving and interventions is evidenced in direct clinical practice, policy planning and administration; community-level and state-level services; private and public sectors; and teaching, research, and scholarship.

Today, social work professionals assist individuals, families, groups, organizations, communities, and society in the areas of aging, child welfare, children and youth services, community organization, criminal justice, crisis counseling, disaster assistance, death and dying / hospice, domestic violence and victim assistance, employee assistance programs, family services, homelessness and shelters, hospitals, juvenile justice, mental health, mental retardation / developmental disabilities, public health, public welfare, schools (elementary and secondary), substance abuse and vocational rehabilitation etc. Within these areas and others, many professional social workers are responsible for administration, budgets and funding, management, policy analysis and planning, program development and supervision with sustainability monitoring.

Many become advocates for change within the systems in which they function; some rally for political action. While professional social work practice is far-reaching in its scope, a changing world continues to present new challenges and avenues to make a difference. For example, in health care, community-based services and managed-care are becoming prevalent and require the special skills of social workers. Poverty, alcohol and drug abuse, and the generational transmission of domestic violence are issues facing nearly all practitioners. Technology is advancing methods of service delivery and allowing for the creation of new approaches to the traditional notions of relationships.

There is a wealth of opportunity to outreach within the profession and there is a greater need for qualified, committed professional social workers. The social work program do impart specialized skills in assessment, interviewing, intake/referral, service planning, case management, crisis intervention, service provision, problem solving, program evaluation, community outreach, advocacy and training, research and networking. The social work program prepares students for advanced social work practice and research in public and private agencies in these fields of specialization and not limited to: the areas are advocacy, leadership and social change; child welfare; community mental health; health care; and school social work. Students are prepared for leadership roles in prevention, intervention, and rehabilitation; program development and analysis; direct service, supervision, planning and administration.

The purpose of this specialization is to prepare students for social work careers that emphasize social change both within organizations and through public advocacy. The social work profession has a long tradition of working toward improving the lives of disadvantaged citizens through advocacy efforts with political officials and others. The profession likewise has worked to improve the provision of human services through the more effective management of agencies, and by advocating for changes within those agencies.

THE OUTREACH IN SOCIAL WORK

Child Welfare: the social work course is designed to help students develop knowledge and skills for effectively delivering social services to children and their families. They advocate on behalf of children, which includes providing case management services, developing community resources, and influencing legislative and agency policy. Students who complete this specialization will have preparation in all aspects of child welfare, including investigations, follow-up services, working with intact families, and prevention.

Community Mental Health: Social workers in the field of community mental health work with individuals, families, and groups in dealing with internal, interpersonal, and environmental problem situations that affect mental health and social functioning. They also plan, administer, and evaluate community mental health service systems. The emphasis in the curriculum is preparing students to provide, coordinate, and administer community-based services for people who encounter emotional stress. Also included are services for substance abusers and for mentally disabled people. Social workers provide more than half of the mental health services in the country.

Health Care: Social workers in the health care field collaborate with other health professionals in providing patient care, and serve to mobilize family, friends, and other supportive networks on the patient's behalf. *They act as a link between health agencies and other community services*. Social workers in this specialization work in hospitals and clinics, as well as in federal, state, and local public health centers, with physicians in private or group medical practices, on home health care teams, and/or with nursing home health planning agencies. Health care social workers are on the faculty of medical schools across the country. Apart from the above outreach programmes trained social workers do involve in various developmental agencies such as NGO's, Industries, Corporate networking agencies, government departments and organizations, national and international developmental agencies and others.

Social Work-Higher Education in India*:* The system offers expanding and challenging opportunities for social work practice and innovation. The social work specialization emphasizes social work services in schools/colleges/universities as a process in *school-community-student relations that focuses on planned system change, consultation, and interdisciplinary teaming by net working and establishing strong linkages with grassroots' and intermediary level* *development agencies*. The specialization prepares social workers for practice in the various settings and includes knowledge and skills to address the most pressing needs of the society.

PARTICIPATION OF CIVIL SOCIETY IN SOCIAL WORK HIGHER EDUCATION

There is need for increasing financial inputs for social work higher education. Currently the Government is subsidizing the higher education by charging low fees to those who can pay. The cost of higher education in social work is not being met by the educational institutions because of subsidy and fee restrictions. There is also a mismatch in the costing at school level and higher education level. There is no single solution for educational affordability, however, a number of solutions exists which together can solve this problem. Fees should have some economic relationship with cost of education; 'differential' fee system based on the paying capacity of students should be introduced.

COPING WITH THE FIELD REALITIES AND SUSTAINABILITY QUESTIONS

The industry / corporate sector, being the direct beneficiary of higher education, should contribute to educational development. Student welfare programmes should be given priority. The present scheme of providing loans to students should be streamlined and made facilitating. Efforts to be made to raise resources for non-transitional sources such as industries and other commercial concerns, which are making use of this highly qualified and trained manpower. The funds from industries and other business houses could be tapped by introducing courses relevant to the needs of industries and by undertaking consultancy research project. Encourage public and private sector enterprises to sponsor a specified number of students, especially in technical and professional fields, whom they can employ after graduation.

Every university should create a corpus fund into which all donations, voluntary contributions, etc. should go. This fund should be deposited in fixed deposit and only interest be drawn from it for development purpose. The need for mobilization of resources from external sources should also be explored.

Universities can start special job and skill-oriented certificate or diploma courses. Some of the leading universities in the West earn enormous amount from their publishing activities. If a university is a storehouse of knowledge, it should disseminate it through its publications. Universities can rent their premises for social and public functions too. Universities should also take the initiative to promote educational tourism. To quote an example from Social Work (MSW) context, the course design itself is targeting the outreach activity by teaching and learning process.

REFERENCES

1. Hilary Lawson, 2001, Practice teaching changing Social Work, Jessica Kingsley publishers, London and Philadelphia.
2. Maria O'Neil MeMahon, 1996, The general Method of social work Practice, Allyn and Bacon publication Boston, London.
3. Murli Desai, 2004, Methodology of Progressive Social Work Education, Rawat Publication, Sathyam Apartments, Sector 3, Jawahar Nagar, Jaipur 302 004.
4. Subhedar I S, 2001, Field work Training in Social work, Rawat Publication, Sathyam Apartments, Sector 3, Jain temple road, Jawahar Nagar, Jaipur 302 004.

3

Adult Education – An Instrument of Poverty Alleviation

Poverty can be defined as a social phenomenon in which a section of the society is unable to fulfill even its basic necessities of life. Poverty in India still remains unabated. The country has hardly been able to establish her identity free from the age old impression 'India is a poor country'. Despite decades long effort most of our population are still struggling below poverty line. The Gandhiji's dream to provide each and every Indian poor an access to basic needs of life is yet to be materialized. Although the planning commission of India has added qualitative parameters to the concept of basic needs, in terms of minimum food, clothing and shelter, our country has failed to provide the same to its citizens.

Poverty scenario in India

Millions of people in India are unable to meet these basic standards, and according to government estimates, in 2007 there were nearly 220.1 million people living below the poverty line.

Nearly 21.1% of the entire rural population and 15% of the urban population of India exists in this difficult physical and financial predicament. The following chart presents the poverty situation:

The division of resources, as well as wealth, is very uneven in India – this disparity creates different poverty ratios for different states. For instance, states such as Delhi and Punjab have very low poverty ratios. On the other hand, 40-50% of the populations in Bihar and Orissa live below the poverty line.

Poverty in India- Fresh figures

Despite sustained high GDP growth in India, latest estimates of global poverty by World Bank suggest that India has more people living below US$ 2 than even sub-Saharan Africa. These new figures should compel political leaders and policymakers to devise fresh strategies to reduce poverty.

None other than the World Bank (WB) has busted the hype about India's post-liberalization success. According to the Bank's new estimates not only is India home to roughly one-third of all the poor in the world, it has a higher proportion of its population living on less than $ 2 a day than even sub-Saharan Africa.

Compared with India's 828 million people, or 75.6% of the population living below US$ 2 a day, sub-Saharan Africa, considered the world's poorest region, ranks better with 72.2% of its population – about 551 million people – below the US$ 2 a day level.

India has 456 million people, or around 42% of its population living below the new international poverty line of $ 1.25 a day. The number of Indian poor constitutes 33% of the global poor – pegged at 1.4 billion people.

New estimates

The new estimates are based on recently re-calculated purchasing power parity (PPP) exchange rates that make comparisons across countries possible. The new PPP has been arrived at as "the average poverty line found in the poorest 10-20 countries," according to the Bank's briefing note.

In other words, nearly five out of 10 Indians live below what the world's poorest countries consider the poverty line.

These sobering figures have emerged from the World Bank's latest estimates on global poverty, and clearly hint at the fruits of economic benefits having failed to trickle down to India's poor.

The data available shows that the rate of poverty decline in India was faster between 1981 and 1990 than between 1990 and 2005. The poverty rate – those below $ 1.25 per day – for India declined from 59.8% in 1981 to 51.3% by 1990, or 8.5 percentage points over nine years. Between 1990 and 2005 it declined to 41.6%, which is a drop of 9.7 percentage points over 15 years, clearly a much slower rate of decline.

Provisions

Right from the independence our Government started a number of poverty eradication programmes. Swarnajayanti Gram Swarojagar Yojana (SGSY), Drought Prone Area Programme (DPAP), Tribal Area Development Programme (TADP), High Yield Variety Programme (HYVP), Minimum Needs Programme (MNP), Training of rural Youth for Self-Employment (TRYSEM) etc. Though some of the above programmes recorded appreciable progress in some areas, by and large all programmes and their approaches were selective, sporadic, sectorial in nature and suffered from several defects.

However there is no denying the fact that our progress is very slow and most corresponding adequately to the extent of our need. Although there is a lot of provision for the poverty stricken masses of our country the former always fails to reach the latter properly. This may be attributed to the procedural and attitudinal rigidities in government machinery, corrupt practices, and lack of proportionate distribution on the part of clients, misuse of government benefits by the clients etc.

It can hardly be said that the government is not doing enough for the poor. There is no doubt in the fact that a lot of need based schemes are in progress for the eradication of poverty and the uplift of the poor. However our achievement is still insignificant. The reasons are tow dimensional. On the one hand governmental schemes are not properly reaching the poor. On the other hand the latter are not able to receive the benefits due to their ignorance or lack of awareness. Thus there is a wide gap between need and supply which in turn allows poverty to prevail as poverty with a little variation from time to time.

Creation of awareness, dissemination of information on government programmes, vocational training and increase the income of the labour may be measures that would help to bridge the gap between the need and supply. This can be achieved through certain specified levels of educational preparation among the masses. Adult education is such a type of education which provides the instruments for liberation form ignorance and important input for human development as the quality of human factors determine the quality of development.

Concept and chronology of Adult Education in India

Adult Education is a package of educational programmes for adults outside the formal educational system aiming at providing more information and better knowledge and skills for improving their life style and also their earning capacity. Adult education helps the adults to become aware of themselves and their society to come to some understanding about the problems which they face and to encourage them to select their own task. Knowledge and skills is then the secondary part of adult education to make available the knowledge and skill they need to tackle the problems which they face and to encourage them to select their own task. Knowledge and skills is then the secondary part of adult education to make available the knowledge and skills they need to tackle the problems. This understanding will come slowly. Action – integral to the acquisition of knowledge and skills will be true encouragement to act in some way or another – thus the adult education has been a major tool and important input for human resource development.

It is possible to discern a pattern and certain cyclical trends in the history of Indian Adult Education. Broadly, there are four cycles which represent the four major approaches and concepts of adult education in India. While the traditional approach to literacy adopted the view that learning the traditional approach to literacy adopted the view that learning to read and write had an innate goodness in itself. Manifested during the face of social education, the life-oriented approaches continue even today. It goes beyond the acquisition of knowledge and the emphasis is on the application of learning to daily living. The work-oriented approach dominated during the phase of functional literacy. Based on Paulo-Freire's philosophy conscientisation, the social change approach made its debut during the phase of NAEP and is continues even today.

Thus recognizing the role of literacy of education in all-round development of the individual and nation as a whole, the Government of India has launched the above programmes and continuously improved in terms of its quality based on the experiences and research findings. To create a learning society by providing for life-long leaning opportunities which may result in the release of creative energies of the people, the National Literacy Mission has been implementing the Continuing Education Programme by establishing Continuing Education Centers and organizing the programmes which are multifarious, for reaching and essential for the upliftment of quality of life.

Role of Adult Education in Poverty Alleviation

Poverty alleviating programmes in the country are the first level of response to overcome the problem of poverty. The second level response consists of meeting the needs of the people through supplementing and complementing the large formal educational system through non-formal and open learning systems of education. Adult education is a type of non-formal education in this direction has an important role in this regard. Some of its important dimensions are discussed in the context of the objective of poverty alleviation.

Increasing Effectiveness of Development Programmes

It is widely recognized that the successful implementation of any developmental programme needs the participation of its target group at various stages of the programme implementation starting from planning to evaluation. Due to their ignorance the people does not come forward to receive the assistance that are offered to them. The access to information is so limited that they do not know about the programme designed to promote their development. Information window is one of the important activities of CECs, provides information about various development schemes formulated by the Government, new agricultural practices, legal rights etc. will ensure that their benefits actually reach the target groups.

Promotion of Employment

Education of the right type increases quality of labour and inculcates a sense of self-confidence among the recipients. Therefore, a right kind of education to remove the mass unemployment and disguised unemployment which are principal causes of mass poverty must be developed. The relevance of functional and vocational training to benefit the lower income groups is much greater in under developed countries where there is marked shortage of labour skills, the adult education should, there cater for these needs through Income Generating Programmes in continuing education centers in simple trades and occupations leading to greater employment opportunities and self-employment avenues.

Strengthening of communication Channels

If the rural and urban poor are insufficiently linked with the modern sectors through effective communication system, the benefits of the industrial growth are unlikely to trickle down for a long time to come, the problem of ensuring access to education for lower income groups is important for reaching the economic development to lower strata of the economy thus strengthening the process of development. The adult education programme with its bias in favour of the poor and the disadvantaged instrument providing educational opportunities through equivalency programmes in continuing education centers.

Awareness Generation

The process of Economic Development makes growing demands on human resources and in a democratic set-up it calls for social values and attitudes where in education enters as an important factor. The adult education facilitates and contributes to economic development not only by skilled manpower for specific tasks of development, but, by creating the requisite attitudes and personality traits among the masses leading to a proper climate for development through the quality of Life Improvement Programmes in Continuing Education Centers.

Mobilization and Co-ordination of the Resources

Non-Government Organisations, Government Development Departments, Universities, Youth Clubs and such other agencies have been able to organize local specific programmes, according to the felt needs of the society. They help in providing infrastructure, motivating people, grass-root level planning etc. The Preraks in the CECs will make the efforts to mobilize money and material resources from these agencies to help the community.

Co-ordination is always seen inadequate in the functioning of various government and NGO's, universities, functionaries and in the implementation of various schemes and programmes. Continuing Education Centers build proper co-ordination among the government, NGOs, the community to concentrate in this aspect for maintaining the momentum.

Motivation of the Learners

The Individual Interest Promotion Programmes organizing in the CECs aims to provide opportunity for individuals to participate in and learn about their chosen social, cultural, spiritual, health, physical and artistic interests motivate these programmes will promote self-reliance, learners to attend the C.E.Cs personal development and self-actualization interests help in the quality of human resources of the society.

To sum up Information and communication technologies today have divided people globally into two groups based on knowledge irrespective of gender, caste and region. While a small section of people in every society are ensuring developing technology, they are also the main beneficiaries of this advancement. Government and Non-Government efforts in civilized societies are directed towards ensuring that the pace of development is accelerated and the benefits accrue to large numbers in society. Adult education in the 21st century will cover education in this direction. The intellectuals, academics, the media, the men and women should show concern to arouse social conscience of mankind to build a new social order free from diseases, hatred, fear and apathy. Slogans like 'Education for all', 'Science for All' and 'Food for All' should be converted into reality.

4

Assessment and Accreditation of Schools

"Excellence of institutions of education is a function of many aspects; self evaluation and self-improvement are important. If a council sets up a mechanism, which will encourage self-assessment in institutions and also assessment and accreditation, the quality process, participation, achievement etc, will be constantly monitored and improved"–The National Policy on Education (NPE)-1986 and Programme of Action (POA)-1992.

Assessment and Accreditation of institutions of education has recognized as the quality ensuring mechanism all over the world. It has become necessary and relevant to our country as we have developed the world's second largest system of education rather rapidly during last 50 years. On the recommendations of the Programme of Action (1992) on the National Policy on Education (1986), the UGC has established the National Assessment and Accreditation Council (NAAC) in 1994 with its head quarters at Bangalore for assessing and grading the institutions of Higher Education. Though the assessment is voluntary, the UGC has already indicated that its plan based developmental support will be related to the outcome of assessment and accreditation.

NAAC's process of assessment and accreditation is neither an inspection to ensure minimum standards nor an exercise of faultfinding. In the Value Judgement continuum the process of assessment is towards the holistic, systematic, data-based, transparent and shared experience for institutional improvement. It is an exercise based on mutual trust.

Assessment refers to the scientific process of obtaining all round information about an institution's progress and achievement, i.e., what and how well the institution has performed during and at the end of a period and assigning a value or grade to the performance. Assessment of the educational institution is a complex procedure that is found to be hotly debated.

Various individuals and organizations define accreditation in different ways. Accreditation, as defined in the Encyclopedia of Education is "a process of quality control and assurance in higher education, whereby, as a result of assessment or inspection or both, an institution or its programmes are recognized as meeting minimum standards". According to Zook and Haggerty (1993), "accreditation is the recognition to an education institution, by some agency or organization, which sets up standards or requirements that must be complied with, in order to secure approval". Accreditation as commonly understood is a mechanism, which provides quality assurance that the aims and objectives of the institution are known to be honestly available, and that the institution has demonstrated capabilities to ensure continued effectiveness of the educational programmes, over the period.

Accreditation is nothing but institutional evaluation and quality certification. Institutional assessment is a planned and organized inquiry by institutional personnel itself into the total working and effectiveness of institutional establishment and operations. This process assesses the institutions (university) in terms of efficiency and effectiveness to realize institutional goals. If planned properly and carried out systematically, institutional assessment study would lead to institutional reformation besides improving public image (reputation) of the institution. The institutional assessment and accreditation studies require honesty, flexibility, open mindedness and commitment to quality and effectiveness among the top decision making authorities and higher officers.

Institutional accreditation today is closely linked to institution's continuing efforts to assess its effectiveness and to ensure the fullest possible realization of its mission and goals. It does not require similarity of aims, uniformity of processes, or comparability among institutions. Rather, it indicates that in the judgement of responsible members of the academic community, an institution's goals are soundly conceived and appropriate, that its educational programmes have been intelligently planned and are competently conducted, and that institution is accomplishing the majority of its goals substantially and has the resources to continue doing so for the foreseeable future.

Institutional accreditation embraces all educational endeavours conducted by an institution regardless of its complexity. Specialized or programmatic accreditation deals with schools, departments, programmes or other segments of institution. To prepare for such evaluations, the process of institutional self-study was introduced. Its guiding principles include broad constituent involvement, can dour and a willingness to take an honestly critical look at all aspects of the institution. A twelve-month to twenty four-month period of self-study precipitates a report that serves to inform visiting team of professional peers and the accrediting agency of the nature and purpose of the institution and to convey the institution's own assessment of its effectiveness. With continual refinement and adaption, self-study and periodical evaluation are now essential features of all institutional and most specialized accrediting.

In India, there is NAAC for assessing and accrediting institutions of higher education. At present there is no such assessing and accrediting body for schools. Again schools are following different types of syllabuses, time-table, programmes, examination patterns etc. There are different types of schools namely; pre-primary, primary, upper-primary, secondary, higher secondary special etc. The school pupils' population in India is in cores. Schools are run under different managements. Rural, semi urban, urban etc schools are available, with different mission and clientele. Well equipped and ill equipped schools are available. Management and funding wise some are governmental and others are private, and some others are in-between. Their size, in terms of pupils' strength, is also quite variable from a couple of hundreds to thousands. Hence assuring quality of all these institutions is a necessity in the interest of public.

The concept of assessment and accreditation is new to our country. When the concept is new and the school education system is so complex, there is a natural reluctance or apprehension about anything new. Reluctance is for trying to experiment themselves and apprehensions are due to their feeling of their own inadequacies and the fear of being rated low in comparison to others. Besides, accepting the concept of quality audit through assessment is expensive in terms of time, money and efforts.

Professional accreditation of institutions is generally seen by academics and others concerned with education, as a desirable provision rather than a requirement like affiliation of colleges by universities or recognition of schools by state Governments concerned or other bodies. Accredited status of an institution or programme is a mark of good standards, a stamp of quality, a certificate of dependability, trustworthiness, and credibility, an expression of responsibility even accountability, a matter of reputation or prestige for the institution of accreditation.

The future of accreditation hinges more directly on the integrity of educational institutions and on the responsibility of their leaders. The benefits of accreditation are (i) fostering of their education through development of criteria and guidelines for assessing institutional effectiveness; (ii) assuring the academic community, the general public, the professions, and other agencies that an institution or programme has clearly defined and appropriate educational objectives, has established conditions to facilitate their achievement, appears in fact to be achieving them substantially, and is so organized staffed and supported that it can be expected to continue doing so; (iii) in providing counsel and assistance to established and developing institutions; and (iv) in protecting institutions from encroachments that might jeopardize their educational effectiveness or academic freedom.

Assessment and accreditation provides a professional approach to look into the working of the institutions, and helps to meaningfully pursue and achieve the constitutional and legal mandates. Keeping in mind the noble constitutional and legal requirements, there is great need to assess and accredit the quality of the various aspects of the schools. The following aspects of the schools may be considered for assessment and accreditation.

5

Curricular Changes in Teacher Education

India is a developing country. We have thousand years of radiation and Culture. Different types of people are living in India. In olden days the educational institutions were called as 'Ashramam' and teacher was called as 'Guru'. Guru is a respectable person in the society after mother and father. According to our Vedas Guru is a third God. In olden days they were given importance for shravana, Dhyana and Asana. All types of information are there in Vedas. Yoga is a greatest gift of India to the world. Yoga has its origin in the Vedas, texts that were heard by ancient sages in their state of meditation, and hence are known as suits. The great sage Vyasa organized the Vedas in a systematic manner. Hence he is known as Veda Vyasa.

Now we are living in the technological world. Vast changes are occurring in day to day life of human being. The effect of Television, Telephone, Radio, Computer, Internet and Mobile is very much in our daily life. Even today also teacher is a role model for the students in the society. Teaching profession is a respectable job in the society. But there are enormous changes were occurred in the system of education.

Western culture is increased. Because of globalization we see everything in the form of commercial. But it is not good. Teacher is a nation builder. The development of any country depends upon its educational system. Any type of development is possible through education. The concept of curriculum can be perceived as a connective link between teacher and student, organized in such a way to achieve goals previously set by the teacher, the learning organization or by the curriculum specialists.

Curriculum is a means to the education. While education is learning, curriculum signifies situations for learning. While education deals with 'how' and 'when', Curriculum deals with 'what' education is a product, curriculum is the plan.

Teacher Education

Teacher education is an integral component of the educational system. It is intimately connected with society and is conditioned by the ethos, culture and character of a nation. The constitutional goals, the directive principles of the state policy, the socio-economic problems and the growth of knowledge, the emerging expectations and the changes operating in education, etc. call for an appropriate response from a futuristic education system and provide the perspective within which teacher education programmes need to be viewed.

When India attained freedom, the then existing educational system was accepted as such because it was thought that an abrupt departure from the same would be disturbing and destabilizing. Thus a predisposition to retain the system acquired preponderance and all that was envisaged by way of changes was its rearrangement. Consequently, education including teacher education largely remained isolated from the needs and aspirations of the people. During the last five decades certain efforts have been made to indigenize the system. The gaps, however, are still wide and visible. The imperatives for building the bridges may be as follows:

- To build a national system of teacher education based on India's cultural ethos, its unity and diversity synchronizing with change and continuity.

- To facilitate the realization of the constitutional goals and emergence of the new social order.
- To prepare professionally competent teachers to perform their roles effectively as per needs of the society.
- To upgrade the standard of teacher education, enhance the professional and social status of teachers and develop amongst them a sense of commitment.

Scenario of Teacher Education

The need for improved levels of educational participation for overall progress is well recognised. The key role of educational institutions in realizing it is reflected in a variety of initiatives taken to transform the nature and function of education — both formal as well as non-formal. Universal accessibility to quality education is considered essential for development. This has necessitated improvement in the system of teacher education so as to prepare quality teachers.

Various Commissions and Committees, Sarvepalli Radhakrishnan Commission (1948), Secondary Education Commission (1953), Kothari Commission (1964-66) etc., are appointed by the Central and the State Governments in recent decades have invariably emphasised the need for quality teacher education suited to the needs of the educational system. The Secondary Education Commission (1953) observed that a major factor responsible for the educational reconstruction at the secondary stage is teachers' professional training. The Education Commission (1964-66) stressed that 'in a world based on science and technology it is education that determines the level of prosperity, welfare and security of the people' and that 'a sound programme of professional education of teachers is essential for the qualitative improvement of education.'

India has a large system of education. There are nearly 5.98 lakh Primary Schools, 1.76 lakh Elementary Schools and 98 thousand High / Higher Secondary Schools in the country, about 1300 teacher education institutions for elementary teachers and nearly 700 colleges of education / university departments preparing teachers for secondary and higher secondary schools. Out of about 4.52 million teachers in the country nearly 3 million are teaching at the primary/

elementary level. A sizeable number of them are untrained or under-trained. In certain regions, like the North-East, there are even under-qualified teachers. As far as in-service education is concerned the situation is not very encouraging. It is estimated that on an average 40% of the teachers are provided in-service teacher education once over a period of five years. Regarding non-formal education, though a number of models are in vogue in various states in the country, much more needs to be done to prepare teachers and other functionaries for the system.

The National Council for Teacher Education (NCTE) as a non-statutory body (1973-1993) took several steps as regards quality improvement in teacher education. Its major contribution was to prepare Teacher Education Curriculum Framework in 1978. Consequently, teacher education curricula witnessed changes in teacher preparation programmes in various universities and boards in the country. A similar effort was made in 1988.

During the last decade, new thrusts have been posed due to rapid changes in the educational, political, social and economic contexts at the national and international levels. Curriculum reconstruction has also become imperative in the light of some perceptible gaps in teacher education. Teacher education by and large, is conventional in its nature and purpose. The integration of theory and practice and consequent curricular response to the requirements of the school system still remains inadequate. Teachers are prepared in competencies and skills which do not necessarily equip them for becoming professionally effective. Their familiarity with latest educational developments remains insufficient. Organised and stipulator learning experiences whenever available, rarely contribute to enhancing teachers' capacities for self-directed lifelong learning. The system still prepares teachers who do not necessarily become professionally competent and committed at the completion of initial teacher preparation programmes. A large number of teacher training institutions do not practice what they preach. Several of the skills acquired and methodologies learnt are seldom.

Definitions of curriculum, from Oliva (1997)

Curriculum is:

- That which is taught in schools
- A set of subjects.
- Content
- A program of studies.
- A set of materials
- A sequence of courses.
- A set of performance objectives
- A course of study
- Is everything that goes on within the school, including extra-class activities, guidance, and interpersonal relationships.
- Everything that is planned by school personnel.
- A series of experiences undergone by learners in a school.
- That which an individual learner experiences as a result of schooling.

Flexibility of the Curriculum

In India there are large number of communities living in the hilly area, the plateau area, the dessert area, plain area and costal area all having their own peculiar individuality, environment customs and needs. Therefore, the same curriculum can't be forced upon all, irrespective of their needs and environment. It must differ from locality to locality and from society to society.

"The destiny of India now being shaped in her class rooms". In the world based on science and technology it is education that determines the level of prosperity, security and welfare of the people (Education Commission 1964-66).

Teacher Education at the Pre-Primary Stage

Objectives

- Enabling student teachers to inculcate among children a desire to know their immediate natural environment, to love and respect it;
- Preparing student teachers to use local resources and local contexts.

Curriculum Content and Transaction

Teacher education curriculum at this stage need to develop awareness about literacy programmes, community dynamics, national and local customs, fairs and festivals and community mode of social living. It may also develop awareness of forces affecting environment including pollution, appreciation of places of historical and cultural significance and special educational features and developmental tasks contained in policies and programmes.

Teacher Education at the Primary Stage

Objectives

- Developing among student teachers skills for teaching integrated environmental studies, integrated social sciences and integrated science and technology;
- Enabling student teachers to inculcate among children a desire to know their immediate natural environment, to love and respect it;

Implications for Pre-service Teacher Education

Curriculum Content and Transaction

It is necessary that student teachers be sensitized to the need for reducing curriculum load, organise appropriate learning experiences which are joyful in nature and related to immediate environment of the learner and help them develop and imbibe desirable values.

Teacher education programmes at this stage shall have to provide subject based orientation. Teaching and learning of mathematics would be woven around the environment of the learners so that environmental concerns are properly integrated. The activities would focus on local culture and environment using the local specific contexts and resources. Student teachers shall have to be provided with experiences to help children develop socio-emotional and cultural aspects. A realistic awareness and perspective of the phenomena occurring in the environment will have to be linked with social or scientific events. This may be accomplished by emphasizing observation, classification, comparison and drawing of inferences, conducted within and outside the classroom.

Need of Curriculum Changes in Teacher Education

India has thousand years of tradition and culture. Educational institutions were called as Ashramam and teacher was called as Guru. A tremendous change was occurred in our daily life. Due to globalization now the educational system is affected totally. Now the educational institutions give importance for technical education. Teacher is a national builder. He has a capacity to change the society. By knowing the importance of technology, communication skills, National Council of Teacher Education (NCTE) introduced a separate subject on technology known as 'Educational Technology' at both B.Ed and M.Ed levels. Computer Education, Communicative English, Personality Development are also introduced at B.Ed. level. Now we are facing so many problems like terrorism, poverty and high-population. We want such type of curriculum which improves peace, non-violence, positive attitude and values in the society. By inculcating these things in teacher education curriculum, we will get positive change in the society. Our National Education Policy (1986) and other Education Committees and Commissions were also given importance for quality teacher education. But it is our duty that to follow such type of curriculum. By conducting national seminars, workshops and conferences it is important to collect eminent scholars attitude towards importance of curricular change in the present scenario. There are many recommendations about curriculum change, but they are not in practice.

Guidelines/Suggestions

- The present curriculum format of teacher education at different levels, pre-primary, elementary and secondary education is generally based, apart from others on Foundation Courses, which includes philosophical, sociological and psychological perspectives of education. The intention is that the teacher must have a conceptual understanding of the field of education, its significant concerns which are relevant for political, social and cultural development of the nation so that the teacher is just not responsible only for performing "knick knacks" of the task of teaching but is also imbued with the perspectives of creating individuals who can apply their minds to the diverse situations that obtain in the field of education. It is the Foundation Courses which provide a lot of scope for being recast to lay focus on discussion on the issues listed in the preceding chapters. Apart from others, it can re-look at the existing curriculum and divide it into appropriate cluster of topics which include the core elements of the NPE and the Constitutional concerns related to non-discrimination. Other areas of equal relevance for development of the ideas are the internship in teaching and working with the community.

- The type of exercises for developing the values related to non-discrimination as given in the chapters on sex/gender, caste/tribe, disability, etc. could become the central themes of co-curricular and extra-curricular activities of the teacher education institutions. It is not the intention to repeat the listing of those activities here in this chapter; a reference can be made to these activities in the appropriate chapters in which they have been listed.
- It could also be helpful to plan orientation programme on teacher education on this theme. The seminars could familiarize the teacher educators with strategies for operationalizing the teaching-learning dimensions relevant to the theme. An effective way to institutionalize the concept is to incorporate it in the elementary and secondary pre-service teacher education curriculum. This could be supplemented by a suitable co-curricular programme which should aim at offsetting some of the shortcomings in the curricular approach especially in terms of attitude and value development.
- What is needed is a vigorous advocacy with state educational agencies, teacher education institutions and university departments of education for conscious inclusion of such components in the curricula.
- In order to overcome the disadvantage of fragmented treatment of the theme, it is suggested that an independent comprehensive unit comprising familiarization with the Constitution of India and its concerns as impinge on education

should be incorporated in the elementary and secondary teacher education courses.

- o In India, evaluation system influences the educational process especially the quality of classroom teaching significantly, and as such a separate unit of educational imperatives of Constitution will ensure due importance and weightage to the theme in the classroom teaching.
- o A great deal depends on the ingenuity and dedication of teachers and teacher educators in achieving anything substantial through education. If the concerns are handled with sincerity and purpose, they could definitely bring about the desired transformation in the educational system through teacher education.

Conclusion

Today we are in a technological world where things are happening fast. Parents and teachers would like to be getting results fast. India has kept pace in science and technology with forward nations but we have shown slower pace in our value system even when we have a strong heritage of human values.

An overview of the context and concerns as discussed earlier, teacher's profile and general and specific objectives would define the boundaries of a curriculum framework. The perceived characteristics of the envisaged curriculum framework would include the following:

- Reflects the Indian heritage, acts as an instrument in the realization of national goals and fulfills aspirations of people.
- Responds to the latest developments in the field of education.
- Establishes integration of theory and practice of education.
- Provides multiple educational experiences to teachers.
- Enables teachers to experiment with new ideas.
- Ensures inseparability of pre-service and in-service education of teachers.
- Sets achievable goals for various stages of teacher education.

According to Swami Vivekananda Teacher gives knowledge and bright future to his students. He always trying to help students and encourages good habits not only in the students but also in the society. Teacher is a backbone for country's development. The influence of teacher is more in the student life. Any type of social development depends upon its educational system. So it is very important to give prime priority for Teacher Education Curriculum. It is very important to give place to science and technology in Teacher Education Curriculum. Then surely India will become powerful and rich country in the world.

6

Educating Children With Learning Difficulty Dyslexia

If we are to teach real peace in this world, and if we are to carry on a real war against war, we shall have to begin with the children. ...M.K.Gandhi

If hope and salvation are to come, they can only come from the children, for the children are the makers of men ...Maria Montessori

We know 'Today's children are tomorrow's citizens'. It is necessary to take care about children. Education is the solution for all types of problems. Through education we can solve all types of problems in the society. Education gives strength, power, character, courage and knowledge. So, it is necessary to give education for all in the world without considering castes, religions and regions.

- Specific Learning Disabilities
- Reading Disability
- Writing Disability
- Nonverbal learning Disability
- Disorders of Speaking and Learning
- Auditory processing Disorder

DYSLEXIA

Dyslexia is a learning disability that manifests primarily as a difficulty with written language, particularly with reading and spelling. It is separate and distinct from reading difficulties resulting from other causes, such as a non-neurological deficiency with vision or hearing, or from poor or inadequate reading instruction.

Evidence suggests that dyslexia results from differences in how the brain processes written and/or verbal language. Although dyslexia is the result of a neurological difference, it is not an intellectual disability. Dyslexia occurs at all levels of intelligence; sub-average, average, above average, and highly gifted.

According to the findings of a University of Hong Kong study, dyslexia affects different structural parts of children's brains depending on the language they read. The study focused on comparing children that were raised reading English and children raised reading Chinese. Using MRI technology researchers found that the children reading English used a different part of the brain then those reading Chinese. Researchers were surprised by this discovery and hope that the findings will help lead them to any neurobiological cause for dyslexia. The word *dyslexia* comes from the Greek words dyes and lexis. People with dyslexia are called *dyslexic* or *dyslectic.*

Causes of Dyslexia

Dyslexia has not been generally recognized as a learning difficulty until the last decade or two. **John Bradford** presents an overview of the latest research on its causes, and suggests further reading.

Dyslexia is brought about either though inherited traits (developmental dyslexia) or by early ear infections such as 'glue ear', which cause hearing loss (acquired dyslexia). Its cause has not been fully established, but the effect is to create lifelong neurological anomalies in the brain. These anomalies bring about varying degrees of difficulty in learning when using words, and sometimes symbols.

Symptoms of Dyslexia

Children or students who are dyslexic have phonological difficulties, that is, they find it difficult to sort out the sounds within words. This means that they have problems with reading, writing and spelling. The majority of dyslexic children have difficulty with text, memory and the sequencing processes of basic mathematics.

At what age does it become a problem?

Children are either born with dyslexia, or they acquire the difficulty during early childhood through hearing loss, but it is when they begin to learn using words and sometimes other symbols at school that it becomes a noticeable problem.

What level of intelligence does it affect?

Dyslexia can occur in children and students of all abilities, and dyslexic people are frequently of average or above average ability. It is found in all socio-economic groups and in every country in the world. If no help is given, it often results in low self-esteem.

Can Dyslexia be cured?

Each dyslexic person's difficulties are different and vary from slight to very severe disruption of the learning process. There is no total cure, but skilled specialist teaching of phonics, sequencing and techniques to raise the person's self-esteem can alleviate the effects of dyslexia.

The neurological differences also give some dyslexic people visual, spatial, physical co-ordination and lateral thinking abilities that enable them to be successful in a wide range of careers. One famous architect's practice gives preference to employing people who are dyslexic because of their strong spatial awareness and lateral thinking abilities.

How many people are affected by dyslexia?

It is estimated that between 4% and 7% of the population are dyslexic.

Are boys affected more than girls?

Roughly equal numbers of boys and girls are affected.

Does dyslexia affect a child's self-esteem?

As literacy skills are so strongly emphasized during the schooling process, dyslexic children experience a great deal of failure which can easily lower their self-esteem and make them feel that they must be stupid.

This is why it is important for dyslexic children to receive as much praise, credits, certificates, gold stars, etc. as the other children. To complete a piece of written work in class is twice as hard as for a non-dyslexic child. It is also important for a dyslexic child to have art, crafts, physical education and sports during their week in school, as these are the only areas in which they may excel and experience a feeling of satisfaction in learning. Having to learn a foreign language - like French - is a virtual impossibility for a dyslexic child, and a sure route to failure: schools need to be flexible and take account of this.

Limited career prospects

Given proper support, dyslexic students are perfectly able to go on to achieve degrees at university and pursue successful careers. Many dyslexic people find success and fulfillment in:

- Creative areas,
- In areas which allow them to use their physical co-ordination skills, and
- In areas that allow them to use their ability to empathize with others.

How can a parent help their dyslexic child?

The most important thing you can do is to build up the damaged confidence and self-esteem of your child. Make sure s/he knows s/he is loved for himself, and that this love is not dependent on how well s/he does at school.

- Make it clear that the child's difficulties are not his fault. Be very encouraging and find things he is good at.
- Praise him for effort - remember how hard he has to try to achieve success in reading, writing and math/s.
- Help with homework from school, or from any special needs lessons.
- Help him to be organized.

- Encourage areas in which he can experience success, such as creative areas and activities such as sports, which involve physical co-ordination.
- Encourage hobbies, interests and out of school activities.

Treatment and intervention

Poor academic achievement can be addressed with a variety of interventions. Although the underlying processing difficulty is usually considered to be a lifelong disorder, academic skills themselves can be improved with targeted interventions. Some (adjustments, equipment and assistants) are designed to accommodate or help compensate for the disabilities while others (specialized instruction) are intended to make improvements in the weak areas. Practice is a particularly important component in developing competence, regardless of the starting point. Children who start out with a weakness in a basic skill, such as reading, may miss out on the necessary practice because of the need to catch up with their chronological age peers. Thus a small weakness can snowball into a larger problem.

Interventions include

Mastery model

- Learners work at their own level of mastery.
- Practice
- Gain fundamental skills before moving onto the next level.

Note: this approach is most likely to be used with adult learners or outside the mainstream school system.

Direct Instruction

- Highly structured, intensive instruction.
- Emphasizes carefully planned lessons for small learning increments.
- Scripted lesson plans.
- Rapid-paced interaction between teacher and students.
- Correcting mistakes immediately.

- Achievement-based grouping.
- Frequent progress assessments.

Classroom adjustments

- Special seating assignments.
- Alternative or modified assignments.
- Modified testing procedures.

Special equipment

- Electronic spellers and dictionaries.
- World processors
- Talking calculators
- Books on tape

Classroom assistants

- Note-takers
- Readers
- Proofreaders

Special Education

- Prescribed hours in a special class
- Placement in a special class
- Enrollment in a special school for learning disabled students

Sternberg has argued that early remediation can greatly reduce the number of children meeting diagnostic criteria for learning disabilities. He has also suggested that the focus on learning disabilities and the provision of accommodations in school fails to acknowledge that people have a range of strength and weaknesses, and places undue emphasis on academic success by insisting that people should receive additional support in this arena but not in music or sports.

Conclusions

Some critics of the concept of learning disabilities and of special education take the position that every child has a different learning style and pace and that each child is unique, not only capable of learning but also capable of succeeding. These critics assert that applying the medical model of problem solving to individual children who are pupils in the school system, and labeling these children as disabled, systematically prevents the improvement of the current educational system.

References

1. Aaron, P.G. (1995). "Differential Diagnosis of Reading Disabilities." School Psychology Review 24(3): 345-60.
2. Bandian, N.A. (1999) Reading disability defined as a discrepancy between listening and reading comprehension: A longitudinal study of stability, gender differences, and prevalence. Journal of Learning Disabilities, 32 (2) 138-148.
3. Marcia A. Barnes; Fletcher, Jack; Fuches, Lynn. Learning Disabilities: From Identification to Intervention. New York: The Guilford Press.
4. Patil L. Harrison; Flanagan, Dawn P. (2005). Contemporary intellectual assessment: theories, tests, and issues. New York: Guildford Press.
5. Sternberg, R.J., & Grigorenko, E.L. (1999). Our labeled children: What every parent and teacher needs to know about learning disabilities. Reading, M.A. Perseus Publishing Group.

7

Preservation of Indian Values and Culture Through Education

"The central task of education is to implant a will and facility for learning; it should produce not learned but learning people. The truly human society is a learning society, where grandparents, parents, and children are students together"- Eric Hoffer *"The aim of education should be to teach us rather how to think, than what to think rather to improve our minds, so as to enable us to think for ourselves, than to load the memory with the thoughts of other men"*- Bill Beattie

Introduction

India is a land of different religions, communities and languages. Though each has its own tradition and culture, they co-exist. 'Unity in diversity' is the greatness of Indian culture. The development of any nation depends mainly on the standards of its educational institutions.

Education is the most powerful and effective instrument for inducing radical changes in the behaviour of students. Education is the process through which an individual is developed into individuality and a person into a personality. Education should be individualized and personalized to the utmost and should constitute preparation for self-learning.

Education, according to Indian tradition, is not merely a means to earn a living, nor is it only a nursery of thought or a school for citizenship. It is an initiation into the life of spirit, a training of human soul in pursuit of truth and the practice of virtue. Aristotle, however, held that education exists exclusively to develop man's intellect in a world of reality, which men can know and understand.

Man and Education

Man has created education, yet it has become indispensable in his life; for man seeks education for betterment of his life, both inward and outward, and even for survival. It is no wonder, therefore that the U.N.O., in its Universal Declaration of Human Rights, proclaims: "Everyone has the right to education" (Article 26). Not only is this, 'educability' now considered as one of the capacities which distinguish man from other species. Man is educable, whereas other animals and birds etc., are not, although some of them can be trained to do certain things. Hirst and Peters rightly state: "We distinguish now between 'training' and 'education', whereas previously people did not. We would not now naturally speak of educating animals and we would never speak in this way of plants. But we do speak of training animals and of training roses and other sort of plants.

Man can, not only create objects, machines, institutions and ideas, but also can envision a life which he can be or become if he wills. To elaborate a little more-man imagines the concept of a chair or a machine with some particular form, qualities or functions and builds it with a degree of perfection, approaching that of the concept, depending on his ability. Similarly man can envision a life with certain qualities: truthfulness, love, tolerance, peace etc., and can become the being he envisions. To explain in the words of Maslow, "being" is "that which the person is" and "becoming", "that which the person could be", Gordon W. Allport can be aptly quoted in this connection. He writes:

"If the prejudiced style of life can be learned and certainly it is not innate-then surely the tentative style or in Gandhi's term, 'equi-minded outlook' can also be acquired".

Thus man can envision lives with different styles, virtues, states etc., and can become like those. Creativity of this kind, envisioning a life and devising ways for becoming the envisioned personality can very well be termed as "creativity in the field of being and becoming".

In ancient India, the highest conception of education was: *Sâ Vidyâ Yâ Vimuktaye*-Learning or education is that which liberates or makes one liberated. Although other aims were there, certainly there had been a stress on 'to-be'-to be a liberated person (jivanmukta) and to be completely free in ultimate sense. In modern age, quite for a long time education has been conceived as that which helps to achieve-mostly outward things. But it seems, there is a revival of the interest in a kind of education that helps 'to be'- kind of person. The emphasis on 'to be'-to be a 'lifelong learner' and to be a 'complete man' by the International Commission on the Development of Education, and naming of their report as 'Learning to Be', symoblises such an interest.

The Concept of Value

According to Cambridge dictionary of philosophy, the value is the worth of something that philosophers discerned these main forms of intrinsic, instrumental, inherent and contributory value.

Values are described as the socially defined desires and goals that are internalized through the process of condition, learning and socialization.

Values are goals set for achievement and they motivate, define and colour all our activities cognitive, affective and co-native. When education builds up true values in the life of our student, it has equipped the ship of students with RADAR and compass to sail clear on the stormy sea of life.

Values reflect different philosophical positions. The concepts of values are closely associated with the concept of man.

According to Jules Henry in "Culture against Man" (1963), values are something that we consider good such as love, kindness, quietness, contentment, fun, honesty, decency, relaxation and simplicity.

According to Carl Rogers in "Freedom to Learn" (1969), valuing is the tendency of a person to show preference.

According to Louis Raths, Merril and Harmin and Sidney B. Simon (1966) in "Values and Teaching", values are due to the out of experiences may come certain and guides to behaviour. These tend to give direction to life.

According to Shepard B. Clough (1960) in "Basic Values of Western Civilization", in a summary states that values have been variously viewed as preferences, criteria, objects and possessions, personality and status characteristics and states of mind that are absolutes, inherent in objects present in man and stages of mind and identical with his behaiour.

According to John Dewey "the value means primarily to prize, to esteem, to appraise, to estimate; it means the act of cherishing something, holding it dear and also the act of passing judgment upon the nature and amounts of values as compared with something else".

According to Parker, "values belong wholly to the inner world of mind. The satisfaction of desire is the real value; the thing that serves is only an instrument. A value is always an experience never a thing or an object".

According to Mukerjee "values are socially approved drives and goals that are internalized through the process of conditioning, learning or socialization and that becomes subjective preferences, standards and aspirations".

According to Alloport's "the term value means the relative prominence of the subject's interest or the dominant interest in personality".

According to Derek Rowntree's (1960), "Dictionary of Education" that the moral and aesthetics, principles, believes and standards that give coherence and direction to a persons decisions and actions. Where such values are held by or are imposed upon the majority of people in a society they may be known as social values.

In statistics, the different quantitative and qualitative in which an entity can be with respect to some variable that is different categories and measurement.

Values simply stated, are the determiners in the man that influence his choices in life and that decide his behaviour.

Values as indicated are inherent, in individual man but they are additionally inherent although perhaps less definably so, in collective man in a given culture that is or in a combination of cultures. Whatever the exact nature of human society, values exist in some form. In a primitive society, they reside in developed society they reside in written documents as well as in the intangible of social mores and expectances.

The Concept of Culture

Culture comes from the Latin word *cultural* stemming from colure, which means to cultivate. There are many various definitions of culture, some define it as the behaviours, ways of life, arts, beliefs and the institutions of a population that are passed down from generation to generation. Another definition of culture can be and has been called the way of life for an entire society which includes codes of manners, dress, language, religion, rituals, norms of behaviour such as law and morality.

Culture has been defined differently by people. The different definitions attached to culture are based on the differences in the orientation of the people. According Ekeh (1989), culture is constructing, used in an attempt to analyze and integrate events and ideas in broad spectrum of areas of society. Culture is complex which includes knowledge, belief, arts, morals, laws, customs, and any other capabilities and habits acquired by man as member of the society.

Schein (2003) defined culture as, "a set of basic solutions – shared solutions to universal problems of external adaptation (how to survive) and internal integration (how to stay together) – which have evolved over time and are handed down from one generation to the next".

Culture is not an abstraction. It evolves by constantly integrating individual and collective choices that are taken in interaction with other, similar wholes. It expresses itself in diverse ways without being reducible to 'works'. Culture is the product of a complex inheritance constantly submitted to scrutiny and the need to adapt a constant conquest to achieve (Jean, 2002).

In the modern day third world countries, absolute kneeing down may be fading as noted by Tardif (2002). He opines that culture is not genetically transmitted rather it takes place by process of absorption from the social environment or through deliberate instruction. This is to say that culture is learned. Such learning does not occur through natural inheritance. Probably that is why Jekayinfa (2002) maintains that the man learns culture through the process of socialization, enumeration, personal experience and through deliberate teaching. It should be noted that learning of culture is a lifelong process. That is, learning of culture is from birth of death. Jekayinfa (2002) further observes that what is learnt differs from society to society and from one stage to another. However, all that is learnt is geared towards the realization of the goal of the society.

Culture is the totality of the way of life of a group of people that has been developed, shaped and practiced over the years. The development of these cultural norms and practices are shaped by the environment and the needs of the people. Over the years as societies develop and modernize, these cultural practices undergo changes to reflect the changing times to better serve the needs of the people. This means that culture is not stagnant. It is constantly undergoing evolutions based on the changes in the environment in which it exists (Baffoe 2005).

According to Obiora (2002) the transformation of culture is gradual and not sudden. Obiora (2002) contends that culture is a continuous process of change. In spite of the change culture continues to give a community a sense of dignity, continuity, security and binds society together. Another attribute of culture is that it is learned, acquired, transmitted or diffused through contact or other means of communication flow from one generation to another. The fact that we are human does not mean we are the same. However, it is noted that every moment, we are being transformed, always growing like the cell in our bodies. Culture changes exactly the same way as the human being change. In other words, culture is dynamic.

Preservation Value and Culture through Education

“Today, it is no longer desirable to undertake educational reforms in piecemeal fashion, without a concept of the totality of the goals and modes of the educational process. To find out how to reshape its component parts, one must have a vision of the whole" (UNESCO, 1972).

The National Policy on Education has laid considerable emphasis on value education by highlighting the need to make education a powerful tool for cultivation and preservation of social and Moral Values. Keeping in view the pluralistic base of our society, the education system besides preserving our cultural heritage has also to nurture our youth to be more adaptable to life in the changing environment. An inter-linking of education and culture has also been emphasized in the Programme of Action for implementation of National Policy on Education.

People say that "Values cannot be taught but caught". Against this belief educationists strongly advocate that values could be taught with sufficient care and caution.

The National Council for Educational Research and Training (NCERT) in its publication documents on Social, Moral and Spiritual Values in Education (1979) has drawn up 84 values to be inculcated through education.

The cultural values need to be identified for standard curricula all over the country. Respect for the old, care for poor and up-privileged and tolerance should be some of the values. Value based inter-personal relations, importance of racial and religious harmony and concern for humanity should form the basis for friendship and cooperation amongst the people.

Fine arts, music, creative writing, puppetry and theatre are to be given due place in the curricula right from school to the university level.

The curriculum should strike a balance between theory and practice. Creative work in fields of music, dance, literature, drama, visual arts is essential to cultivate the inherent tolerance of children.

Value/moral education should be thought as a compulsory subject up to the high school level. It should be made an examinable subject at the school level. Evaluation of value education should be based on compassion, self-reliance, respect and honesty.

Language is an importance medium for inculcating, fostering and propagating of moral values and national cultural heritage. Education through mother tongue needs to be ensured.

Co-curricular activities play a very significant role in preserving different values in the students. For all-round development of personalities of the students co-curricular activities are considered to be very important now-a-days. Previously the term "extra-curricular activities" was used for outdoor activities and other cultural programmes organized in the school. But now-a-days this term has been discarded keeping in view the importance of these activities. In many progressive schools there is an allotment of certain periods for these co-curricular activities in their regular time table.

Through these activities, many values can be inculcated profitably. Co-curricular activities form an integral part of the modern school curriculum. They should be made more and more purposive and fruitful as well as value oriented with the democratic base and purposeful pursuit. This can be done, provided children have an opportunity of having living experience of moral life through these activities.

In programmes of outdoor activities, the children are taken out of the school to the areas of adventure, appreciation of art and culture and the places of historical values. They can be brought avenues in the training of initiative, team-work, self-discipline and learn much about our cultural heritage and historical details. Besides games and sports, there are several outdoor activities, namely, NCC, Scouting & Guiding, Mountaineering, Trekking, Excursion, Field trips etc., which may serve the purpose of inculcation of desired values among the students and formation of character.

Almost in all the schools and colleges various festivals are organized at different levels. Festivals may be classified into three heads:

1. National Festivals
2. Religious Festivals
3. Birth/Death anniversaries of great persons.

Besides these, there are so many occasions like Sports Day, Teachers' Day, Parents' day, Annual Day, UNO Day, etc., in the school. Through these activities, the qualities of leadership, self-discipline, co-operation, team-work, etc., can be easily developed. Through these activities, new dimension can be given to the personalities of the students.

Conclusion

Values and culture are two faces of a single coin. They are co-existing. Through culture we can preserve values. Today there is lot of degradation of values in every walk of human life. Individuals are crazy for material wealth. Money making is the main motive of the majority of the individuals even through immoral ways. Proper foundation will be laid on Moral Values at the initial stages of the child. Schools and colleges are the institutions which can shoulder the responsibility of inculcating Moral Values among the people and students. Through games and sports, essay writing, elocution, quiz competition, drama and seminars and conferences we can inculcate and protect our values and culture.

References

1. Allport, G.W. (1951): "New Knowledge in Human Values", Houghton Mifflin Co., Boston.
2. Allport, G.W. Vernon. P.E. and Lindzey, G (1951): "A Manual of Study of Values", Houghton Mifflin Co., Boston.
3. Baffoe M. (2005). "These obsolete customs and & traditions must be scrapped"! www.ghanaweb.com.
4. Carl Rogers (1969): "Freedom to Learn", Merill, Ohio.
5. Jean T. (2002). The hidden dimension of globalization: What is at stake geoculturally? Global Policy Forum, New York, ATTAC May 29.
6. Jean, T (2002). "Intercultural dialogues and cultural security". September 2005 planat Agora, www.planetagora.com.
7. Ministry of Education (1964): "Report of the Committee on Religious and Moral Instructions", GoI, New Delhi.
8. Ministry of Education (1964-66): "Report of the Indian Education Commission", Kothari Commission.

9. Ministry of Education (1966): “Education and National Development”, NCERT, New Delhi.

10. Ministry of Education (1971): “Report of the Indian Education Commission”, NCERT.

11. Obiora, A. L. (1996). “Feminism, globalization and culture after Beijing” Paper presented at a Symposium Organized by Indiana Journal of Global Legal Studies.

12. Seshadri, C.S. (1981): “The Concept of Moral Education Column”, Comparative Education Vol. 17, No.3.

8

Preservation of Medicinal Plants by Tribes Through Education in India

All of you know that 'Health is Wealth' and 'A Sound Mind in a Sound Body'. A person has a lot of money and relatives without health he can't enjoy the life. A patient knows the value of health. Man is a greatest animal in the world. Because of Education, Science and Technology he has been becoming a strongest person in the world. Because of internal and external environmental effects sometimes we got diseases. With the help of practiced knowledge we can treat diseases by using medicinal plants.

Medicinal Plants in India

Human beings have been utilizing plants for basic preventive and curative health care since time immemorial. Recent estimates suggest that over 9,000 plants have known medicinal applications in various cultures and countries, and this is without having conducted comprehensive research amongst several indigenous and other communities (Farnsworth and Soejarto 1991).

Medicinal plants are used at the household level by women taking care of their families, at the village level by medicine men or tribal shamans, and by the practitioners of classical traditional systems of medicine such as Ayurveda, Chinese medicine, or the Japanese Kampo system. According to the World Health Organization, over 80% of the world's population, or 4.3 billion people, rely upon such traditional plant-based systems of medicine to provide them with primary health care (Bannerman et. al. 1983).

India is the home of several important traditional system of health care like Ayurveda. This system depends heavily on herbal products. Several millions of Indian households have been using through the ages nearly 8000 species of medicinal plants for their health care needs. Over one and half million traditional healers use a wide range of medicinal plants for treating ailments of both humans and livestock across the length and breadth of the country. Over 800 medicinal plant species are currently in use by the Indian herbal industry.

Herbal History in Indian Context

The Rig-Veda, the oldest document of human knowledge mentions the use of medicinal plants in the treatment of man and animals. Ayurveda gives the account of actual beginning of the ancient medical science of India, which according to western scholars was written between 2500 to 600 B.C. Charaka and Susruta wrote around 1000 B.C. Charaka concentrates more on medicine while Susruta deals with surgery in details along with therapeutics.

Tribes in India

The Indian sub-continent is inhabited by 88.2 million tribal populations belonging to over 577 tribal communities that come under 227 linguistic groups. They inhibit varied geographic and climatic Zones of the country. Their vocation ranges from hunting, gathering, cave dwelling nomadic to societies with settled culture living incomplete harmony with nature.

The tribal people are the real custodians of the medicinal plants. Out of 45,000 species of wild plants, 7500 species are used for medicinal purposes. The World Health Organization (WHO) has been promoting a movement for *'Saving plants for saving lives'*. This is because of the growing understanding of the pivotal role medicinal plants play in providing herbal remedies to health maladies.

Forests have been their dear home and totally submitted themselves to forest settings. Their relationship with the forest was symbolic in nature. They have been utilizing the resources without disturbing the delicate balance of the eco-system. Tribal thus mostly remained as stable societies and were unaffected by the social, cultural, material and economic evolutions that were taking place with the so called civilized societies. But this peaceful co-existence of the tribal has been disturbed in recent years by the interference in their habitats. Traditional communities living close to nature have, over the years acquired unique knowledge about the use of living biological resources. Modernisation, especially industrialization and urbanization has endangered the rich heritage of knowledge and expertise of age old wisdom of the traditional communities.

A study on the utilization of local tribal revealed that they hold precious knowledge on the specific use of a large number of agents of wild plant and animal origins, the use of many are hitherto unknown to the outside world.

Preservation of Medicinal Plants by Tribes through Adult Education in India

According to 2001 census the literacy rate of schedule castes was 54.69% and that of. Schedule tribe was 47.10% as against the national average of 64.84%. We know majority of the tribes living in the deep forest area. They are for away from the rural and urban communities. Now a day also majority of tribal communities have no current facility. They do not using modern technology in the field of cultivation. Their livelihood is also different. The tribal children are not interest to come the school. Majority of the medicinal plants are occurring in the deep forest. The following steps are necessary to preserve medicinal plants.

- Educate all types of people in the tribal area.
- Provide advanced technology for tribes.
- Tell the importance of medicinal plants for world people.
- Increase Teacher-Student ration in the tribal community area.
- Collect valuable medicinal plants with the help of tribes in the deep forest area.

- Give training about photography for tribes for documentation of medicinal plants and herbal products.
- Provide all types of facilities with advanced communication system.
- Conduct awareness programmes about diseases and un-believable things.
- Give lectures about modern world, universe, marketing system and population in the world.
- Give encouragement for cultivation of medicinal plants.
- Arrange medicinal plans garden in the forest.
- Conduct seminars, workshops and exhibitions about medicinal plants both in the agency and rural/urban areas.

Preservation of Medicinal Plants by Farmers through Education in India

We know India is a developing country. The majority of the people occupation in India is cultivation. 70 per cent of the total population is living in the rural area and their main occupation is cultivation. The farmers' gives importance for food based agriculture. Because of globalization and industrialization and economic reforms, the attitude of the farmer is also changed, the State and Central Governments encouraging the farmers for cultivation of medicinal plants by giving subsidy. The recent allocations in the XI five year plan over Rs. 970 Crores (from 93.50 Crores during X Plan) for the sector is an indication on the importance given by the Government for the development of medicinal plants in the country.

According to National Medicinal Plants Board and Department of AYUSH there are 344 Medicinal plants garden in India. Through these institutions/gardens it is possible to give training for farmers about cultivation of medicinal plants.

The literacy rate of rural people in India is 58.74%. It is very less when compared to national average 64.84%. We know education is a solution for all types of problems. The following steps are important in the preservation of medicinal plants in India by the farmers.

- Educate all the people in the villages.

- Provide advanced technology in the field of agriculture, transport and communication system.
- Provide good market system for their products.
- Arrange regular awareness programmes about cultivation of medicinal plants for farmers.
- Tell the importance of medicinal plants.
- Tell the value of medicinal plants in the international market.
- Establish Ayurved colleges in the rural areas.
- Give subsidy for farmers and provide good marketing system.
- Arrange medicinal plants garden in the rural areas.
- Conduct workshops, seminars and exhibitions.

Uses of Medicinal Plants

Since ancient times, plants have been an exemplary source of medicine. Ayurveda and other Indian literature mention the use of plants in treatment of various human ailments. India has about 45000 plant species and among them, several thousands have been claimed to possess medicinal properties.

There has been resurgence in the consumption and demand for medicinal plants. These plants are finding use as pharmaceuticals, neutraceuticals, cosmetics and food supplements. Even as traditional source of medicines and they continue to play pivotal rule.

The World Health Organization (WHO) estimated that 80% of the population of developing countries still relies on traditional medicines, mostly plant drugs, for their primary health care needs. Also, modern pharmacopoeia contains at least 25% drugs derived from plants. Many other are synthetic analogues built on prototype compounds isolated from plants. Demand for medicinal plant is increasing in both developing and developed countries due to growing recognition of natural products, being non-toxic, having no side-effects, easily available at affordable prices. Medicinal plant sector has traditionally occupied an important position in the socio cultural, spiritual and medicinal arena of rural and tribal lives of India.

Saving the Plant Is Saving the Life

According to the text of Vishnu Samhita, causing any harm to the plants/animals is a sin. Even purloining of parts/ products of any of these living beings is a crime. The sinner/ criminals are liable to chastisement in this life and also after death. The punishments are of diverse nature:-pecuniary, corporal, expiatory and donation of specific articles to Brahmins.

Conclusions

Since ancient times, plants have been an exemplary source of medicine. Ayurveda and other Indian literature mention the use of plants in treatment of various human ailments. India has about 45000 plant species and among them, several thousands have been claimed to possess medicinal properties. It is our duty to preserve all these medicinal plants for the purpose of future generation. Through Adult Education only it is possible.

- Educate all types of tribes in India.
- Educate all type of people in the society.
- Establish some more Medicinal Plants Boards in the rural and forest areas.
- Take care about marketing system of medicinal plants.
- Conduct awareness programmes about medicinal plants every month regularly.

Reference

1. Andrew Chevallier. "The Encyclopedia of Medicinal Plants- A Practical Reference Guide to Over 550 Key Herbs and Their Medicinal Uses".
2. Barua, I. and R. Phukan. 1990. "Socio-religious aspects of Health among Sonowal Kachari". The Eastern Anthropologist, 55: 4.
3. Bhasin, Veena. 1997. "Medical Pluralism and Health Services in Ladakh." J. Soc. Sci., 1: 43-69.
4. Bhasin, Veena. 1997. "The Human Settlements and Health Status of People of Sikkim", (Pp. 153-187), in K.C. Mahanta (ed.), People of the Himalayas: Ecology, Culture, Development and Change. Delhi:Kamla-Raj Enterprises.

9

Role of Higher Educational Institutions in Promotion of Rural Human Resources

The development of any nation depends mainly on the standards of its educational institutions. Education is the most powerful and effective instrument for inducing radical changes in the behaviour of students. Education is the process through which an individual is developed into individuality and a person into a personality. Education should be individualized and personalized to the utmost and should constitute preparation for self-learning.

First Higher Educational Institution

Education has been around for as long as man has been, though its structure and perception has varied over centuries and civilizations. The beginning of historically-documented higher education began with the Nanjing University founded in 258 AD in China which is generally believed to be the oldest higher education institution in the world, later becoming the first modern Chinese university in the early 1920s.

During the Vedic and Upanishadic period, India had some of the prominent institutions of higher education, which attracted scholars from distant places located in different parts of the world to come to India in pursuit of knowledge. The ancient universities of Takshashila and Nalanda, which survived till the end of the fifth and twelfth Century AD respectively, imparted knowledge in different areas according to the requirements of the contemporary society.

In the knowledge economy, the objectives of a society changes from fulfilling the basic needs of all round development to empowerment. The education system instead of going by text-book teaching will be promoted by reactive, interactive self learning, both formal and informal, with focus on values, merit and quality. The workers instead of being skilled or semi-skilled will be knowledgeable, self-empowered and flexibly skilled. Finally, the economy will be knowledge driven and not industry driven.

All fields of human activity, including education, have been influenced by the process of globalization clubbed with unexpected advancements in information and communication technology. Within the various sectors of education, higher academic and technical education has been affected the most. It is now increasingly realized that knowledge is universal and its creation and dissemination cannot be confined within national boundaries. The world is now like a global village, and continuous international interaction has become an essential component of human survival. The globalization of economy has led to internationalization of higher education, not merely for economic benefits, but also for increased social interaction and promotion of international understanding. The main aim of primary educational institutions is to develop four skills. Whish are listening, speaking, reading and writing.

Importance of Education

Education means the gradual process of acquiring knowledge. Education is a preparation for life. Swami Vivekananda, the great thinker and reformer of India had remarked: “We want that education by which character is formed, strength of mind is increased, intellect is expanded and by which one can stand on one’s own feet. Education is the manifestation of the perfection already in man.” The great Nobel Laureate and writer Rabindra Nath Tagore was one of the earliest educators to think in terms of the global education village, and his educational model has a unique sensitivity and aptness for education within multi-racial, multi-lingual and multi-cultural situations.

Development through Educational Institutions

Independent India has witnessed an upsurge in the growth of higher education. Yet from an international perspective, we are relatively slow, despite being steady in registering advancements in learning. Today India has the second largest education system in the world, next only to the USA. Yet, the total number of students represents hardly six percent of the relevant age group, i.e. 18-23 years, which is much below the average of developed countries which is about 47 percent. The gap is glaring. Hence the phenomenal challenge. The journey from being 'Good' to being 'Great' appears to be long and arduous.

India is a developing country. 70% of people are living in the villages. The rural area literacy percentage is very low when compared to urban area literacy rate. The main occupation of Indians is cultivation. The duty of higher educational institutions is to introduce courses which help to improve the rural people socio-economic status in the society. Through education it is possible to change the world. Because of globalization now world become a village. We get any type of information within the seconds. Educational institutions have prominent role in the development of rural people in the society.

The development of India depends mainly on the development of villages. But today the state and central governments are not taking good steps to develop villages. The economic positions of farmers are not good. The suicide attempts of farmers are increasing. The unemployment percentage is also increasing. By introducing new agricultural and self-employment courses in the vocational institutions it is possible overall development of rural areas.

Dr. A P J Abdul Kalam, while envisioning India of 2020, recently observed - "Spirit of Inquiry, creativity, entrepreneurial and moral leadership are the capabilities central to nation building in a democracy. Educators should develop in our children these capacities and make them autonomous learners who are self-directed and self-controlled."

Earlier all over the world, education, especially higher education, was available only to a privileged few. In the context of a knowledge society and the goals of sustainable development, higher education needs to percolate to the masses, not only just in terms of quantity, but also quality. In the last few years, this shift has been slowly taking place. Still, glaring deficiencies remain in the access to higher education, overall development of the student, sensitivity to human needs and equality in our society.

Also come into play, concerns in higher education that come with globalization and rapidity of change like fast rate of obsolescence of knowledge, quality, competitiveness of education services, networking of institutions and innovations and new practices in delivery. Combined with this are the concerns for sustainable development of the world.

Conclusion

The higher educational institutions have a prominent role in the development of rural areas. Through education it is easy to motivate people in the society. Education gives knowledge, wealth and health. Education is a part in our daily life. Through education it is possible to learn new things. The higher educational institutions duty is to give training for adults in the society to proper utilization of sources in the nature. India has a large number of human resources in the world after China. It is necessary to establish some higher educational institutions in our country. It is also educational institution duty to motivate people to use advanced technology in the field of agriculture and self-employment fields like poultry and architecture etc.

10

Impact of Globalization on Teacher Education

A teacher who establishes rapport with the taught, becomes one with them, learns more from them than he teaches them. He who learns nothing from his disciples is, in my opinion, worthless. Whenever I talk with someone I learn from him. I take from him more than I give him. In this way, a true teacher regards himself as a student of his students. If you will teach your pupils with this attitude, you will benefit much from them ... M.K. Gandhi.

Education has been around for as long as man has been, though its structure and perception has varied over centuries and civilizations. Now we are living in the highly scientific and technological world. Enormous changes are occurring in the day to day life of human beings because of globalization, privatization and liberalization. Education is seen as central to economic competitiveness, the reduction of poverty and inequality, and environmental sustainability. So, it is necessary to provide education for all; then only India will become developed country by 2020.

Globalization

Globalization is a term describing the increasing interdependence, integration and interaction among people, companies and corporations in disparate locations around the world. This umbrella term refers to a complex medley of economic, trade, social, technological, cultural and political relationships. The term has been used as early as 1944; however Theodore Levitt is usually credited with its first use in an economic context.

In defining and explaining globalization, Nsibambi (2001), incorporated five concepts. He defined globalization as "a process of advancement and increase in interaction among the worlds, countries and peoples facilitated by progressive technological changes in locomotion, communication, political and military power, knowledge and skills, as well as interfacing of cultural values, systems and practices". He noted that globalization is not a value-free, innocent, self-determining process. It is an international socio-politico-economic and cultural permeation process facilitated by policies of governments, private corporations, international agencies and civil society organizations. It essentially seeks to enhance and deploy economic, political, technological, ideological and military power and influence for competitive domination in the world. Globalization is the worldwide process of homogenizing prices, products, wages, rates of interest and profits. Globalization relies on three forces for development: the role of human migration, international trade, and rapid movements of capital and integration of financial markets.

From the culture point of view, David (2002), states that globalization is the process of harmonizing different cultures and beliefs. Globalization is the process that eroding differences in culture and producing a seamless global system of culture and economic values (Castells, 1997). The harmonization, according to Awake (2002), is achieved due to advancement in communication and countries are increasingly being forced to participate. Therefore, globalization can be viewed as a process of shifting autonomous economies into a global market. In other words, it is the systematic integration of autonomous economies into a global system of production and distribution.

The world of separate nation-states is said to be ending enabling the process of globalization to run its logical course. The new technology, based on the computer and satellite communication have indeed revolutionized our traditional conception of the media, both print and electronic. Books, newspapers, radio, television and video programme are now being transposed into the multimedia world of the cyber space and available to all people of the world wherever they may live. Ajayi (2001) remarks that globalization is about competition and struggle for dominance which encourages more than anything else, the continuation and expansion of western imperialism in the new millennium.

Importance of Education

During the Vedic and Upanishadic period, India had some of the prominent institutions of higher education, which attracted scholars from distant places located in different parts of the world to come to India in pursuit of knowledge. The ancient universities of Takshashila and Nalanda, which survived till the end of the fifth and twelfth Century AD respectively, imparted knowledge in different areas according to the requirements of the contemporary society.

The importance of education is quite clear. Education is the knowledge of putting one's potentials to maximum use. One can safely say that a human being is not in the proper sense till he is educated. This importance of education is basically for two reasons. The first is that the training of a human mind is not complete without education. Education makes man a right thinker. It tells man how to think and how to make decision.

The second reason for the importance of education is that only through the attainment of education, man is enabled to receive information from the external world; to acquaint him-self with past history and receive all necessary information regarding the present. Without education, man is as though in a closed room and with education he finds himself in a room with all its windows open towards outside world.

Education means the gradual process of acquiring knowledge. Education is a preparation for life. Swami Vivekananda, the great thinker and reformer of India had remarked: "We want that education by which character is formed, strength of mind is increased, intellect is expanded and by which one can stand on one's own feet. Education is the manifestation of the perfection already in man." The great Nobel Laureate and writer Rabindra Nath Tagore was one of the earliest educators to think in terms of the global education village, and his educational model has a unique sensitivity and aptness for education within multi-racial, multi-lingual and multi-cultural situations.

Development through Educational Institutions

Independent India has witnessed an upsurge in the growth of higher education. Yet from an international perspective, we are relatively slow, despite being steady in registering advancements in learning. Today India has the second largest education system in the world, next only to the USA. Yet, the total number of students represents hardly six percent of the relevant age group, i.e. 18-23 years, which is much below the average of developed countries which is about 47 percent. The gap is glaring. Hence the phenomenal challenge. The journey from being 'Good' to being 'Great' appears to be long and arduous.

India is a developing country. 70% of people are living in the villages. The rural area literacy percentage is very low when compared to urban area literacy rate. The main occupation of Indians is cultivation. The duty of higher educational institutions is to introduce courses which help to improve the rural people socio-economic status in the society. Through education it is possible to change the world. Because of globalization now world become a village. We get any type of information within the seconds. Educational institutions have prominent role in the development of rural people in the society.

The first citizen of India today, Dr.A P J Abdul Kalam, while envisioning India of 2020, recently observed - "Spirit of Inquiry, creativity, entrepreneurial and moral leadership are the capabilities central to nation building in a democracy. Educators should develop in our children these capacities and make them autonomous learners who are self-directed and self-controlled." Earlier all over the world, education, especially higher education, was available only to a privileged few. In the context of a knowledge society and the goals of sustainable development, higher education/teacher education needs to percolate to the masses, not only just in terms of quantity, but also quality. In the last few years, this shift has been slowly taking place. Still, glaring deficiencies remain in the access to higher education, overall development of the student, sensitivity to human needs and equality in our society.

Also come into play, concerns in teacher education that come with globalization and rapidity of change like fast rate of obsolescence of knowledge, quality, competitiveness of education services, networking of institutions and innovations and new practices in delivery, combined with this are the concerns for sustainable development of the world.

Role of Teacher in Building Modern India

The role of the modern teacher is not confined to teaching alone. He/she is expected to participate in the development programmes of the community life. The question arises as to how this could be integrated with the teacher education programmes. Mudaliar Commission (1952-53) Report stated rightly, "we are convinced that the most important factor in the contemplated education reconstruction is the teacher-his personal qualities, his educational qualifications, his professional training and the place that he occupies in the school as well as in the community". On similar lines Kothari Commission (1964-66) stated that, "Nothing is more important than securing a sufficient supply of high quality recruits to the teaching profession, providing them with the best possible professional preparation and creating satisfactory conditions of work in which they can be fully effective".

The importance of the teachers in the Educational Programme of a country is too great. The greatness of a country does not depend on lofty buildings, gigantic projects and large armies, but on the quality of its citizens. If a nation has young men of sterling character and unimpeachable patriotism, she is found to make rapid progress in all fields. Young men are entrusted to the care of the teacher and it is therefore the sacred duty of the teacher to impart the right type of knowledge and make them good citizens. It is the teacher who impresses his children with his personality.

The teacher, a national integrator as he is, is the backbone of society, particularly so in the remote villages. He stands as an outstanding figure among the illiterate and semi-literate families. He is their friend, Philosopher and guide. The teacher actively shares the responsibility of reconstructing a social order, with all the cherished values and traditional beliefs, which are being eroded by the surge of new ideals and practices. He acts as a social reformer and counsellor to the community.

Impact of Globalization on Teacher Education

In the knowledge economy, the objectives of a society changes from fulfilling the basic needs of all round development to empowerment. The education system instead of going by text-book teaching will be promoted by reactive, interactive self learning, both formal and informal, with focus on values, merit and quality. The workers instead of being skilled or semi-skilled will be knowledgeable, self-empowered and flexibly skilled. Finally, the economy will be knowledge driven and not industry driven.

All fields of human activity, including education, have been influenced by the process of globalization clubbed with unexpected advancements in information and communication technology. Within the various sectors of education, teacher education has been affected the most. It is now increasingly realized that knowledge is universal and its creation and dissemination cannot be confined within national boundaries. The world is now like a global village, and continuous international interaction has become an essential component of human survival. The globalization of economy has led to internationalization of higher education including teacher education, not merely for economic benefits, but also for increased social interaction and promotion of international understanding.

Positive impact of Globalization on Teacher Education

1. A number of teacher educational institutions were increased.
2. Usage of technology increased in the educational institutions.
3. Information and communication technology were increased.
4. Teacher educational institutions were established in rural areas.
5. Government and private partnership in the field of teacher education.

6. Extension of internet facilities even to rural areas educational institutions.
7. Teachers are less worried for government jobs as MNC's and private or public sector are offering more lucrative jobs.
8. Free education for bright students.

Negative impact of Globalization on Teacher Education

1. Indian youths leaving education in mid-way and joining MNC's.
2. There has been an increase in the violence, particularly against women in the educational institutions.
3. Quality in education is decreasing (liberalization).
4. Degradation of values.
5. More availability of cheap and filthy material (CD's or DVD's of Hollywood movies, porn movies, sex toys, foreign channels like MTV) in the name of liberalization. It affects the psychology of teachers. Some teachers are miss-behaving with students.
6. Values of teacher are decreasing.

Conclusion

It is left to one's discretion to use a knife either to cut a fruit or to kill a person/animal. In the modernized and globalized world, it is necessary to be very cautious. Every single step should be taken with utmost care. It is the first duty of policy makers, politicians, officials and leaders to give priority for mother society and well being of their people. Globalization undoubtedly offers great opportunities for growth and development. However, no one can deny that its benefits are unevenly shared and its costs are unevenly spread among, across and within countries. This is particularly true with respect to developing and underdeveloped countries. In spite of economic reforms the rates of unemployment and poverty in India are still high. Both in concept and practice, while globalization has positive, innovative, dynamic aspects, it also has negative, disruptive and marginalizing aspects (UNDP HDR 1999). Nsibambi (2001) suggested that globalization must be seen as a change process full of opportunities and challenges that must be carefully and skilfully harnessed and managed to ensure human development.

Teacher is a national builder. According to Indian philosophy teacher is a third god. It is very important to take care about teacher education. Through education only it is possible to preserve values and culture. Through education it is possible to solve any types of problems in the society.

It is apt to quote Mahatma Gandhi "I do not want my house to be walled in on all sides and my windows to be stuffed. I want the cultures of all the lands to be blown about my house as freely as possible. But, I refuse to be blown off my feet by any".

References

1. David F. (2002). Why National Pride Still Has a Home in the Global Village. Global Policy Forum. New York. The Scotsman May 18.
2. Gandhi, M. K. (1977), "*The Collected Works*, Ahmedabad: Navajivan.
3. Kumar, K. (1994), 'Mohandas Karamchand Gandhi' in Z. Morsy (ed.) *Thinkers on Education Volume 2*, Paris: UNESCO.
4. Nsibambi, A (2001). "The effects of globalization on the state in Africa: Harnessing the benefits and minimizing the costs. Paper presented at UN General Assembly, second committee: Panel discussion on globalization and the state, November 2, 2001.
5. Ruggie, John Gerard (1993), "Territoriality and Beyond: *Problematizing Modernity in International Relations*," International Organization 47; 139-74.
6. Scholte, Jan Aart (2000), "*Globalization: A Critical Introduction*" (New York: St. Martin's).

11

Importance of Values in Teacher Education

The past is beyond recovery. We are not sure of the future. The given moment is the right time. Do not delay; do right action......*Sri Sathya Sai Baba.*

Introduction

The development of any nation depends mainly on the standards of its educational institutions. Education is the most powerful and effective instrument for inducing radical changes in the behaviour of students. Education is a powerful instrument of national development-social, economic and cultural. The teacher occupies pivotal position in the system of education. Teaching has been one of the oldest and most respected professions in the world.

According to Indians Teacher is the third god. Today we are living in the technological world. India developed in the fields of Science and Technology. It is possible to know each and everything within seconds throughout the world. Today's children are tomorrow's citizens. It is necessary to give quality and value based education to each and every student in the society. Then only all children will become good citizens in the future.

Values

Values are the guiding principles, decisive in day to day behaviours as also in critical life situations. Values are a set of principles or standards of behaviour. Values are regarded desirable, important and held in high esteem by a particular society in which a person lives. Thus values give meaning and strength to a person with character by occupying a central place in his life. Values reflect one's personal attitudes and judgments, decisions and choices, behaviour and relationships, dreams and vision. They influence our thoughts, feelings and actions. They guide us to do the right things.

Values are the guiding principles of life which are conductive to all round development. They give direction and firmness to life and bring joy, satisfaction and peace of life. Values are like the rails that keep a train on the track and help it move smoothly, quickly and with direction. They bring qualities to life.

Value Education

Value education means inculcating in the children a sense of humanism, a deep concern for the well being of others and the nation. This can be accomplished only when we instill in the children a deep feeling of commitment to values that would build this country and bring back to the people pride in work that brings order, security and assured progress.

Through value education, we like to develop the social, moral, aesthetic and spiritual sides of a person which are often undermined in formal education. Value education teaches us to preserve whatever is good and worthwhile in what we have inherited from our culture. It helps us to respect the attitude and behaviour of those who differ from us. Value education does not mean value imposition or indoctrination.

Value education has the capacity to transform a diseased mind into a very young, fresh, healthy, natural and attentive mind. The transformed mind is capable of higher sensitivity and a heightened level of perception this leads to fulfillment of the evolutionary role in man and in life. Values in general, could be classified broadly under five headings personal, social, moral, spiritual and behavioural.

Education in general and value education in particular occupies a prestigious place in the modern context of the contemporary society. The problem of value education of the young has assumed increasing prominence in educational discussions during recent times. Parents, teachers, administrators and society at large are concerned of about values and value education of children.

"The destiny of India is now being shaped in her class rooms". This is the opening sentence of the Kothari Education Commission report (1964-66). What kind of destiny has been actually shaped during the last sixty years? There are thousands of schools without primary needs. The position of teacher's economic condition is also poor when compared to USA teachers.

Nature of Values

- Values relate to the aims of human life. For the achievement of aims man frames certain notions and these notions are called values.
- Our conduct is motivated by our values.
- Value is the act of cherishing something. A person who values justice will spend a lot of energy in search for it.
- Values are masterminds which give direction to one's strivings. Values represent feelings, wants, interests, attitudes, preferences and opinions about what is right, just fair or desirable.

Classification of Values

There are so many classifications of values. According to Plato's classification, there are three types of values: (1) Truth, (2) Beauty and (3) Goodness.

Gandhi's Classification

In order to create new social order Gandhiji introduced Nai Talim in the year 1937, which is popularly known as Basic Education.

1. Truth

2. Non-violence
3. Freedom
4. Democracy
5. Sarva Dharma Smabhava
6. Equality
7. Self-realisation
8. Purity of ends and means
9. Self-discipline
10. Suddhi

The numbers of values are unlimited. The NCERT listed 83 values. It is unmanageable to deal with so many values in schools. Under the Sathya Sai Organization, these 83 values are classified and grouped under the five well known prime values. These five are: Sathya (Truth), Dharma (righteousness), Prema (Love in its broadest Sense), Shanti (Peace) and Ahimsa (Non-violence in various forms and actions, thoughts, feelings etc).

We have the constitution of India which we are bound to follow: major values embedded there in are (1) Justice, Equality, liberty and Fraternity and (2) Democracy, Secularism, and Social Justice. Next we have individual and personal values: Cleanliness, Neatness, Punctuality, Regularity, Industriousness, Health care, honesty, Self respect, Self reliance etc.

We must add values necessary for Peace and Harmony. These are concern and compassion for others, co-operation, self-sacrifice, national integrity and unity and world/ universal brotherhood. For all values, the approach has to be through a spirit of enquiry, persuit of truth, logical thinking, open mindedness, sharing and a scientific bent of mind.

Characteristics of a Real Teacher

Teacher is a national builder. He has a power to change the society. In the 13th chapter of the "Bhagavad-Gita" the characteristics of a real teacher are laid down as follows: absence of pride, free from hypocrisy, non-violence, forgiving nature, straight forwardness, service of the preceptor, purity of mind and body, steadfastness and self-control. Centuries ago in this land of Vedas the teacher devoted all his time for the upliftment of his pupils in all directions-knowledge, morals, values etc. He was called the 'Guru or Acharya'.

According to V.S.Mathews "No system of education, no syllabus, no methodology, no text book can rise above the level of its teachers. If a country wants to have quality education it must have quality teachers". So, it is necessary to give importance for values in the teacher education.

Teacher Education

"Values are to be caught and not taught', is a very old saying. It was perhaps true in days gone by when parents at home and leaders in community in various walks of life were all value-based people. Therefore younger children and growing adolescents could catch values of elderly people and either by imitation or by special efforts developed appropriate values accepted and respected in society. Much water has flowed under the bridge since then and there is a grave deterioration both among parents and community leaders in terms of their being value models for the younger generation. We cannot therefore expect values to be caught from undesirable situations and persons in society. In today's world, therefore values have got to be taught in addition to being caught from selected situations and personalities.

According to V.S.Mathews "No system of education, no syllabus, no methodology, no text book can rise above the level of its teachers. If a country wants to have quality education it must have quality teachers". So, it is necessary to give importance for values in the teacher education.

Let we observe the teacher education system in the state of Andhra Pradesh, India. There are 24 Government D.Ed. colleges for the academic year 2006-07 with 2565 students, 324 B.Ed. colleges with 36009 students, 3B.Ed. institution in distance mode with 1500 students, 17 Telugu Pandit colleges with 1700 students, 10 Urdu Pandit Colleges with 480 students, 35 Hindi Pandit colleges with 2090 studens, 5 D.P.Ed. colleges with 400 students, 7 B.P.Ed. colleges with 435 students and 20 M.Ed. colleges with 457 students both in Government and Private sectors.

It is necessary to take care in the framing of teacher education curriculum. Teacher is a national builder. So, it is important to give good quality and value based education to the teacher in teacher education. It is necessary to provide all types of labs and library facilities to improve quality education in teacher education.

Need for value based Teacher Education

Today we are in a technological world where things are happening fast. Parents and teachers would like to be getting results fast. India has kept pace in science and technology with forward nations but we have shown slower pace in our value system even when we have a strong heritage of human values. India was quoted by great visionaries and saints as a punya bhumi. Swami Vivekananda reiterated in his powerful words: " *If there is any land on this earth that can lay claim to be the blessed punya bhumi, to be land to which souls on this earth must come to account for karma, the land to which every soul is wending its way Godward must come to attain its lost home, the land where humanity has attained its highest towards gentleness, towards generosity, towards purity, towards calmness, above all, the land of introspection and of spirituality-It is India.*" Thus value Education has been elucidated by swamiji. From such a state, we are in the Pythonic Grip of deepening Value crisis. How unfortunate it is!!!

How can we overcome this? When can we become capable of training the young citizens to be the carriers of the noble human resources? What value, value has changed to? Present scenario and surroundings looms large with terroristic acts, violence, negative thoughts, anti-social acts, many an immoral qualities are all seen everywhere and the world looks a big booming , buzzing confusion . Such is the case in all fields, braving such conditions the wise men of our country has been trying to put forth issues like a national system of education and a national policy of education which should focus & bridge the gaps that are widening .

The NPE (1986) and subsequently the POA's have been emphasising the faith in *vidya dadati vinayam, vinayat yati patratam, patratwat dhanamapnoti, dhanat dharmam tataha sukham*- it is learning and knowledge that gives capability to earn, and earning the ability to do dharma for a noble cause and this results in gaining peace. The analysts and educationists of our country have consciously changed the curriculum and prioritized universalisation of primary education, the girl child education, and inculcating value-based education in their recent policy recommendations like - the Eshwarbhai Patel's; Ramamurthy commission; Prof.Yashpal's commission and the present focus on the same issues through the national curriculum framework. All these commissions, reports and recommendations have one thing in common and that is, changing curriculum at different levels for capacity building among teachers. Further, recent studies and analysis of evaluation of achievements at different levels have clearly shown the quality concerns and that teacher factor and his /her performance is poor but his responsibilities are more and there is need to train teachers in several of the new techniques & bring him to the frontline in this task of building a national system of education with a focus on value education. Thus educating the whole child and developing values assumed importance in recent years.

Implementation Process

The following points may be considered for implementing the value education in in-service and pre-service teacher training programmes and at different stage of educational institutions.

In-service Teacher Training

As a first step, three training camps may be arranged for teachers- (1) coaching camp, (2) evaluation camps and (3) refresher courses. A minimum of two teachers from each school must be covered by this programme. The above programmes for the teachers should be in such a way that it kindles the vast potentialities lying dormant in a teacher resulting in the teacher developing his/her own ways of imparting VE. These courses should enable the teacher to have his perspective in all the activities of school viz. classes on subjects, sports and games, cultural activities, youth festivals and all other extra-curricular activities. **In other words, moral education will not get confined to one moral class only.**

A teacher's manual of guidelines may be prepared, based on the values listed above, containing portions from the existing textbooks that deal with values, to help them give a special thrust to values while teaching the students.

Progammes

- Conduct periodically essay writing, elocution, storytelling, poems recital, quiz on value-based subjects.
- Teach life stories of eminent characters in the epics and history, poems that would spur national fervour and devotion, patriotic songs, environmental hygiene etc.
- Motivate children to write short notes on value-based topics from the school library books. This will also encourage the development of reading habit.
- Organize special programmes on value-based subjects on every January 26, August 15 and October 2, and give awards to all the participants in the form of leaflets/pamphlets/books containing value-oriented articles and stories.
- Conduct a class exclusively for moral instruction, based on Gandhian lines, in every school once a week to focus the student's attention on the observance of a proper code of conduct and good behaviour at home, in school, in public places, and while moving about in the society.
- Begin the classes every day with a universal peace prayer.
- Display every day, messages and sayings of Mahastmas and great thinkers related to values at a prominent place in the schools under the caption 'Thought for the Day'. Such sayings may be read out and explained in the morning school assembly.
- Invite distinguished persons to talk to the students and parents on the need for importance of leading a value-based life.
- Organize occasionally common gatherings of students of government, aided and unaided schools to bridge the gap in the level of their awareness and absorption capacity.
- Institute recognition and bravery awards for those students whose assimilation of values outshines that of their fellow-students.

- Observe once a year a Parents' Day; to enable the children to express their abiding love, reverence and gratitude for all that their parents have been doing for them.
- Celebrate Teachers' Day in the true spirit to enable children to remember with great reverence and abiding gratitude what their teachers have done for them.
- Arrange debates, speeches and skits on the life and teachings of outstanding national leaders, who can be considered as role models for the young generation.

Outdoor camps

- Conduct periodical outdoor camps for selected children from a group of schools. This is an easy way to enable the children to understand the gifts of nature and to study the infallible laws of nature.
- In this context, it may be most appropriate to arrange for at least one outdoor self-contained campsite in each of the approximately 50 districts in the country. This site may also provide facilities for nature cure, organic farming and yoga as it is felt that there is growing importance given to this in many countries and therefore, students may be trained in this at an early age itself. Such a facility would basis in the outdoor camps that may be conducted every weekend in each district.

Conclusion

According to Sarvepalli Radhakrishnan teacher is a national builder. He has a power to change the society. It is government duty to provide quality education for prospective and in-service teachers. Teacher is a back bone for national development. Through education we can change the world. Teacher is a good resource to develop values in the society. Without teacher the education have no meaning. Value oriented education is necessary for today's situation.

References

1. Achievement of B.Ed. Students, Dr. C. Manchala, Discovery Publishing House, New Delhi – 110002.

2. Value Education in India, Usha Rai Negi, Editor, Published by association of Indian Universities, AIU House, 16 Kotla Mark, New Delhi – 110 002, 2000.

3. Value Education, Dr. Venkataiah, Editor, APH Publishing Corporation, 5, Ansari Road, Daryaganji, New Delhi – 110 002, First Edition, 1998.

12

Inculcation of Ethics Through Education and Globalization Effects on Ethics

Introduction

Now we are living in the technological modern world. Science and Technology have a prominent role in the development of the any nation in the world. India is a developing country in the world. Indian economy is the fourth largest economy in the world. According to 2001 census the literacy rate of India is 64.84%. It is very less when compared to developed county in the world. The Planning Commission made a survey for finding out the number of persons below poverty line and estimated that 18.96% of the total peoples live below poverty line as of the year 1993-94. It is necessary to take care about poor and illiteracy.

ETHICS

Ethics is a major branch of philosophy, encompasses right conduct and good life. It is significantly broader than the common conception of analyzing right and wrong. A central aspect of ethics is "the good life", the life worth living or life that is satisfying, which is held by many philosophers to be more important than moral conduct. The major problem is the discovery of the **summum bonum**, the greatest good.

Ethics are related to institutions and rights. The Universal Declaration of Human Rights and human rights accordingly stem from ethics even if no moral grounds can be adduced. Yet moral grounds are to be found everywhere, including science. From the point where, in the name of ethics, science itself does not fall outside this domain, morals, similarly, do not lie outside the realm of ethics as ethics are a profoundly human, secular construction in so far as they represent a conscious choice or plan and a legal endeavour in terms of the law. The confusion that exists between rights and values on the one hand and between morals and ethics on the other lie at the heart of the debate on universal ethics, that is to say, universal ethics based on recognition of human rights.

Morals are linked to the very definition of ethics. Moral principles are extremely diverse. As it happens, morals, historically speaking, have come to be increasingly connected with religion as human society has developed. Therefore, the moral debate has also become a religious one and, as many religious phenomena do not lie beyond the scope of laws, between majorities and minorities, nor the ideological choices involved, it may be difficult to find the same moral values for all societies. Moral values are very diverse. A number of values are universal.

In generally, values may be classified as;

- Personal Values
- Social Values
- Moral Values
- Spiritual Values and
- Behavioural values.

All these values are necessary for all types of persons in the society.

Why Ethics?

To enable young people to appreciate themselves and others, and to take greater responsibility for their actions and for the world around them.

Ethics and Economics

There are three ways in which ethics enters economics. First, economists have ethical values that help shape the way they do economics. This builds into the core of economic theory a particular view of how the economy does work and how it should work. Second, economic actors (consumers, workers, business owners) have ethical values that help shape their behavior. Third, economic institutions and policies impact people differentially and thus ethical evaluations, in addition to economic evaluations, are important.

Economists have Ethical Values

The issue of ethical value judgments in economics is at least as old as the John Neville Keynes argument which divided economics into three areas: positive (economic theory), normative (welfare economics), and practical (economic policy). The first deals with 'what is', the second with 'what ought to be', and the third with how to get from one to the other. Although the majority of economists admit that ethical values permeate welfare economics and economic policy, they proceed with some confidence in the belief that their work in pure and applied economic theory is ethically neutral. Methodologists studying the question are more cautious.

Ethics in the relationship between developed and less developed countries dictates that the developed countries treat the less developed countries fairly, aware of their disadvantaged economic position, and acknowledging that taking advantage of one's own economic power inevitably will hurt the poor within developing countries.

What is unethical?

- Economic institutions, rules, practices which disadvantage the poor will be viewed as unethical
- Ethical behavior requires "progressivity": the poor should benefit disproportionately
- Hypocritical behavior viewed as unethical
- Advisers who are not "fully honest" viewed as unethical

Ethics and Globalization

The world has been utterly transformed in recent years by a phenomenon affecting us all, what we call globalization. Although there was a time when it was possible for citizens of one country to think of themselves as owing no obligation to the people of other nations, admittedly that was long ago. Today national borders have less meaning as issues of trade, environment, and health, along with incredible technological advances of the last century, have left us with a legacy of connectedness we cannot ignore.

We know globalization involves complete economic liberalization, i.e., opening doors to big businesses. Multinational corporations are at the forefront. Globalization wants the governments around the world to create an environment that is as conducive as possible to its growth of business. Regional groupings like APEC, GATT and WTO are totally committed to the same goal. The connection between big businesses, governments and regional and international institutions to create an environment for globalization is not an accident. It has historic roots in colonization, and as such, the dominant forces behind globalization are based in the developed world. Nonetheless, it would be wrong to describe globalization today as a replica of the Western colonial experience only. This is because one of the centers of power is based in Japan. Other centers of control in Northeast and Southeast Asia are emerging.

In reflecting on the good and bad sides of globalization we find that whatever good has come out of it is actually a by-product. The very motive, maximizing profit is responsible for its bad sides. So, globalization may well be one of the most serious challenges ever to the integrity of human civilization. Since society and culture hold some positive aspects it is important that it is not completely rejected. Ethics and moral standards should be injected into some economic activities as a short-term and medium-term strategy. The market should be regulated by ethical principles. The challenge is to devise ethical economically-sound policies built into the globalization process that are in keeping with values. I mean, the economic dimensions of globalization are not the only factors that need reconsidering. Culture should be guided by moral universal values whereby a strong ethic of restraint is within one culture is applied to prevent the dominance of another culture. The internationalization of the ethical values within the consciousness of the individual and the community could be the only hope for humanity. It is almost impossible to effectively censor all information through the Internet, satellite, etc. The individual who derives his/her value-system should be guided by time-honoured principles of what is right and wrong. Such individuals are the real antidotes to the bad effects of globalization.

Positive aspects of Globalization

- Foreign Direct Investment (FDI) has helped to reduce poverty by creating jobs and improving incomes.
- The expansion of trade and foreign investment has accelerated social mobility and strengthened the middle class.
- New communications and information technology have helped disseminate knowledge in many fields of study and disciplines.
- Communication is cheaper and easier. Costs of telephone calls as well as travel have fallen. This makes it easier to understand one another. Communities although heterogeneous, can be more cooperative now that are more means of understanding each other.
- Globalization makes it possible for humanity to have compassion for each other when calamities, natural or man-made, affect others.
- Issues such as human rights and public accountability are brought to the fore.
- The rights of women are highlighted and the problems many women face are now addressed.

Negative aspects of Globalization

- Environmental degradation due to unrestrained activities of multinational corporations whose sole aim is to multiply profits.
- Although poverty has been reduced to a certain extent, new economic disparities have been created. There are stark regional disparities in poverty.

- Basic necessities in life are set aside in favour of profits. Many developing countries have been occupied with facilitating foreign investment in industries that are lucrative to foreign markets and discarding the most fundamental needs of the people.
- Globalization aids the removal of national controls over cross-border financial flows. Dramatic outflows of capital from one country to another have caused havoc in some currencies, particularly in Southeast, and South Asia including Bangladesh.
- Advances in technology aggravated by the outflow of capital to low cost production sites in the developing countries has caused growing unemployment in the developed countries, which is an cause offence to human dignity.
- Globalization has popularized the consumer culture. Consumerism has given birth to materialism where people are more interested in what they have rather than the essential aspects of humanity.
- Global consumerism is now forming a homogeneous global culture where rich indigenous cultures of many developing countries are being replaced by cultures with vibrant economies.
- Formal education systems are emphasizing technical and managerial skills responding to market demands and leaving aside traditional academic subjects. This means that education is nothing more than acquiring specific skills and techniques to do business and less emphasis on development of social or basic sciences.
- Although the IT boom has given rise to an expanse of information there is a lot of information that is useless and meaningless causing people to be pre-occupied with unimportant things.
- Double standards are present in the human rights aspect of the present world where they are used as part of many governments' policy but only when it suits them.

Because of globalization we have some advantages and disadvantages. We are human beings. Take good things and leave bad things. The policies of some developed countries are not good for developing countries. The ethical value decreases day by day. The business person gives more important for profit only. Organizational ethics is very important.

Centre for Globalization

The Yale Center for the Study of Globalization uses a variety of means to explore globalization and promote the flow of ideas pertinent to our core issues. The activities organized by the YCSG are designed to interconnect in ways that will further the Center's mission and enable us to achieve our goals. It is necessary to establish this type of centre in our university also. In the modern generation also computer literacy is very low in our community. It is very sad thing that our students have no interest to learn computer education. It is very necessary in the scientific and technological world.

Inculcation Ethics though Education

Value education means inculcating in the children a sense of humanism, a deep concern for the well being of others and the nation. This can be accomplished only when we instill in the children a deep feeling of commitment to values that would build this country and bring back to the people pride in work that brings order, security and assured progress.

Value education has the capacity to transform a diseased mind into a very young, fresh, healthy, natural and attentive mind. The transformed mind is capable of higher sensitivity and a heightened level of perception this leads to fulfillment of the evolutionary role in man and in life By saying autobiography of good persons like Gandiji, Vivekananda, Ramakrishna Paramahamsa, Ramananda, Tagore and Sathya Sai Baba, we can easily inculcate values in the students and in the people. Thinking with love is truth Feeling with love is peace Acting with love is right conduct Understanding with love is non-violence -Sathya Sai. According the Sathya Sai Baba the following five values are necessary for students.

- Right Conduct
- Peace
- Truth

- Love
- Non-Violence

Gandhi's Values

In order to create new social order Gandhiji introduced Nai Talim in the year 1937, which is popularly known as Basic Education.

1. Truth
2. Non-violence
3. Freedom
4. Democracy
5. Sarva Dharma Samabhava
6. Equality
7. Self-realization
8. Purity of ends and means
9. Self-discipline
10. Suddhi

If there is no place for values education in the curriculum, we can inculcate values through other subjects like Social Sciences & Technology. Learning takes place through lesson plans based on practical, meaningful and fun activities using the five components of:

- **Stories** - about life, identity & relationships;
- **Quotations, poems and prayers**;
- **Songs and music**;
- **Silent sitting** - exercises leading to inner calm and peace;
- **Activities** e.g. drama, discussion, games, role play, community service, etc.

Conclusions

Swamy Vivekananda said *"We want that education by which character is formed, strength of mind is increased, the intellect is expanded, and by which one can stand on one's own feet"*. It is true. It is our Government duty to give such type of education for each and every student in the country. Through education only we can solve all types of problems. Through education it is easy to motivate people about Ethical value and Moral values and human rights. Education gives knowledge, strength and creativity. India is a fourth largest economy in the world. The youth population is also very high. By proper using of science & technology and human & natural resources India will become developed country in the world.

We must protect the forests for our children, grandchildren and children yet to be born. We must protect the forests for those who can't speak for themselves such as the birds, animals, fish and trees.

References

1. Amrtya Sen. 'On Ethics and Economics'.
2. Peter Singer. 'One World-The Ethics of Globalization', 2004.
3. Value Education in India, Usha Rai Negi, Editor, Published by association of Indian Universities, AIU House, 16 Kotla Mark, New Delhi – 110 002, 2000.
4. Value Education, Dr. Venkataiah, Editor, APH Publishing Corporation, 5, Ansari Road, Daryaganji, New Delhi – 110 002, First Edition, 1998.

13

Inculcation of Human Values Through Education

Introduction

"If human values take root in the educational system, the emerging individuals will have the following attributes: They will want peace & justice in a world that acknowledges the rule of law and in which no nation or individual need live in fear; Freedom and self reliance to be available to all; The dignity & work of every person to be recognized & safeguarded; All people to be given an opportunity to achieve their best in life; and They will seek equality before the law and the equality of opportunity for all" .....Sathya Sai.

Now we are living in the Modern, Scientific and Technological world. Science and Technology have brought enormous changes in the society. The attitudes of the people are also changes in the day to day life of human beings.

Man is a unique creation in this universe that under certain parameters is free to make his own destiny. Now, if man has to make his destiny, the question of values in life comes up. He has to think naturally as to what should be the guiding norms of life process. It is therefore clear that the guiding factors for man, which provide the prime motivating force behind his thought, emotion and action, have to be moral and spiritual. The socio-cultural and spiritual life of man has to bring peace, progress and welfare for both the individual and the society. This is precisely the reason why the modern society is worried about the deterioration of values.

Having diagnosed the present problem, we have to find the remedy for this situation before there is further deterioration of values in the wider interest of the mankind. With the help of Science (Exhibitions) and Technology (Print & Electronic Media and Mass Media) including social awareness programmes we can inculcate the values in the people.

Importance of Values

In today's multi-cultural and multi-racial society, with its changing social norms and expectations, it can be difficult for a young person to know what is right. To enable young people to appreciate themselves and others, and to take greater responsibility for their actions and for the world around them. Sri Sugunendra Tirtha Swamiji of Puthige Math has said that it is necessary to give importance to human values in the present era of globalization.

Classification of Values

In generally, values may be classified as;

- Personal Values
- Social Values
- Moral Values
- Spiritual Values and
- Behavioural values.

All these values are necessary for all types of persons in the society.

Inculcation of Values through Education

Thinking with love is truth Feeling with love is peace acting with love is right conduct Understanding with love is non-violence -Sathya Sai

According the Sathya Sai Baba the following five values are necessary for students.

- **Right Conduct**
- **Peace**
- **Truth**
- **Love**
- **Non-Violence**

These values are specific because they are in line with a human being's make up. They are also heavily interrelated (e.g. right conduct is action with love and according to conscience).These five values are inter-related and inherent in human beings, raising them above the level of the animal kingdom.

Right Conduct

Information is received through the five senses i.e. smell, taste sight, touch and hearing. When this information is referred to the conscience, the resulting action will be beneficial. Every action is preceded by thought. If the thought is consciously seen and noted, aims to help and is unselfish, the action will be good for oneself and others. If our mind is busy, or we are daydreaming, the action may be useless, clumsy or harmful to ourselves or others.

Right conduct is also concerned with how we look after and use our bodies. The body needs to careful maintenance to be strong, healthy and well co-coordinated to serve us in performing the tasks of life. Students need to understand the importance of exercise, such as gymnastics, yoga and sports combined with good rest. Good thoughts and good company (which includes everything imbibed by the five senses) are essential for healthy and well balanced development. Right conduct is taught through: Silent Sitting, Storytelling and Group Activities.

Truth

The desire to know truth has prompted mankind to ask some of the great questions such as: Who am I? What is the purpose of life? How can I know my inner self/ God/ the Creator of the universe? How can I live fully in the present moment?

Learning to speak the truth is a first and vital step in the formation of a strong character. Voicing an untruth is an anti-social act and causes confusion in the mind of both the speaker and listener and leads to anti-social behaviour. Telling lies hurts us as well as others in a subtle, but very real way.

One great distinction between humankind and the rest of the animal kingdom is the ability to choose how to behave, rather than just to follow the lower instincts (the law of the jungle). A human being is also able to recognize past, present and future and to take note of changes occurring over time.

A quotation used in the lesson to stimulate thought and questions may later come to mind to provide guidance and choice in a life situation. Short Term Pain for Long Term Gain: Choosing to refer to this higher level of awareness and to consciously exercise moderation in our behaviour leads to better health and greater contentment. The value of truth can also be taught through story telling which promotes curiosity, optimism, fairness to all and noble ideals. It also aids the understanding of the value of honest speech and self-analysis.

Love

Love is not an emotion, affected by the sub-conscious mind, but is a spontaneous, pure reaction from the heart.

It is the power of love which causes one person to wish happiness for another and take pleasure in their well-being. A beneficial energy (love) is directed towards the other person. As this energy flows through our own body first, it also enhances our own health.

It is the power of love which causes one person to wish happiness for another and take pleasure in their well-being. A beneficial energy (love) is directed towards the other person. As this energy flows through our own body first, it also enhances our own health. Love is unconditional, positive regard for the good of another. It is giving and unselfish. Love is essential if children are to grow up healthy in mind and body. Love is the unseen undercurrent binding all the four values.

When the mind is turned away from selfishness, the ‘heart’ opens, and love flows. Love is energy, not an emotion, and is inherent in every breath. It is the motive force of the physical body and is enhanced through breathing exercises. The component of group singing in the Programme promotes harmony, co-operation and joyfulness. In singing a child may experience the sweetness of love. Love may also be fostered through storytelling and activities which provide young people with the opportunity to care for other people, animals, plants and objects.

Values Related to Love

Non-Violence

For the non-violent person, the whole world is his family When the former four values are practiced (i.e. the conscious mind is keenly aware, love is flowing, there is peace and actions are right) life is lived without harming or violating anything else. It is the highest achievement of human living encompassing respect for all life -living in harmony with nature, not hurting by thought, word or deed.

Non-violence can be described as universal love. When truth is glimpsed through intuition, love is activated. Love is giving, rather than grasping and in allowing our stream of desires to subside, inner peace develops and right conduct is practiced. This results in nonviolence i.e. the non-violation of the natural laws which create harmony with the environment.

In working through the lessons that comprise these components, the importance of the triple partnership (Student, Teacher and Parents) for education becomes apparent:

- Teachers will inspire children in their schools, if they are value conscious adults
- Parents' example affects the conduct of their children, and
- Children when reaching a certain age need self-discipline to balance their generally natural exuberance.

Conclusions

According to our Indian tradition and culture teacher is the third God. He has a pivotal role in the process of teaching and learning. He is a guide, philosopher, mother, father, god, architecture and model. Education is the solution for all types of problems. With the help of education we can solve any types of problems in the society. Through education it is easy to inculcate values in the students and in the people. Without human values we can't survive in the world in the peaceful manner and we can't enjoy life. So give importance for human values.

References

1. National Institute of Child Health and Human Development. (2000). The National Reading Panel: Reports of the Subgroups.
2. Value Education in India, Usha Rai Negi, Editor, Published by association of Indian Universities, AIU House, 16 Kotla Mark, New Delhi – 110 002, 2000.
3. Value Education, Dr. Venkataiah, Editor, APH Publishing Corporation, 5, Ansari Road, Daryaganji, New Delhi – 110 002, First Edition, 1998.

14

Inculcation of Organizational Ethics in Management Students Through Education

If you want to build a ship, then don't drum up men to gather wood, give orders, and divide the work. Rather, teach them to yearn for the far and endless sea-Antoine de Saint-Exupery.

Introduction

India is a developing country. We have thousands years of tradition and culture. 'Unity in diversity' is the greatness of Indian culture. According to the latest World Developing Report of World Bank, Indian Economy is the fourth largest economy in the world. The population of India is 1,129,866,154 (July 2007 est.). The literacy of India is 61 %.(73% male and 48% female literacy) according to 2000 report. Adult literacy rate is 61.3% for the age group 15 years and above. Youth literacy rate is 76.4% (2000-2004) for the age group 15-24 years. There are 268.42 million illiterates in India (2000). The unemployment rate in India is 10.1% out of the total population (2004).

The Planning Commission made a survey for finding out the number of persons below poverty line and estimated that 18.96% of the total peoples live below poverty line as of the year 1993-94. It is necessary to take care about poverty and illiteracy. By minimizing poverty ratio and increasing literacy ratio, we will reach the developed country position in the future. Because of globalization it is easy for government to do these things with the help of corporate companies. Today they are participating seriously in social service activities. We have largest youth population in the world. It is necessary to take care about them. Then only they will become good citizens in the future.

Organizational Ethics

Organizational ethics is a tool that shapes an organization as a community. In every organization, there is something that works well, which can serve as a foundation for significant progress toward a desired future. Organizational ethics pays special attention to the best of an organization's past and present to ignite its collective imagination of what might be. It builds from what is working well now toward where the organization and its stakeholders truly desire to go. Organizational ethics sees an organization as a community to be valued and explored. It strives to quicken and intensify existing individual capabilities and organizational capacities, extend their number and scope, organize them so that their conflicts will be harmonized, and mobilize their energies of will and intellect to bring them to self-realization. Organizational integrity is the end sought. It is a dynamic state of being and process; it both shapes and improves. It is about moving the organization toward its guiding image of the future.

Organizational ethics is one of the most important, yet perhaps one of the most overlooked and misunderstood concepts in corporate America and schools of business. Organizational ethics initiatives have not been effectively implemented by many corporations, and there is still much debate concerning the usefulness of such initiatives in preventing ethical and legal misconduct. Simultaneously, business schools are attempting to teach courses and/or integrate organizational ethics into their curricula without general agreement about what should be taught, or how it should be taught. Ethics has been termed the study and philosophy of human conduct, with an emphasis on the determination of right and wrong.

For managers, ethics in the workplace refers to rules (standards, principles) governing the conduct of organization members. Most definitions of ethics relate rules to what is right or wrong in specific situations. For present purposes, and in simple terms, organizational ethics refers to generally accepted.

Importance of Organizational Ethics

As the speed of decision making in organizations increases we are becoming more dependent on our values to guide our judgments. Although rules are still important in guiding ethical decision making, they can also be a burden to developing timely and innovative responses.

On the other hand organizations have seldom had greater exposure to ethical risk. Contemporary organizations, and the products and services they produce are more complex and more likely to have unforeseen consequences in production, delivery, and consumption. When mistakes happen in an increasingly interdependent world the repercussions can be far reaching. Whether the issue is employee, consumer, or public safety, or fairness in the way we treat our stakeholders, organizations which are proactive in addressing ethical concerns are much better positioned to deal with problems once they arise. The benefits of being proactive are enormous: improvements in organizational reputation, stakeholder good will, employee recruitment and retention, organizational effectiveness, and cost savings associated with minimizing ethical mistakes.

Organizational ethics is important in developing ethical leadership. An individual's personal values and moral philosophies are but one factor in decision-making processes involving potential legal and ethical problems. True, moral rules can be related to a variety of situations in life, and some people do not distinguish everyday ethical issues from those that occur on the job. Of concern, however, is the application of rules in a work environment.

Employees with only limited work experience sometimes find themselves making decisions about product quality, advertising, pricing, hiring practices, and pollution control. The values that they bring to the organization may not provide specific guidelines for these complex decisions, especially when the realities of work objectives, group decision making, and legal issues come into play. Many ethics decisions are close calls. Years of experience in a particular industry may be required to know what is acceptable, and what is not acceptable.

Inculcation of Organizational Ethics in Management Students through Education

The development of any nation depends mainly on the standards of its educational institutions. Education is the most powerful and effective instrument for inducing radical changes in the behaviour of students. Education is a powerful instrument of national development-social, economic and cultural. The teacher occupies pivotal position in the system of education. Teaching has been one of the oldest and most respected professions in the world.

Education is the process of instruction aimed at the all round development of boys and girls. Education dispels ignorance. It is the only wealth that cannot be robbed. Learning includes the moral values and the improvement of character and the methods to increase the strength of mind.

In this era of global economy, education has emerged as significant important factor of economic development. The general opinion is that countries at which invest more on education will have higher growth rates of national economy since educated people may provide more productivities. Therefore, many people tend to seek sophisticated and excellent education in order to obtain technically competent. However, the current concern is that the ethical behaviour of business has become a major issue in the workplace. The major reason of this concern is that some educated people have deficient in understanding their responsibilities in managing a company and interacting in society. The illustrations of this include political and business scandals, sexual harassment. It is necessary to overcome these things. With the help of moral and ethical education, it is possible to change the behaviour of the management students (any type of students).

We know *'today's children are tomorrow's citizens'*. In the same manner today's management students are tomorrow's managers, executive officers, policy makers and professors. By inculcating organizational ethics through education, the management students will become good citizens in the future. Then, India will become developed county in the world. Value and Ethics oriented education is necessary for management students. It is better if there is any separate ethics subject in the curriculum.

The six ethical decision-making steps are as follows: Issue clarification, Stakeholder analysis, Values identification, Issue resolution, Addressing objections, and Resolution implementation. Social responsibility is critical for organization's to succeed ethically and to be seen as good corporate citizens.

The organizational ethics programs are recommended by

- The World Bank
- The Organization for Economic Cooperation and Development
- The U. S. Federal Sentencing Guidelines
- The Public Service of Canada's Modern Management Program

Excellent ethics programs contain the following characteristics in one form or another

- Goals clear and linked to a realistic time-frame.
- Finances, other indicators of support
- Well-planned design, with ethics in mind
- Relevance for employees' work, linking the desired goals to the work
- Ethical program consistency and accountability
- Measurable outcomes with documentation

Through Organizational Ethics education it is easy to give answers to the following questions

- How to design a comprehensive and successful ethics program tailored to your organizational environment?
- How to avoid common pitfalls in designing and sustaining ethics programs?
- How to measure program effectiveness and conduct social audits?

- How leaders and managers can shape and sustain organizational ethical culture?
- How to recognize ethical problems and apply situation specific ethical decision making tools to resolve such problems?
- How to develop customized ethical awareness sessions for employees, managers and different communities of practice?
- How to align the organization with ethical initiatives?
- How to identify and reduce ethical risks?
- What are the sources and differences in personal, cultural, and organizational ethical values?
- What employees value and why some ethics programs are counterproductive?

Stages of Moral Development

Stages of Moral Development have been proposed by Lawrence Kohlberg. Kohlberg contended that different people make different decisions when confronted with similar ethical situations because they are at different stages of what he termed cognitive moral development (Kohlberg 1969). He believed that people progress through the following three stages:

- The pre-conventional stage of moral development, in which individuals focus on their own needs and desires.
- The conventional stage of moral development, in which individuals focus on group-centered values and conforming to expectations.
- The principled stage of moral development, in which individuals are concerned with upholding the basic rights, values, and rules of society.

Conclusions

There is no universal agreement on the correct moral philosophy to use in resolving ethical and legal issues in the workplace. Moreover, research suggests that employees may apply different moral philosophies in different decision situations (Fraedrich and Ferrell 1992). And, depending on the situation, people may even change their value structure or moral philosophy when making decisions.

Individuals make decisions under pressure and may later feel their decisions were less than acceptable, but they may not be able to change the consequences of their decisions.

Education is a solution for all types of problems in the society. Through education it is easy to motivate any type of person in the society. By inculcating organizational ethics in the curriculum of management students, we can get a lot of change in the behaviour of the management students in the society. Write valuable quotations in the campus of companies and colleges.

References

1. Charlotte McDaniel(2004), 'Organizational Ethics-Research and Ethical Environment' Ashgate Publishing Ltd
2. *Economic Survey 2004-05*, Economic Division, Ministry of Finance, Government of India, quoting UNDP Human Development Report 2004.
3. National Institute of Child Health and Human Development (2000). The National Reading Panel: Reports of the Subgroups.
4. Robert Allen Peterson, O. C. Ferrell, 'Business Ethics: New Challenges for Business Schools and Corporate Leaders.
5. UNESCO Institute for Statistics: Literacy rates, youth (15-24) and adult (15+), by region and gender (September 2006 Assessment).

15

Poverty, Education and Health in India

Introduction

Poverty is hunger. Poverty is lack of shelter. Poverty is being sick and not being able to see a doctor. Poverty is not having access to school and not knowing how to read. Poverty is not having a job, is fear for the future, living one day at a time. Poverty is losing a child to illness brought about by unclean water. Poverty is powerlessness, lack of representation and freedom. Education and Health are two faces of an Economic Growth coin. Through education it is possible to minimize or eliminate poverty in the society with good health.

Poverty and Its Reduction in India

Poverty eradication has been a key objective of India's development strategy. Both economic growth and the specific target of poverty eradication have been tied together as major development tools (Gupta, 1995). 'Growth with social justice' has been the main strategy of development since the beginning of the 1970s, though in recent years the relative focus tends to shift in favour of growth. 'Balancing of economic growth and social development' has been a difficult challenge. Along with strategies for growth a large number of poverty alleviation programmes have been launched, some of which originated in the 1960s.

Table-1: Poverty Line in India

Poverty Line in India (Rs per capita per month)		
Year	**Rural**	**Urban**
1973-74	49.63	56.76
1983-84	89.50	115.65
1993-94	205.84	281.35
1999-200	327.56	454.11
2005-06	365.00	580.00

Table-2: Incidence of Poverty in India

Incidence of Poverty in India (Population below poverty line)						
	Rural		**Urban**		**Total**	**No. of People**
	%	No (mln)	%	No (mln)	%	No (mln)
1970-71	57.30	251.70	45.90	50.10	55.10	301.80
1983-84	45.65	251.90	44.79	70.90	44.48	322.89
1987-88	39.10	231.40	40.10	78.70	39.30	310.10
1993-94	32.27	244.03	32.26	76.33	35.97	320.36
1999-2000	27.89	193.27	23.62	67.01	26.10	260.25

Source: National Human Development Report 2001 (New Delhi: Government of India, Planning Commission, 2001).

According to government estimates, in 2007 there were nearly 220.1 million people living below the poverty line. Nearly 21.1% of the entire rural population and 15% of the urban population of India exists in this difficult physical and financial predicament.

India has made significant progress in reduction in poverty over the years. The percentage of population below the poverty line has declined from 55 per cent in 1970-71 to 26 per cent by 1999-2000. But still 260 million people are estimated to be living below the poverty line – 193 million in rural areas and 67 million in urban areas, some of whom may have been living in 'chronic poverty' in 1999-2000. During the 30 year period, i.e., between 1971 and 1999-2000, in absolute numbers the number of people in poverty could be reduced by a meager 40 million. Increase in population has been a big hindrance to several development efforts, including to the poverty alleviation programmes. It is important to note, according to these official estimates, that a substantial decline in the number of poor has happened only between 1993-94 and 1999-2000.

Programmes launched to reduce poverty

- Integrated rural development programmes that include provision of subsidy and bank credit for productive employment opportunities
- Training rural youth for self employment (TRYSEM)
- Development of Women and Children in Rural Areas (DWACRA)
- Supply of Improved Toolkits to Rural Artisans
- Drought Prone Area Programme
- Self employment and Wage employment programmes
- Creation of Rural Infrastructure (roads, etc.,) for employment generation
- Employment assurance schemes,
- Social Security programmes – national social assistance programme – that include old age pension scheme, family and maternity benefit schemes, food and nutrition security, public distribution system etc
- Land reforms

HEALTH

"If wealth is lost nothing is lost

If health is lost something is lost

If character is lost everything is lost" - M. K. Gandhi.

Approximately 1.2 billion people in the world live in extreme poverty (less than one dollar per day). Poverty creates ill-health because it forces people to live in environments that make them sick, without decent shelter, clean water or adequate sanitation. The total health expenditure in India for the year 2001-02 was Rs.

1,057,341 million, which accounted for 4.6 per cent of its gross domestic product. As a proportion to total health expenditure, public expenditure constituted 20.3 per cent, private sector expenditure 77.4 and external support 2.3 per cent. Health care provider data reveal that 70 per cent of the financial resources is flowing to health care providers in the for profit private sector. Another 23 per cent of resources are spent on public providers of health care services.

Table-6: Per Capita Expenditure on Health in India

Per Capita Expenditure on Health in India (1993-1994 to 2003-2004)		
	Real	
Year	Health Expenditure (Rs. In Core)	Per Capita Expenditure
1993-1994	7938.36	89
1994-1995	7921.58	87
1995-1996	8521.14	91.82
1996-1997	8876.16	93.83
1997-1998	9772.64	101.38
1998-1999	10884.42	110.73
1999-2000	12068.52	120.56
2000-2001	12078.79	118.54
2001-2002	11795.52	113.75
2002-2003	12790.28	121.23
2003-2004	13091.7	122.01

(**Source:** Planning Commission, Govt. of India)

The Indian Finance Minister said in his Budget 2007-08 speech, all districts to complete preparation of District Health Action Plans by March 2007; major emphasis to be on mother and child care and on prevention and treatment of communicable diseases; convergence sought to be achieved among various programmes such as immunization, ante natal care, nutrition and sanitation through Monthly Health Days (MHD) organised at Anganwadi centers; 320,000 Associated Social Health Activists (ASHAs) recruited with over 200,000 given orientation training; 90,000 link workers selected by the States; AYUSH systems being mainstreamed into health delivery system at all levels; increase in allocation for NRHM from Rs.8,207 crore to Rs.9,947 crore.

Education

"Economic development naturally makes growing demands on human resources and in a democratic set-up it calls for values and attitudes in the building up of which the quality of education is an important element" (Government of India, 1956, p. 500).

"Education is the most important single factor in achieving rapid economic development and technological progress ... in all branches of national life education becomes the focal point of planned development" (Government of India, 1961, p. 573).

The State shall endeavour to provide, within a period of ten years from the commencement of this Constitution, for free and compulsory education for all children until they complete the age of fourteen years. (Article- 45).

The role of education in development has been recognised ever since the days of Plato. Education, Plato believed, is indispensable to the economic health of a good society, for education makes citizens 'reasonable men'. Since education has high economic value, Plato argued that a considerable part of the community's wealth must be invested in education. Major contribution to the discussion on the relationship between education and economic growth was made first by Adam Smith, followed by a long honourable tradition of classical and neo-classical economists until Alfred Marshall (1890) who emphasised that "the most valuable of all capital is that invested in human beings". However, "in line with the biased postwar approach it was largely forgotten" (Myrdal, 1968, p. 167), and no systematic study on the contribution of education to economic growth could be found in the literature, until Schultz's (1961) Presidential Address to the American Economic Association in 1960, which created what is later aptly described as "human investment revolution in economic thought" (Bowman, 1966). Schultz's pioneering research followed by a mammoth growth of research in the area of Economics of Education, and the untiring research has clearly established that education is not merely a consumption activity, but for the most part an investment. It leads to the formation of human capital, comparable to physical capital, making a significant contribution to economic growth.

Synchronising with the human investment revolution in economic thought, many countries around the world, and more particularly the newly independent developing countries expanded their educational systems and made heavy investments in education. The rates of growth of educational systems in many countries exceed the rates of economic growth. This is not surprising, as "during the process of economic modernisation the rate of increase in human capital is higher than that of reproducible physical capital" (Schultz, 1986, p. 5). India stands as an outstanding classic example of massive expansion of educational systems among the third world countries. In the post-independent India, particularly since the inception of the plan era (since 1951), an educational explosion has taken place, which may be described as an "educational miracle". The 'miracle' is particularly important when one examines in the context of the colonial legacy.

The 73rd and the 74th amendments to the Constitution had placed greater role on local bodies on the development of education, among others. Elementary education has been made a fundamental right with the 86th amendment to the Constitution in 2002. Several foreign aided projects have been launched in primary education since the mid-1990s. Some of these efforts, including decentralization, specifically aimed at not only improving the education situation, but also targeted at reducing poverty and empowerment of the poor.

Table -3: Growth of Education in India

Growth of Education in India					
Year	Primary	Upper Primary	Secondary & Higher Secondary	Higher: University	Higher: Colleges
Institutions					
1950-51	209,671	13,596	7,416	27	578
1960-61	330,399	49,663	17,329	45	1,819
1970-71	408,378	90,621	37,051	82	3,277
1980-81	494,503	118,555	51,573	101	6,943
1990-91	560,965	151,456	79,796	184	5,748
2000-01*	638,738	206,269	126,047	254	10,152
2002-03*	651,382	245,274	137,207	304	15,000
Enrolment		in 10 million		in thousands	

1950-51	1.92	0.31	0.15	174
1960-61	3.50	0.67	0.34	557
1970-71	5.70	1.33	0.76	1956
1980-81	7.38	2.07	1.10	2752
1990-91	9.74	3.40	1.91	4924
2000-01*	11.38	4.28	2.76	8399
2002-03*	12.24	4.69	3.32	9516
Teachers (in thousands)				
1950-51	538	86	127	24
1960-61	742	345	296	62
1970-71	1060	638	629	190
1980-81	1363	851	926	244
1990-91	1616	1073	1334	271
2000-01*	1896	1326	1761	350
2001-02*	1928	1488	1777	

* Provisional

Source: Selected Educational Statistics 2001-2002; Annual Report, UGC 2002-03 for enrolment and teachers in higher education.

The above table shows the growth of Education in India from 1950 to 2003.

Table-5: Educational Level in India

S.No.	India/ State	Educational Level	Population Persons	 Males	 Females
1	India	Total	1,028,610,328	532,156,772	496,453,556
2	India	Illiterate	467,922,531	195,623,056	272,299,475
3	India	Literate	560,687,797	336,533,716	224,154,081
4	India	Literate but below Matric/secondary	381,798,166	220,614,002	161,184,164
5	India	Matric/secondary but below graduate	117,432,082	76,056,459	41,375,623
6	India	Technical diploma or certificate not equal to degree	3,666,680	2,900,839	765,841
7	India	Graduate and above other than technical degree	32,615,751	21,891,181	10,724,570
8	India	Technical degree or diploma equal to degree or post-graduate degree	5,054,396	3,642,127	1,412,269

Source: Census of India 2001.

Major Issues

- 27.5 per cent of Indians live below the national income poverty line
- More than 60 per cent of women are chronically poor, as are 43 per cent of Scheduled Tribes and 36 per cent of Scheduled Caste groups
- More than 90 per cent of the overall workforce is employed in the informal economy; for women, it is even higher, at 96 per cent
- 48.6 per cent of farmer households are in debt, and only 27 per cent access formal credit
- 296 million people are illiterate and 233 million are undernourished, particularly children younger than age 3.
- Educational expenses formed 3% of total consumer expenditure in rural India and 5% in urban India.
- Post-elementary education makes a significant contribution to reduction in absolute as well as relative poverty.
- Medical expenses formed 7% of total consumer expenditure in rural India and 5% in urban India.
- In 2004-05, 5% of the Indian rural population belonged to households with monthly per capita consumer expenditure (MPCE) in the range "Rs.0-235", that is, spending less than Rs.8 per person per day on consumption.
- Another 5% of the Indian rural population belonged to households with monthly per capita expenditure in the range "Rs.235-270", that is, spending about Rs.8-9 per person per day on consumption.
- Maternal mortality – an indicator not only of the quality of maternal health care services but also of the general level of empowerment of women – stands at 301 per 100,000 live births, compared to a target of 108 per 100,000.

Source: Poverty Estimates for 2004-2005, Government of India, NSS 61st round 2004-05, Government of India, New Delhi.

Poverty, Health, Education and Development

Poverty is a state of deprivation. In absolute terms it reflects the inability of an individual to satisfy certain basic minimum needs for a sustained healthy and a reasonably productive living. The proportion of population not able to attain the specified level of expenditure is then segregated as poor. Poverty is hunger. Poverty is lack of shelter. Poverty is being sick and not being able to see a doctor. Poverty is not being able to school and not knowing how to read.

In India Rao (1964; see also Rao, 1970) and the Education Commission (1966) are first of their kind to have emphasized the links between education and development. Though the earlier research in India and abroad concentrated more on the role of education in economic growth, the impact of education on poverty and well being of the masses was also clearly recognized and of late this began receiving more serious attention in the wider framework of human development.

Available research in the last couple of decades (e.g., Fields, 1980a, 1980b; Tilak, 1978, 1986, 1989a, 1994) clearly shows that education and poverty are inversely related: the higher the level of education of the population, the lower would be the proportion of poor people in the total population, as education imparts knowledge and skills that are associated with higher wages.

Economics of Education is abundant with studies that firmly established the correlation between education and earnings – earnings rising with increase in education levels, not rarely but almost universally and quite steeply and systematically, in case of the general population and also of sub-groups of the population – males, females, rural, urban, socially backward sections, etc. (Psacharopoulos and Tilak, 1992). As Blaug (1972) noted, the universality of this relationship is well recognized beyond doubt.

In addition to this direct effect of education, the effect of education on poverty could be indirect through its fulfillment of basic needs like better utilization of health facilities, shelter, water and sanitation, and its effects on behaviour of women on decisions relating to fertility, family welfare and health etc., (Noor, 1980; Cochrane, 1988; Jeffery and Basu, 1996) which in turn enhance the productivity of the people and yield higher wages, taking them above the poverty line.

The relationship between health and poverty or health and development is complex multifaceted and multidirectional. Poverty in its various dimensions could be a manifestation, as well as a determinant of an individual's health. In its most basic from – as a state of food deprivation and nutritional inadequacy – poverty has a direct bearing of the morbidity and longevity of people. How does health relate to development? The first point to is that the enhancement of health is a constitute part of development; second given other things good health and economic prosperity tend to support each other. Better health, also contributes directly to economic growth as it reduces production losses on account of illness of workers or, potentially, also in terms of higher work productivity for healthy workers.

Improvements in educational attainments have invariably been accompanied by improvement in health and longevity of the population and in their economic well-being. Educated people are likely to be more productive and hence better-off. They are also likely to contribute more to a country's economic growth. Lack of education robs an individual of a full life. It also robs society of a foundation for sustainable development because education is critical to improving health, nutrition and productivity. Income poverty may pull children from out of the school system, thus denying them the opportunity of participating in school education, even at the basic level, as evidenced in the third world country situations.

It is known fact that illiteracy, one of the key factors contributing to poverty is a fall out of the poor participation of children in elementary education. Some of the main issues of human deprivation are hunger, illiteracy, epidemics and the lack of health services or safe water. Improving health outcomes not only improves well-being but also increases income – earning potential. Increasing education not only improves well-being-it also leads to better health outcomes and to higher incomes. Health, along with education, is seen as one of the key ultimate goals of development and increasingly seen as a dimension of poverty in its own right.

Suggestions and Conclusions

India is a developing country. We have lot of human resources after China. In the recent years we find that economic growth is also high. Still we are facing poverty, ill health and illiteracy. Health and Education are two faces of an economic growth coin. Though growth tends to reduce poverty, significant improvements in health status are also necessary for poverty to decrease. Also, economic growth and health status are positively correlated and have a two-way relationship, suggesting that better health enhances growth by improving productivity and higher growth allows better human capital formation. Health expenditure is an important determinant of both higher growth and better health status, and is therefore a key tool available to policy-makers. Among other exogenous variables, literacy and industrialization seem to improve both health outcomes and growth, and to reduce poverty.

Reference

1. Barro, R. (1996), "Health and Economic Growth", Annex I of the Convocatoria para propuestas de investigation sober Inversion en Saludy Crecimiento Economic de la Organizacion Pan-American de la Salud.
2. Census of India 2001, Government of India, New Delhi.
3. Dev, S. Mahendra and Jos Mooij (2002), "Social Sector Expenditure in the 1990s: An Analysis of Central and State Budget", Economic and Political Weekly, Vol. 37 No. 9, March 2.
4. Indrani Gupta and Arup Mitra (2004). "Economic Growth, Health and Poverty: An Exploratory Study for India" Overseas Development Institute.
5. Janadyala B. G. Tilak (2005). "Post-Elementary Education, Poverty and Development in India".
6. NSS 61st round 2004-05, Government of India, New Delhi.
7. Planning Commission of India-2008, Government of India, New Delhi.

8. Poverty Estimates for 2004-05, Government of India, New Delhi.
9. Saravalingam, A., Siva Kuma, M. (2004). "A Study about Poverty, Health, Education and Human Development in India".

16

Role of Teachers in Building Modern India

Introduction

Education means an all round drawing out of the best in child and man – body, mind and spirit...... Mahatma Gandhi.

The development of any nation depends mainly on the standards of its educational institutions. Education is the most powerful and effective instrument for inducing radical changes in the behaviour of students. Education is a powerful instrument of national development-social, economic and cultural. The teacher occupies pivotal position in the system of education. Teaching has been one of the oldest and most respected professions in the world.

According to Indians Teacher is the third god. Today we are living in the technological world. India developed in the fields of Science and Technology. It is possible to know each and everything within seconds throughout the world. Today's children are tomorrow's citizens. It is necessary to give quality and value based education to each and every student in the society. Then only all children will become good citizens in the future.

About India

India is a developing country. We have thousands years of tradition and culture. 'Unity in diversity' is the greatness of Indian culture. According to the latest World Developing Report of World Bank, Indian Economy is the fourth largest economy in the world. The **population** of India is **1,129,866,154** (July 2007 est.). The **literacy** of India is **61 %.(** 73% male and 48% female literacy) according to 2000 report. **Adult literacy** rate is **61.3%** for the age group 15 years and above. **Youth literacy** rate is **76.4%** (2000-2004) for the age group 15-24 years. There are **268.42 million illiterates** in India (2000). The **unemployment** rate in India is **10.1%** out of the total population (2004). The Planning Commission made a survey for finding out the number of persons **below poverty line** and estimated that **18.96%** of the total peoples live below poverty line as of the year 1993-94.

Indian Education System and Teacher

"Of all the different factors which influence the quality of education and its contribution to national development; the quality, competence and character of teachers are undoubtedly the most significant......."Kothari Education Commission (1964-66)

Mahatma Gandhi in his debate with British Parliamentarian Philip Hartog in 1931 is said to have described the indigenous Indian education system as 'The Beautiful Tree'. And the root of this beautiful tree of Indian education was the nourishing relationship between the teacher and the student. The acharya or the guru was not merely an instrument for transmission of knowledge, he /she was an all-pervasive influence on the life and character of the student. The guru was a father, mother, friend, counsellor, motivator, role model and spiritual guide, all rolled into one.

Teacher plays an important role in the field of education. Today's education is child-centered. But the child centered education cannot be successful without the teacher. The teacher is the maker of the future of the child. The children of today are the citizens and leaders of tomorrow. It means that the teacher is the maker of the leaders or rulers of the nation.

Like a master architect, the teacher has a very thorough knowledge of all the details essential to his work. He knows the real nature of the objectives of his work and the ends to be attained. Besides an understanding of the nature of the outcomes desired, he understands the nature of the different kinds of learning experiences necessary to attain them. He also knows how to organize and direct such learning experiences. Further, to do this satisfactorily he knows how to use effectively the best teaching techniques and devices available. He guides learning and gives suggestions and directions to the students in order to make them able to attain the desired knowledge. In any system of education, teacher has a pivotal role to play. The responsibility of making the education work successful lies with the teacher. He is undoubtedly the key point in all educational programmes and the quality of education depends on the quality of teachers.

The teacher today is required to be able to cope up with the aspirations of rising generations of youth and the changing needs of the society and has to play a multidimensional role.

Teaching has always been considered to be essential for preservation and development of all intellectual life. Among other agencies, teachers are considered to be the major transmitters of accumulated knowledge and experience of human race from one generation to the next. The very foundation of the social order rests on citizens who are taught and trained in the classroom with or without walls. Teachers thus, determine to a great extent the character and destination of a nation.

Values and Teacher

Now we are living in modern and technological world. A lot of changcs arc occurring in thc day to day lifc of human bcings bccausc of Science and Technology. Because of westernization a lot of changes are occurring in the tradition and culture of the today people. Teacher has a pivotal role to preserve all these things and he is the first person to preserve all these things.

Values are the guiding principles, decisive in day to day behaviours as also in critical life situations. Values are a set of principles or standards of behaviour. Values are regarded desirable, important and held in high esteem by a particular society in which a person lives. Thus values give meaning and strength to a person with character by occupying a central place in his life. Values reflect one's personal attitudes and judgments, decisions and choices, behaviour and relationships, dreams and vision. They influence our thoughts, feelings and actions. They guide us to do the right things.

Value education means inculcating in the children a sense of humanism, a deep concern for the well being of others and the nation. This can be accomplished only when we instill in the children a deep feeling of commitment to values that would build this country and bring back to the people pride in work that brings order, security and assured progress.

Through value education, we like to develop the social, moral, aesthetic and spiritual sides of a person which are often undermined in formal education. Value education teaches us to preserve whatever is good and worthwhile in what we have inherited from our culture. It helps us to respect the attitude and behaviour of those who differ from us. Value education does not mean value imposition or indoctrination.

Values are the guiding principles of life which are conductive to all round development. They give direction and firmness to life and bring joy, satisfaction and peace of life. Values are like the rails that keep a train on the track and help it move smoothly, quickly and with direction. They bring qualities to life.

Role of Teacher in Building Modern India

The role of the modern teacher is not confined to teaching alone. He/she is expected to participate in the development programmes of the community life. The question arises as to how this could be integrated with the teacher education programmes. Mudaliar Commission (1952-53) Report stated rightly, "we are convinced that the most important factor in the contemplated education reconstruction is the teacher-his personal qualities, his educational qualifications, his professional training and the place that he occupies in the school as well as in the community". On similar lines Kothari Commission (1964-66) stated that, "Nothing is more important than securing a sufficient supply of high quality recruits to the teaching profession, providing them with the best possible professional preparation and creating satisfactory conditions of work in which they can be fully effective".

The importance of the teachers in the Educational Programme of a country is too great. The greatness of a country does not depend on lofty buildings, gigantic projects and large armies, but on the quality of its citizens. If a nation has young men of sterling character and unimpeachable patriotism, she is found to make rapid progress in all fields. Young men are entrusted to the care of the teacher and it is therefore the sacred duty of the teacher to impart the right type of knowledge and make them good citizens. It is the teacher who impresses his children with his personality.

The teacher, a national integrator as he is, is the backbone of society, particularly so in the remote villages. He stands as an outstanding figure among the illiterate and semi-literate families. He is their friend, Philosopher and guide. The teacher actively shares the responsibility of reconstructing a social order, with all the cherished values and traditional beliefs, which are being eroded by the surge of new ideals and practices. He acts as a social reformer and counsellor to the community.

Conclusion

According to *Swami Vivekananda* "We want that education by which character is formed, strength of mind is increased, and the intellect is expanded, and by which one can stand on one's own feet.

1. Technology based 'Teacher Education' is necessary for trainee teachers in India.
2. Give more importance for Teachers after Doctors.
3. Education is the solution for all types of problems. So, it is necessary to educate all types of persons in the society.
4. Advanced Technology and Lab facility is necessary for all types of teachers.

Reference

1. Kothari Education commission (1964-66): It is also known as. "Indian Education Commission", with Kothari as its chairman, Report P.46.

2. Mathews, V.S: From 'An Evaluative Study of Primary School Teacher Education Programme in Andhra Pradesh" by K.Chandra Sekhar (2000) unpublished Ph.D. thesis, Dept. of Education, S.V.University, Tirupati, India, P.2.

3. Mehrotra, R.N. (2006): "Teacher and Teaching" – A trend report in Sixth Survey of Educational Research (1993-2000) volume-I. PP.13-53; published by NCERT, Sri Aurobindo Marg, New Delhi-110016; May 2006.

4. Mudaliar Commission 91952-53): It is also known as 'Secondary Education Commission' headed by Mudaliar.

5. Saxena N.R., Mishra B.K., Mohanthy R.K. 'Teacher Education', Surya Publications, Near Govt. Inter College, Meerut, First Edition, 1998.

6. Secondary Education Commission (1952-53): It is also known as 'Mudaliar Commission' headed by Mudaliar.

7. Value Education in India, Usha Rai Negi, Editor, Published by association of Indian Universities, AIU House, 16 Kotla Mark, New Delhi – 110 002, 2000.

8. Value Education, Dr. Venkataiah, Editor, APH Publishing Corporation, 5, Ansari Road, Daryaganji, New Delhi – 110 002, First Edition, 1998.

17

Educational School Psychology in the Pursuit of Human Well-being

Introduction

Now we are living in the technological modern world. With the help of science and technology we have developed in all fields. India is a developing country. We have lot of human resources after China. But the literacy rate is very low when compared to other developed and developing countries in the world. India is a rich country, but Indians are poor. With the help of science and technology and by utilizing all sources in the proper way it is possible to India to become a developed country in the world. In the modern world people living with high tension. The student in schools and colleges are also living with high tension because of heavy competitions. It is necessary to introduce psychology as a general subject in all the classes both at school and college levels. Yoga and meditation is also necessary for each and every one in the world.

Definition of Education

- *Education is the learning of human souls to what is best, and making what is best out of them? - John Ruskin*

- *Education is a weapon, whose effect depends on who holds it is his hands and at whom it is aimed.- Joseph Stalin*

The word **education** is derived from the **Latin educare**, meaning **"to raise", "to bring up", "to train", "to rear"**. Education means the gradual process of acquiring knowledge. Education is a preparation for life. Education is also defined as the profession of teaching (especially at a school or college or university).

Importance of Education

India is a union comprised of twenty eight states and seven Territories. The Constitution provides directives regarding the development of education throughout the country. The areas in which the respective central and state governments have domain have been identified in the Constitution as the *central* list, *state* list and *concurrent* list. Until the late 1970s, school education had been on the *state* list, which meant that states had the final say in the management of their respective school systems. However, in 1976, education was transferred to the *concurrent* list through a constitutional amendment, the objective being to promote meaningful educational partnerships between the central and state governments. Today, the central government establishes broad education policies for school curricula development and management practices. These serve as guidelines for the states.

Generally, at the start of a very young age, children learn to develop and use their mental, moral and physical powers, which they acquire through various types of education. Education is commonly referred to as the process of learning and obtaining knowledge at school, in a form of formal education. However, the process of education does not only start when a child first attends school. Education begins at home. One does not only acquire knowledge from a teacher; one can learn and receive knowledge from a parent, family member and even an acquaintance. In almost all societies, attending school and receiving an education is extremely vital and necessary if one wants to achieve success.

Educational Psychology

Educational psychology is the study of how humans learn in educational settings, the effectiveness of educational interventions, the psychology of teaching, and the social psychology of schools as organizations. Although the terms "educational psychology" and "school psychology" are often used interchangeably, researchers and theorists are likely to be identified as educational psychologists, whereas practitioners in schools or school-related settings are identified as school psychologists. Educational psychology is concerned with the processes of educational attainment among the general population and sub-populations such as gifted children and those subject to specific disabilities

Educational psychology can in part be understood through its relationship with other disciplines. It is informed primarily by psychology, bearing a relationship to that discipline analogous to the relationship between medicine and biology. Educational psychology in turn informs a wide range of specialities within educational studies, including instructional design, educational technology, curriculum development, organizational learning, special education and classroom management. Educational psychology both draws from and contributes to cognitive science and the learning sciences. In universities, departments of educational psychology are usually housed within faculties of education, possibly accounting for the lack of representation of educational psychology content in introductory psychology textbooks.

Uses of Educational Psychology

For finding Individual differences and Disabilities

Each person has an individual profile of characteristics, abilities and challenges that result from learning and development. These manifest as individual differences in intelligence, creativity, cognitive style, motivation, and the capacity to process information, communicate, and relate to others. The most prevalent disabilities found among school age children are attention-deficit hyperactivity disorder (ADHD), learning disability, dyslexia and speech disorder. Less common disabilities include mental retardation, hearing impairment, cerebral palsy, epilepsy, and blindness.

Although theories of intelligence have been discussed by philosophers since Plato, intelligence testing is an invention of educational psychology, and is coincident with the development of that discipline. Continuing debates about the nature of intelligence revolve on whether intelligence can be characterized by a single, scalar factor (Spearman's general intelligence), multiple factors (as in Sternberg's triarchic theory of intelligence and Gardner's theory of multiple intelligences), or whether it can be measured at all. In practice, standardized instruments such as the Stanford-Binet IQ test and the WISC are widely used in economically developed countries to identify children in need of individualized educational treatment. Children classified as gifted are often provided with accelerated or enriched programs. Children with identified deficits may be provided with enhanced education in specific skills such as phonological awareness.

For Social, Moral and Cognitive Development

To understand the characteristics of learners in childhood, adolescence, adulthood, and old age, educational psychology develops and applies theories of human development. Often cast as stages through which people pass as they mature, developmental theories describe changes in mental abilities (cognition), social roles, moral reasoning, and beliefs about the nature of knowledge.

For example, educational psychologists have researched the instructional applicability of Jean Piaget's theory of development, according to which children mature through four stages of cognitive capability. Piaget hypothesized that children are not capable of abstract logical thought until they are older than about 11 years, and therefore younger children need to be taught using concrete objects and examples. Researchers have found that transitions, such as from concrete to abstract logical thought, do not occur at the same time in all domains. A child may be able to think abstractly about mathematics, but remain limited to concrete thought when reasoning about human relationships. Perhaps Piaget's most enduring contribution is his insight that people actively construct their understanding through a self-regulatory process.

Piaget proposed a developmental theory of moral reasoning in which children progress from a naive understanding of morality based on behavior and outcomes to a more advanced understanding based on intentions. Piaget's views of moral development were elaborated by Kohlberg into a stage theory of moral development. There is evidence that the moral reasoning described in stage theories is not sufficient to account for moral behavior. For example, other factors such as modeling (as described by the social cognitive theory of morality) are required to explain bullying.

Developmental theories are sometimes presented not as shifts between qualitatively different stages, but as gradual increments on separate dimensions. Development of epistemological beliefs (beliefs about knowledge) has been described in terms of gradual changes in people's belief in: certainty and permanence of knowledge, fixedness of ability, and credibility of authorities such as teachers and experts. People develop more sophisticated beliefs about knowledge as they gain in education and maturity.

Psychology and Teacher

Teacher is a national builder. He has a power to change the world through education. According to our Indians teacher is a third god. Teacher plays a prominet role in the development of society. Educational Psychology is a main subject in teacher education at D.Ed., B.Ed., and M.Ed. levels. It is necessary for each and every teacher to know about psychology. Because it is necessary to know the behaviour of the students in the class. Teacher has different roles like father, advisor, councellor, administrator and well wisher. The future of any country is in the hands of teachers. So it is necessary to give importance for teacher education. So our government introduced psychology subject in teacher education curriculum. After undergoing the course, the student teacher.

1) Explains psychology and its relationship with Education.
2) Classifies different branches of psychology and explains their significance.
3) Explains the importance of heredity and environment and its influences in educational process.
4) Explains the different aspects of the development of the child.
5) Explains the growth and human beings and their behaviour.
6) Describes the individual aspects of the development of the child.

7) Explains the primary needs of the children.
8) Explains the secondary needs of the children.
9) Explains the theories of learning and the factors influencing learning.
10) Explains the concept of socialization.
11) Explains the different types of learning.
12) Understands the concept of motivation and the steps to be taken to motivate the children.
13) Explains attention and its uses.
14) Develops skill of observation, listening, responding and understanding.
15) Describes memory, remembering and forgetting and identifies conditions of good memory.
16) Describes the effects of different methods used for learning process.
17) Explains thinking process and its uses-perception, conception, apperception for different ages.
18) Explains the role of creativity and its development.
19) Explains the meaning of intelligence and understands the changing concept of intelligence.
20) Enhances personality development of pupils.
21) Describes the mental hygiene and mental health.
22) Understands exceptional children and their significance.
23) Practices guidance and counseling for school pupils.

Conclusion

Educational psychology is an application of the principles of psychology for effective learning and modification of behaviour on desirable dimensions. Knowledge of educational psychology makes a teacher effective in motivating the pupils in their learning. In short it is an inseparable part of strategy in education. Education gives knowledge, wealth and health. Education is a solution for all types of problems in the society. Through education only it is possible overall development of a person in the society. Through education it is easy to know about behavour of the students and persons in the society with the help of psychology. So it is necessary to study psychology all persons in the society in the modern world. Educational Psychology helps the overall development of the student.

References

1. Educational psychology a cognitive view by Asubel, D.P.
2. Element of educational psychology by Bhatia, H.R.
3. Educational psychology by Cole, E.C. and Bruce, W.F.
4. Psychology applied to teaching by Bichler, R.F.

18

Female Education in India-community Participation

INTRODUCTION

The development of any nation depends on its' standards of educational institutions. Education is the most important instrument for human resource development. Education of girls therefore, occupies top priority amongst various measures taken to improve the status of the girl child. Efforts have been made over the four and half decades of planned development to enroll more girls in schools to continue their education as long as possible. The National Policy on Education (NPE) envisages that education would be used as a strategy for achieving a basic change in the status of women. High priority has been accorded to primary school education in the various five years plans to fulfill the requirements under Article 45 of the constitution for universals, free and compulsory elementary education upto the age of 14 years. Recognizing the need for a literate population and provision of elementary education as a crucial input for nation building, the government's stand was reiterated in the NPE and the Programme of Action 1992, to work towards provision of education of satisfactory quality to all children up to 14 years.

Sarva Shiksha Abhiyan (Education for all) is a wonderful programme in the development of elementary education in India.

The government has resolved to make the right to free and compulsory elementary education a Fundamental Right and to enforce it through suitable statutory measures. Universalisation of Elementary Education (UEE) has been accepted as a national goal since 1950. In order to achieve the goal, concerted efforts have been made and as a result, the elementary education system in India has become one of the largest in the world. Universal access, universal retention and universal achievement are the broad parameters to achieve UEE.

FEMALE LITERACY IN INDIA

We got independence on 1947. After completing sixty years of independent also we can't reach 60 per cent of female literacy. It indicates that some more encouragement and importance are necessary towards female literacy programmes.

Table-1

LITERACY RATES (%AGE), 1951 TO 2004-05

Census year	Persons	Males	Females	Male-Female gap in literacy rate
1951	**18.33**	27.16	8.86	18.30
1961	**28.30**	40.40	15.35	25.05
1971	**34.45**	45.96	21.97	23.98
1981	**43.57**	56.38	29.76	26.62
1991	**52.21**	64.13	39.29	24.84
2001	**64.84**	75.26	53.67	21.59
2004-05*	**67.84**	77.00	57.00	20.00

- NSS 61st Round Survey Report No. 517, 2004-05.Page 24.

Literacy rate of female was 8.86 per cent in 1951 where as male literacy rate was 27.16 per cent in the same year. The rate of literacy gap between male and female was 18.30 per cent. After fifty years the literacy rate of female was 53.67 where as male literacy rate was 75.26 per cent. The rate of literacy gap between male and female was 21.59 per cent. The rate of literacy gap was increased from 18.30 in 1951 to 21.59 in 2001, i.e., 3.29 per cent of literacy gap was increased in the last fifty years. But in the case of female literacy rate, it was increased and increasing year by year.

ENROLMENT OF FEMALE STUDENTS (I-XII)

The enrolment of female students from Class I to Class XII was showed in the table-2.

Table-2

ENROLMENT BY STAGES OF SCHOOL EDUCATION ALL CATEGORIES OF STUDENTS 1950-51 TO 2005-06

(Figures in millions)

YEAR	Primary(I –V)			Middle/Upper Primary(VI-VIII)			Sec./Sr. Sec./Inter/ Pre-Degree(IX-XII)		
	Boys	Girls	Total	Boys	Girls	Total	Boys	Girls	Total
1950-51	13.8	5.4	**19.2**	2.6	0.5	**3.1**	1.3	0.2	**1.5**
1955-56	17.1	7.5	**24.6**	3.8	1.0	**4.8**	2.2	0.4	**2.6**
1960-61	23.6	11.4	**35.0**	5.1	1.6	**6.7**	2.7	0.7	**3.4**
1965-66	32.2	18.3	**50.5**	7.7	2.8	**10.5**	4.4	1.3	**5.7**
1970-71	35.7	21.3	**57.0**	9.4	3.9	**13.3**	5.7	1.9	**7.6**
1975-76	40.6	25.0	**65.6**	11.0	5.0	**16.0**	6.5	2.4	**8.9**
1980-81	45.3	28.5	**73.8**	13.9	6.8	**20.7**	7.6	3.4	**11.0**
1985-86	52.2	35.2	**87.4**	17.7	9.6	**27.1**	11.5	5.0	**16.5**
1990-91	57.0	40.4	**97.4**	21.5	12.5	**34.0**	12.8	6.3	**19.1**
1991-92	58.6	42.3	**100.9**	22.0	13.6	**35.6**	13.5	6.9	**20.4**
1992-93	57.9	41.7	**99.6**	21.2	12.9	**34.1**	13.6	6.9	**20.5**
1993-94	55.1	41.9	**97.0**	20.6	13.5	**34.1**	13.2	7.5	**20.7**
1994-95	60.0	45.1	**105.1**	22.1	14.3	**36.4**	14.2	7.9	**22.1**
1995-96	60.9	46.2	**107.1**	22.7	14.8	**37.5**	14.6	8.3	**22.9**
1996-97	61.4	46.8	**108.2**	22.9	15.2	**38.1**	15.3	8.7	**24.0**
1997-98	62.3	48.0	**110.3**	23.6	15.9	**39.5**	13.1	9.3	**25.4**
1998-99	62.7	49.0	**111.7**	23.9	16.5	**40.4**	16.6	10.1	**26.7**
1999-00	63.6	50.0	**113.6**	24.3	17.0	**41.3**	17.2	10.8	**28.0**
2000-01	64.0	49.8	**113.8**	25.3	17.5	**42.8**	19.9	10.7	**27.6**
2001-02	63.6	50.3	**113.9**	26.1	18.7	**44.8**	18.4	12.1	**30.5**
2002-03	65.1	57.3	**122.4**	26.3	20.6	**46.9**	19.5	13.7	**33.2**
2003-04	68.4	59.9	**128.3**	27.3	21.5	**48.7**	20.6	14.4	**35.0**
2004-05	69.7	61.1	**130.8**	28.5	22.7	**51.2**	21.7	15.4	**37.1**
2005-06	70.5	61.6	**132.1**	28.9	23.3	**52.2**	22.3	16.1	**38.4**

Source: Time Series of India-2007

In the year 1950-51 the enrolment of female student at primary level (class I-V) was 5.4 million; at middle and upper primary level (class VI-VIII) was 0.5 million and at secondary/senior secondary/ intermediate/pre-degree level was 0.2 million. From the above table we conclude that the enrolment of female students was increased year by year except 1992-93. In the year 2005-06 the female enrolment was 61.6 million at primary level (I-V); 23.3 million at middle and upper primary level and 16.1 million at secondary/senior secondary/intermediate/pre-degree level. It is necessary to take actions to increase enrolments of female students at middle and upper primary and intermediate levels.

PERCENTAGE OF GIRLS' ENROLMENT TO TOTAL ENROLMENT

The percentage of girls' enrolment to total enrolment was given in the table-3. The rate of girls' enrolment was increased year by year expect some years (2000-01, 2003-04, 2004-05 and 2005-06 at primary level; 1991-92, 2003-04, 2004-05 and 2005-06 at higher education) at all four levels.

Table-3

PERCENTAGE OF GIRLS'ENROLMENT TO TOTAL ENROLMENT BY STAGES 1950-51 TO 2005-06

YEAR	Primary I-V	Upper Primary VI-VIII	Sec./Sr.Sec/ Intermediate (IX-XII)	Hr. Education (Degree& above level)
1950-51	28.10	16.10	13.30	10.00
1955-56	30.50	20.00	15.40	14.60
1960-61	32.60	23.90	20.50	16.00
1965-66	36.20	26.70	22.00	20.40
1970-71	37.40	29.30	25.00	20.00
1975-76	38.10	31.30	26.90	23.20
1980-81	38.60	32.90	29.60	26.37
1985-86	40.30	35.60	30.30	33.00
1990-91	41.50	36.70	32.90	33.30
1991-92	41.90	38.20	33.80	32.30
1992-93	42.60	38.80	33.90	33.20
1993-94	42.70	39.10	34.30	33.50
1994-95	42.90	39.30	35.90	34.00
1995-96	43.10	39.50	36.10	36.00
1996-97	43.20	39.90	36.40	36.70
1997-98	43.50	40.30	36.50	37.50
1998-99	43.90	40.80	37.80	38.80
1999-00	44.02	41.09	38.70	38.70
2000-01	43.70	40.90	38.60	39.40

2001-02	44.10	41.80	39.50	39.90
2002-03	46.80	43.90	41.30	40.10
2003-04	46.70	44.00	41.10	39.70
2004-05	46.70	44.40	41.50	38.90
2005-06	46.60	44.70	42.00	38.30

Source: Time Series of India-2007.

DROP-OUT RATES OF FEMALE STUDENTS

The drop-out rate of female students was showed in the table-4. In the year 1960-61 the drop-out rate of girls at primary (I-V) was 70.90 per cent, it was decreased to 21.77 per cent in the year 2005-06. The drop-out rate at elementary level (I-VIII) was decreased from 85.00 per cent in 1960-61 to 48.98 per cent in the year 2005-06. In the case of secondary level (I-X); the drop-out rate was decreased from 76.90 per cent in the year 1990-91 to 63.56 per cent in the year 2005-06. From the given table it is clear that drop-out rate was high at higher classes.

Table-4

DROP-OUT RATES OF ALL CATEGORIES OF STUDENTS -1960-61 TO 2005-06

YEAR	Primary(I –V)			Elementary (I-VIII)			Secondary (I-X)		
	Boys	Girls	Total	Boys	Girls	Total	Boys	Girls	Total
1960-61	61.70	70.90	**66.30**	75.00	85.00	**80.00**	N.A	N.A	N.A
1970-71	64.50	70.90	**67.70**	74.60	83.40	**79.00**	N.A	N.A	N.A
1980-81	56.20	62.50	**59.35**	68.00	79.40	**73.70**	N.A	N.A	N.A
1990-91	40.10	46.00	**43.05**	59.10	65.10	**62.10**	67.50	76.90	**72.20**
1992-93	43.80	46.70	**45.25**	58.20	65.20	**61.70**	70.00	77.30	**73.65**
1995-96	41.40	43.00	**42.20**	56.60	61.70	**59.15**	66.70	73.70	**70.20**
1996-97	39.70	40.90	**40.30**	54.30	59.50	**56.90**	67.30	73.70	**70.05**
1997-98	37.50	41.50	**39.50**	53.80	59.30	**56.55**	66.60	73.00	**69.80**
1998-99	40.90	42.30	**41.75**	54.20	59.20	**56.70**	64.50	69.80	**67.15**
1999-00	39.80	41.00	**40.40**	53.30	57.70	**55.50**	64.90	69.90	**67.40**
2000-01	39.70	41.90	**40.80**	50.30	57.70	**54.00**	66.40	71.50	**68.95**
2001-02	38.40	39.90	**39.15**	52.90	56.90	**54.90**	64.20	68.60	**66.40**
2002-03	35.85	33.72	**34.78**	52.28	53.45	**52.86**	60.72	64.97	**62.84**
2003-04	33.74	28.57	**31.15**	51.85	52.92	**52.38**	60.98	64.92	**62.95**
2004-05	31.81	25.42	**28.61**	50.49	51.28	**50.88**	60.41	63.88	**62.14**
2005-06	28.71	21.77	**25.24**	48.67	48.98	**48.82**	60.10	63.56	**61.83**

Source: Time Series of India-2007.

WHY FEMALE EDUCATION IS IMPORTANT?

The primary education enrolment rates of girls have a positive impact on economic well-being of women, their families and society in the long run. Since the mother carries the main burden of looking after the health of her child, how well she does this task depends on the knowledge and confidence that she gains from education. Higher levels of schooling for girls increase children's chances of getting immunized and are therefore increase their chances of survival.

Female literacy rate correlates with lower fertility and infant mortality rates. The mother's education appears to reduce the negative effects of poor community sanitation and hygiene. Educated women generally marry late and likely to practice family planning and have smaller families. Education empowers women, it increases women's status in the community and leads to greater input into family and community decision making. Perhaps more importantly, education provides girls with a basic knowledge of their rights as individuals and citizens. Having knowledge and decision-making power can place women on a more equal footing with their male counterparts. Education also provides people with knowledge and skill especially in the areas of health, nutrition, water and sanitation, and the environment. Girl's education is a necessary condition to ensure that development efforts will be sustained. Therefore girls education is necessary for overall development of any country.

PARTICIPATION

Participation means that people are closely involved in the economic, social, cultural and political processes that affect their lives People may, in some cases, have complete and direct control over these processes-in other cases, the control may be partial or indirect. The important thing is that people have constant access to decision-making and power. Participation in this sense is an essential element of human development.

COMMUNITY PARTICIPATION

Community participation in public affairs goes back to the beginning of human society and the concept has taken new significance as societies have grown in size and complexity. In literature its origin can be traced to Aristotle. According to Aristotle participation was essential to development. According to him the best state was one where there was broad participation with no class domination. The need for participation of people in different areas has been the central theme of many scholars. Detokeville, J.S. Mill, Robert Owen, Rousseall Bentham and Karl Marx were great advocates of participation of the citizen. The literature on development shows that followers of various

Approaches i.e., structural-functional approach, comparative history approach, social process approach, political approach etc. all emphasized the significance of people's participation in the development process. Community participation is an integral part of area development planning.

The involvement of the people in the planning process becomes necessary so that the plan is more responsive to the local needs, reflects more accurately the local perceptions and produces a sense of ownership and responsibility. Such community participation is of particular relevance for mobilizing community resources in which participation is viewed as a facilitator or a desired plan output, to sort any differences in the planning and implementation stages, to speed up the process of implementation, and to complement and supplement the efforts of the government in the development process. Achieving successful public participation in local level development is no easy task. It is being realized now that unless people are involved in the process of development, no real improvement will take place. Therefore there is a need for an effective local level institution to energize and involve the public in managing and controlling their resources. The local leaders of the community, teachers, students, people's representatives, beneficiaries' groups, non-governmental organizations, farmers' groups, self help groups, users groups, research institutions etc., need to be actively involved in the various stages of the planning. People's participation in the developmental schemes can be assured if the programmes are based on the felt needs of the people.

COMMUNITY PARTICIPATION IN EDUCATION

The District Primary Education (DPED) is another thrust area in primary education. The DPED is distinct from conventional project as it takes a holistic view of elementary education, emphasizes decentralized management, community mobilization and undertakes district and population specific planning. It emphasizes on building an integrated and locally relevant curriculum. A number of other externally assisted projects such as- Uttar Pradesh Basic Education Programme, Bihar Education Project, Shiksha Karmi and Lok-Jambish Project in Rajasthan, Mahila Samakhya Project. Mahila Samakhya Programme is a direct outcome of the commitment to affirmative action in support of women's education mandated in the National Policy on Education.

Women Sangh as have taken an active lead in the area of girl child education. In U.P. Centers called Udan Khatolas, Hindola or Buransh cater to children who have dropped out, never gone to school and to pre-schoolers. In Karnataka, some Sanghas are running Balwadis with no financial assistance from Mahila Samakhya except the initial setting up and training to the workers. These Sanghas are playing active role in enrolling children into primary schools. The Bal Mitra Kendras for girls have been started in Andhra Pradesh to cater to the needs of girls. An important feature of these kendras is the focus on establishing and creating a sense of partnership and ownership in this activity among the Sangha women, parents play important role in selection of teachers, monitoring the centers and contribution to teacher's fees. At present, 590 voluntary agencies are running 38,900 centers in the country, under Experimental and Innovative programmes, new strategies on a pilot basis for micro-planning survey training, material development, education for the disabled and working children health education, running of non Formal education are taken up. In addition, NGOs are running District Resource Units for providing resource support to the programme. The Bal Bhavan Society of India through its Bal Bhavan Kendras helps the children to explore their inner potential by giving opportunities for expression of ideas through various mediums. Article 243G (11th Schedule) of the constitution provides necessary power and functions to Panchyati Raj Institutions to plan and implement schemes for socio-economic development including primary and secondary school education.

The Central Advisory Board of Education (CABE) Committee has proposed a broad framework for education management in the light of 73rd Constitution amendment. A crucial feature of the framework is the provision for a village level panchayat standing committee in case of single panchayat and a village education committee in the case of group of panchayat. The Constitution of the committee was specified : the number of members had to be not less than seven and not more than 15 apart from the chairman or panchayat member and the headmaster of the primary school, a representative of the Schedule Castes and Tribes, a parent and an Anganwadi worker were to be included. The committee was expected to have the power to check attendance registers and report on among the other things, regularity of students, teacher's attendance and school functioning. While such measures to involve people's institutions in the education process are welcome steps there is need to revitalise these committees.

STRATEGIES FOR PARTICIPATION

Participation must begin at the lowest level. There must be real opportunities for participative decision-making and community should be involved from the earliest planning to the implementation, monitoring and evaluation.

- A separate educational scheme should be formulated by giving priority for parents of female children.
- A mechanism should be evolved to involve representatives of panchayatiraj institutions, voluntary agencies, youth club, mahila mandals and other local level institutions to prepare micro planning at the village, block and district level. Special emphasis should be given to elicit women's participation.
- A village education committee should be formed with the involvement of elected representatives of panchayats and other local level people's institutions. The school teacher should facilities the meeting. The discussion outcome should be recorded by the teacher.
- An education register should be maintained and updated based on the household survey.
- Monitoring and evaluation are essential to provide feedback in order to identify the problems and constraints in implementation. Community participation is essential not only to know how many but who benefits from education. If help

to determine which need and whose needs are met. It is increasingly gaining ground that the best monitoring system is one in which beneficiaries do some checking themselves.

- People's perceptions about a number of issues related to school education management example - time, holiday curriculum etc. should receive due consideration.
- Teacher, Pupil and People (TPP) meetings should be arranged regularly.
- The community inputs along with school inputs should be identified properly and responsibilities should be fixed.
- The people's institutions like Youth club, mahila mandals and local NGO's should be effectively involved along with Anganwadi Workers of the area at various stages.
- Vidya committees should be appointed in each and every village for proper utilization of funds and to minimize drop-outs.
- Women elected representatives should made responsible for ensuring full enrolment of girls in the village.

ACTION NEEDED TO IMPROVE FEMALE EDUCATION

To increase enrolment of female students the following actions are necessary.

- Ancillary facilities like drinking water, urinals and lavatories should be provided in schools.
- Awareness programme should be conducted to parents of female students.
- Community and rural people's institutions should be mobilized to create a positive climate for girls' education among rural people.
- Dropout rate is higher amongst girls, still higher among rural girls and highest among tribal girls. Therefore special efforts may be made by the community and people's institutions to check the problems of dropouts.
- Efforts should be made to sensitize the education structure and innovative projects with region culture specific issues should be developed.

- Importance of education should be explained to parents.
- Mass media should be utilized for projecting positive image of girl child and gender sensitization campaign for community should be initiated. The school teacher should also be oriented towards gender issues.
- Mid-day meals, books, uniform etc., should be more available for all female students especially in rural areas.
- Plan of action should be created at village level for the success of government programmes.
- Scholarship, bicycles should be given to improve women enrolment.
- Support facilities should be provided to parents to enable girls to continue schooling.
- The role of non-governmental organizations should be increased for better enrolment and continuation of female education.
- Vidya committees should be taken responsible for ensuring enrolment and attendance of girls should be attempted.

References

1. Ali, Aruana Assaf, (1975) 'The Necessity for Education Parassar' Vol. 2 No. 4 P.P. 10-14.
2. Bhatt .B.D. and Sharma S.R. 1980 Women's Education and Social Development, Kaushika Publication Delhi.
3. Census of India -2001.
4. Chattopadhyay, Kamla Devi (1929) The Awakening of Indian Women's, Calcutta.
5. India- Ministry of Community Development and Co- operation.
6. Leela Kumari (1984) Development of Women's Education in Uttar Pardesh Since 1950 to 2000.
7. National Action Plan-India, Ministry of Human Resource Development, Government of India, New Delhi.
8. NSS 61st Round Survey Report No. 517, 2004-05.Page 24.

9. Pandey Balagi (1985) Women Education Social Scientist .Oct – Nov. Volume 13 P.P. 11-19.

10. Ramchandra P. and others (1963) Women's and Education, Tata institute of Social Dev.

11. Rao S.S. (1975) The Changing Indian Women's Yojana Vol XIX No- 6 15th Sept P.P. 12-15.

12. Women's Role in Community Development, Delhi Pub (1961).

19

Forms of Domestic Violence and Development of Women Through Education

However much a mother may love her children, it is all but impossible for her to provide high-quality child care if she herself is poor and oppressed, illiterate and uninformed, anemic and unhealthy, has five or six other children, lives in a slum or shanty, has neither clean water nor safe sanitation, and if she is without the necessary support either from health services, or from her society, or from the father of her children - Vulimiri Ramalingaswami, "The Asian Enigma."

Women constitute almost half of the population in the world. But the hegemonic masculine ideology made them suffer a lot as they were denied equal opportunities in different parts of the world. The rise of feminist ideas has, however, led to the tremendous improvement of women's condition throughout the world in recent times. Access to education has been one of the most pressing demands of theses women's rights movements. Women's education in India has also been a major preoccupation of both the government and civil society as educated women can play a very important role in the development of the country.

1. *India has world's largest number of professionally qualified women.*
2. *India has largest population of working women in the world.*
3. *India has more number of doctors, surgeons, scientists, professors than the US.*

What is Domestic Violence?

Domestic violence is controlling behaviour and includes all kinds of physical, sexual, economic, psychological and emotional abuse within all kinds of intimate relationships. The perpetrators of domestic violence or abuse are usually men and the victims or survivors are usually women and children that they know. It includes:

- Punching and slapping.
- Kicking and hair pulling.
- Biting and pinching.
- Pushing and shoving.
- Being forced to have sex.
- Being beaten or cut with other objects.
- Disrespect, neglect and emotional blackmail.
- Verbal abuse and swearing.
- Being prevented from going out or seeing people – being isolated.

Forms of Domestic Violence

The following are the forms of Domestic Violence:

1. Physical Abuse
2. Sexual Abuse
3. Psychological Abuse
4. Emotional Abuse
5. Financial Abuse

1. Physical Abuse

Physical abuse is the most visible form of abuse and most likely (with sexual abuse) to give rise to criminal charges. Injuries include black eyes, cut lips, bruising, fractures, deafness, blindness, internal bleeding, missing teeth, persistent ill health, miscarriages, and injuries to a fetus and death. Injury sites are often concealed by clothing or hair. It can include slaps, shoves, pushing, being thrown across the room or down the stairs, kicking, stamping, strangulation, burns and scalds, being attacked with weapons such as knives, household objects, firearms etc internally as well as externally.

2. Sexual Abuse

Sexual Abuse in an abusive relationship is another form of violence, control and degradation. It includes rape, sexual assaults (including with implements), enforced prostitution, enforced sexual practices including being forced to watch or engage in pornography.

3. Psychological Abuse

Psychological abuse examples include "Jeckyll and Hyde" behaviour, preventing contact with friends and families, constant belittling and humiliating things being said, claims that children will be removed if anyone is told of abuse, controlling behaviours, deliberately enforcing dependency, constant statements that the victim is mentally ill etc.

4. Emotional Abuse

Emotional abuse is an attack on victims' personality and well being and is often described as worse than physical violence. It may be referred to as "mind-games". It frequently amounts to the abuser assuming a tight and unhealthy control of all members of the family, which may become increasingly isolated in the community.

Examples include threats of violence to all members of family, constant criticism of the victim saying she is ugly, ignorant or worthless, using the children as ammunition, family life and mood being dictated by abuser (abuser-centric) continual questioning, humiliation in public, playing on community and cultural fears, threats to have the children removed, threats to kill or have deported, threat that the abuser will commit suicide, threats and actual violence to family pets etc.

5. Financial Abuse

Financial Abuse is essentially the deprivation of and / or the control of money whether earned or benefits.

An abuser may refuse to pay bills or prevent the victim from having any control over the family finances. The abuser may steal money belonging to the victim or children. Essential services such as gas and electricity may be cut off. The mother may be forced to support the children solely on what she can earn without assistance or child benefit if this is claimed by the abuser. An abuser may deliberately spend money on him or sell the woman's possessions and family furniture.

Crime against Women in India

1. One crime against women every three minutes
2. One rape every 29 minutes
3. One dowry death case every 77 minutes
4. One case of cruelty by husband and relatives every nine minutes
5. Once suicide every 4 hours

Source: National Crime Records Bureau

The main problems of Indian women

- **Malnutrition:** India has exceptionally high rates of child malnutrition, because tradition in India requires that women eat last and least throughout their lives, even when pregnant and lactating. Malnourished women give birth to malnourished children, perpetuating the cycle.
- **Poor Health:** Females receive less health care than males. Many women die in childbirth of easily prevented complications. Working conditions and environmental pollution further impairs women's health.
- **Lack of education:** Families are far less likely to educate girls than boys, and far more likely to pull them out of school, either to help out at home or from fear of violence.

- **Overwork:** Women work longer hours and their work is more arduous than men's, yet their work is unrecognized. Men report that "women, like children, eat and do nothing." Technological progress in agriculture has had a negative impact on women.
- **Unskilled:** In women's primary employment sector - agriculture - extension services overlook women.
- **Mistreatment:** In recent years, there has been an alarming rise in atrocities against women in India, in terms of rapes, assaults and dowry-related murders. Fear of violence suppresses the aspirations of all women. Female infanticide and sex-selective abortions are additional forms of violence that reflect the devaluing of females in Indian society.
- **Powerlessness:** While women are guaranteed equality under the constitution, legal protection has little effect in the face of prevailing patriarchal traditions. Women lack power to decide who they will marry, and are often married off as children. Legal loopholes are used to deny women inheritance rights.

India has a long history of activism for women's welfare and rights, which has increasingly focused on women's economic rights. A range of government programs have been launched to increase economic opportunity for women, although there appear to be no existing programs to address the cultural and traditional discrimination against women that leads to her abject conditions.

Government Role to Minimize Domestic Violence in India

Overall, a crime against women is committed every three minutes in India, according to India's National Crime Records Bureau. Despite the scale of the problem, there had been no specific legislation to deal with actual abuse or the threat of abuse at home. Domestic violence, under the new law, includes "actual abuse or the threat of abuse whether physical, sexual, emotional or economic," a statement from the federal ministry of women and child development said.

"We have been trying for long to protect women from domestic violence. In India alone, around 70% of women are victim of these violent acts in one or the other form," junior minister for women and child development Renuka Chowdhury told the Press Trust of India news agency. They say a bill alone will not help in preventing domestic abuse; what is needed is a change in mind sets.

In January 1992, the National Commission for Women (NCW), was set up as a statutory body under the National Commission for Women Act, 1990 (Act No. 20 of 1990 of Govt.of India) to review the constitutional and legal safeguards for women; recommend remedial legislative measures, facilitate redressed of grievances and advise the Government on all policy matters affecting women.

There are so many government and non-government organizations are working for the benefits of women. Both Central and State governments are continuing so many programmes for the development of women in the country.

Female Literacy in India

According to last census held in 2001, the percentage of female literacy in the country is 54.16%. The literacy rate in the country has increased from 18.33% in 1951 to 65.38% as per 2001 census. The female literacy rate has also increased from 8.86% in 1951 to 54.16%. It is noticed that the female literacy rate during the period 1991-2001 increased by 14.87% whereas male literacy rate rose by 11.72%. Hence the female literacy rate actually increased by 3.15% more compared to male literacy rate.

Factors Responsible for Poor Female Literacy Rate

Historically, a variety of factors have been found to be responsible for poor female literate rate, viz.

- Gender based inequality.
- Social discrimination and economic exploitation.
- Occupation of girl child in domestic chores.
- Low enrolment of girls in schools.
- Low retention rate and high dropout rate.

The main strategies adopted by the Government for increasing female literacy in the country include

- National Literacy Mission for imparting functional literacy
- Universalisation for Elementary Education

- Non-Formal Education

History of Women's Education in India

Although in the Vedic period women had access to education in India, they had gradually lost this right. However, in the British period there was revival of interest in women's education in India. During this period, various socio religious movements led by eminent persons like Raja Ram Mohan Roy, Iswar Chandra Vidyasagar emphasized on women's education in India. Mahatma Jyotiba Phule, Periyar and Baba Saheb Ambedkar were leaders of the lower castes in India who took various initiatives to make education available to the women of India. However women's education got a fillip after the country got independence in 1947 and the government has taken various measures to provide education to all Indian women. As a result women's literacy rate has grown over the three decades and the growth of female literacy has in fact been higher than that of male literacy rate. While in 1971 only 22% of Indian women were literate, by the end of 2001 54.16% female were literate. The growth of female literacy rate is 14.87% as compared to 11.72 % of that of male literacy rate.

Importance of Women's Education in India

Women's education in India plays a very important role in the overall development of the country. It not only helps in the development of half of the human resources, but in improving the quality of life at home and outside. Educated women not only tend to promote education of their girl children, but also can provide better guidance to all their children. Moreover educated women can also help in the reduction of infant mortality rate and growth of the population.

Obstacles

Gender discrimination still persists in India and lot more needs to be done in the field of women's education in India. The gap in the male-female literacy rate is just a simple indicator. While the male literary rate is more than 75% according to the 2001 census, the female literacy rate is just 54.16%. Prevailing prejudices, low enrollment of girl child in the schools, engagements of girl children in domestic works and high dropout rate are major obstacles in the path of making all Indian women educated.

According to the Women and Child Development study, 45 percent of Indian women are slapped, kicked or beaten by their husbands. India also had the highest rate of violence during pregnancy. Of the women reporting violence, 50 percent were kicked, beaten or hit when pregnant. About 74.8 percent of the women who reported violence have attempted to commit suicide. It shows the importance of education. Educated woman has more strength and power to face the challenges when compared to uneducated woman.

Kumud Sharma of the Centre for Women's Development Studies in New Delhi traced the correlation between education and domestic violence to patriarchal attitudes. "Educated women are aware of their rights," she said. "They are no longer willing to follow commands blindly. When they ask questions, it causes conflicts, which, in turn, leads to violence. In many Indian states, working women are asked to hand over their paycheck to the husband and have no control over their finances. So, if they stop doing so or start asserting their right, there is bound to be friction."

It is necessary to establish some more colleges and universities in India. The number of Residential Schools for SC/ST and BC's is not sufficient today. So, increase the number of these schools in the both rural and urban areas. Today's children are tomorrow's citizens. Take care about future generation. Then only India will become developed country in the future.

Conclusions

Now we are living in the modern and technological world. Women are also entering in all the fields like men for doing job. Educated women have better opportunity compared to uneducated women in the society. They are facing so many problems in the society. With the help of education and law and order it is easy to escape from those problems. So it is necessary to educate all types of women in the society. Education gives strength, wealth, health and power to the individual.

According to Swami Vivekandanda: *"We want that education by which character is formed, strength of mind increased and intellect is expanded, and by which one can stand on one's own feet".* The plight of women in medieval India and at the starting of modern India can be summed up in the words of great poet *Rabindranath Tagore: "O Lord Why has you not given woman the right to conquer her destiny? Why does she have to wait head bowed, By the roadside, Waiting with tired patience, Hoping for a miracle in the morrow?"*

References

1. Census of India, (2001), Government of India, New Delhi.
2. Child and Women Development Report, (2006), Ministry of Women and Child Development, Government of India, New Delhi.
3. National Crime Records Bureau, (2007), Government of India, New Delhi.
4. National Family Health Survey, (2006), Government of India, New Delhi.
5. National Institute of Child Health and Human Development. (2001). The National Reading Panel: Reports of the Subgroups.
6. UNESCO Institute for Statistics: Literacy rates, youth (15-24) and adult (15+), by region and gender (September 2006 Assessment).

20

Impact of Education on Domestic Violence and Development of Women Through Education

You can tell the condition of a nation by looking at the status of its women- Jawaharlal Nehru

Literary education is of no value, if it is not able to build up a sound character- Mahatma Gandhi

Education has been regarded as the most significant instrument for changing women's subjugated position in the society. It not only develops the personality and rationality of individuals, but qualifies them to fulfill certain economic, political and cultural functions and thereby improves their socio-economic status. One of the direct expectations from educational development in a society is the reduction in the inequality among individuals and that is why Education was included as the basic right of every human being in the Universal Declaration of Human Rights. The constitution of UNESCO also directs its efforts to achieve 'The ideal of equality of educational opportunity without regard to race, sex or any distinction, economic or social'.

Domestic Violence (sometimes referred to as domestic abuse or spousal abuse) occurs when a family member, partner or ex-partner attempts to physically or psychologically dominate another. Domestic violence often refers to violence between spouses, or spousal abuse but can also include cohabitants and non-married intimate partners. Domestic violence occurs in all cultures; people of all races, ethnicities, religions, sexes and classes can be perpetrators of domestic violence. Domestic violence is perpetrated by both men and women, occurring in both same-sex and opposite-sex relationships.

What Is Domestic Violence?

Domestic violence is controlling behaviour and includes all kinds of physical, sexual and emotional abuse within all kinds of intimate relationships. The perpetrators of domestic violence or abuse are usually men and the victims or survivors are usually women and children that they know. It includes:

- Punching and slapping
- Kicking and hair pulling
- Biting and pinching
- Pushing and shoving
- Being forced to have sex
- Being beaten or cut with other objects
- Disrespect, neglect and emotional blackmail
- Verbal abuse and swearing
- Being prevented from going out or seeing people – being isolated
- Lying, harassment and putting pressure on you through threats

1:4 women experience domestic violence at some point in their lives and 1:10 will be experiencing domestic violence today

Women Violence in Different States of India

Over 37 per cent married women in the country were victims of physical or sexual abuse by their husbands with Bihar topping the list. Women in Himachal Pradesh faced less violence at home compared to other states in the country. The latest National Family Health Survey-III found that 37.2 per cent women had experienced violence and cited lack of education as the key reason behind their woes. "Women with no education were much more likely than other women to have suffered spousal violence. However, spousal abuse also extends to women who have secondary or higher secondary level education, with 16 per cent reporting abuse," the survey said.

The survey showed that countrywide more women face violence in rural areas (40.2) as compared to those in the urban areas (30.4).

In Bihar, women in urban areas fared worse than those in rural areas. While 62.2 per cent underwent the trauma in urban areas, it was 58.5 per cent women in villages.

It is followed by Rajasthan (46.3) Madhya Pradesh (45.8), Tripura (44.1), Manipur (43.9), Uttar Pradesh (42.4), Tamil Nadu (41.9), West Bengal (40.3) and Arunachal Pradesh (38.8).

Among the metros, the fairer sex was better off in Delhi (16.3) and Mumbai (19.5) recorded relatively low percentage as compared to Chennai (40.6) and Kolkata (26.7).

Nearly, 17 per cent women in Goa have experienced violence, with 17.2 women in rural areas at the receiving end as compared to 16.4 per cent women in urban areas.

In Chhattisgarh, a total of 30 per cent women suffered at the hands of their husbands, while in Jharkhand, the figure was 37 per cent. About 40.8 per cent women in Jharkhand villages found the going tough as compared to 24.6 per cent in the urban areas.

In the hill state of Uttarakhand, nearly 28 per cent women experienced violence, with those in villages (29.8) fared worse than their urban counterparts (22.8). After Himachal Pradesh, women fared relatively better in Jammu and Kashmir (12.6), Meghalaya (13.1), Nagaland (15.4), Sikkim (16.5) and Kerala (16.4).

Other states where women find themselves vulnerable are Assam (39.6), Arunachal Pradesh (38.8), Orissa (38.5), Maharashtra (30.7), Andhra Pradesh (35.2), Haryana (27.3), Gujarat (27.6) Punjab (25.4), Mizoram (22.5) and Karnataka (20).

Crime against Women in India

- One crime against women every three minutes
- One rape every 29 minutes
- One dowry death case every 77 minutes
- One case of cruelty by husband and relatives every nine minutes
- Once suicide every 240 minutes.

Source: *National Crime Records Bureau*

Child Violence

Children are the nation's assets. A happy child will make his/her home and the country happy. The future of any country depends upon the right upbringing of its children, for which a congenial environment and adequate opportunities for wholesome development are essential.

According to UNICEF's "The State of the World's Children," report for 2006, one-third of the world's children lack adequate shelter, 31% lack basic sanitation and 21% have no access to clean, potable water. Illness, malnutrition, and premature death are common when children lack the most basic protection.

A government commissioned survey has found that more than 53 per cent of children in India are subjected to sexual abuse, but most don't report the assaults to anyone.

The survey, released last April and which covered different forms of child abuse physical, sexual and emotional as well as female child neglect, found that two out of every three children have been physically abused.

Parents and relatives, persons known to the child or in a position of trust and responsibility were mostly found to be the perpetrators of child sexual abuse in the country. According to the women and child development ministry-sponsored report, which assumes greater significance in the backdrop of the Nithari killings that brought into focus the issue of children's safety, those in the age group of 5-12 years reported higher levels of abuse.

While releasing the survey, Women and Child Development Minister Renuka Chowdhury said, "Child abuse is shrouded in secrecy and there is a conspiracy of silence around the entire subject. The ministry is working on a new law for protection of children's rights by clearly specifying offences against children and stiffening punishments."

The survey carried out across 13 states and with a sample size of 12,447, revealed that 53.22 per cent of children reported having faced one or more forms of sexual abuse, with Andhra Pradesh, Bihar, Assam and Delhi reporting the highest percentage of such incidents. In 50 per cent of child abuse cases, the abusers were known to the child or were in a position of trust and responsibility and most children did not report the matter to anyone.

The survey, sponsored by WCD ministry and carried out by the NGO Prayas in association with UNICEF and Save the Children, found that more than 50 per cent children were subjected to one or the other form of physical abuse and more boys than girls were abused physically. The first-ever survey on child abuse in the country disclosed that nearly 65 per cent of school children reported facing corporal punishment beatings by teachers mostly in government schools.

Of children physically abused in families, in 88.6 per cent of the cases, it was the parents who were the perpetrators. More than 50 per cent had been sexually abused in ways that ranged from severe such as rape or fondling to milder forms of molestation that included forcible kissing.

The study also interviewed 2,324 young adults between the ages of 18 and 24, almost half of whom reported being physically or sexually abused as children. When it comes to emotional abuse, every second child was subjected to emotional assault and in 83 per cent of the cases, parents were the abusers.

Children living with domestic violence may

- Express behavioural problems.
- Be more likely to truant or have difficulties at school.
- Turn to alcohol or drugs.

- Self-harm or attempt suicide.

According to the **NSPCC** (National Society for the Prevention of Cruelty to Children) of Children living with domestic violence:

- 100% are emotionally abused.
- 48% are psychologically abused.
- 26% are physically abused.
- 13% are accidentally injured.
- 7% are sexually abused.

Recent figures from the International Labour Organisation (ILO) show that

- Globally, 1 in 6 children work.
- 218 million children aged 5 - 17 are involved in child labour world wide.
- 126 million children work in hazardous conditions.
- The highest numbers of child labourers are in the Asia/Pacific region, where there are 122 million working children.
- The highest proportion of child labourers is in Sub Saharan Africa, where 26% of children (49 million) are involved in work.

Development of Women through Education

Education is the process of instruction aimed at the all round development of boys and girls. Education dispels ignorance. It is the only wealth that cannot be robbed. Learning includes the moral values and the improvement of character and the methods to increase the strength of mind.

Once the first Prime Minister of India, Jawaharlal Nehru said, "you can tell the condition of a nation by looking at the status of its women". This is absolutely true. Woman of any nation is the mirror to its civilization. If women enjoy good status it shows that the society has reached a level of maturity and sense of responsibility while a decadent image conjures up if the opposite is true. The story of Indian women is as old as the history of Indian civilization.

Kumud Sharma of the Centre for Women's Development Studies in New Delhi traced the correlation between education and domestic violence to patriarchal attitudes. "Educated women are aware of their rights," she said. "They are no longer willing to follow commands blindly. When they ask questions, it causes conflicts, which, in turn, leads to violence. In many Indian states, working women are asked to hand over their paycheck to the husband and have no control over their finances. So, if they stop doing so or start asserting their right, there is bound to be friction."

Female Literacy in India

According to last census held in 2001, the percentage of female literacy in the country is 54.16%. The literacy rate in the country has increased from 18.33% in 1951 to 65.38% as per 2001 census. The female literacy rate has also increased from 8.86% in 1951 to 54.16%. It is noticed that the female literacy rate during the period 1991-2001 increased by 14.87% whereas male literacy rate rose by 11.72%. Hence the female literacy rate actually increased by 3.15% more compared to male literacy rate.

Women Universities in India

- **Andhra Pradesh-** Sri Padmavati University, Tirupati
- **Delhi-** Lady Shri Ram College for Women, Lajpat Nagar
- **Maharashtra-**SNDT Women's University, Mumbai
- **Rajasthan-**Banasthali Vidyapith, Banasthali

It is necessary to establish some more universities and colleges for women in India. Education is a solution for any type of problem in the society. Education gives strength, power and character. Education helps to improve economic position also in the society.

Table 1: Number of Women Job Seekers

Year	Number of Women (in lacs)	Percentage to total
1999	99.3	24.6
2000	104.5	25.3
2001	108.8	25.9
2002	106.0	25.9
2003	107.5	26.0
2004	106.1	26.0

The number of women job seekers has increased from 99.3 lacs in 1999 to 106.1 lacs in 2004. Thus the percentage of women job seekers to the total job-seekers has also increased from 24.6per cent in 1999 to 26.2per cent in 2004.

Number of Educated Women Job Seekers as on December 2004 was 7537.7 thousand. Educated Women at the end of 2004 accounted for 25.8per cent of the total educated job-seekers.

Table 2: Number of Educated Women Job Seekers

Year	Number of Women	Percentage to total
2000	7911.7	27.1
2001	8525.6	28.1
2002	7921.4	26.8
2003	8032.4	26.6
2004	7537.7	25.8

Vision of National Commission for Women

Dr. Girija Vyas took over as Chairperson of the National Commission for Women on 16th February, 2005.

The Indian Women of Today Culturally rooted globally oriented Healthy, Educated, and Self Reliant Secure in her Home and Safe outside with Access to all the Rights of a Citizen with Opportunity to Contribute in all walks of life.

Modern Indian Women

The status of women in modern India is a sort of a paradox. If on one hand she is at the peak of ladder of success, on the other hand she is mutely suffering the violence afflicted on her by her own family members. As compared with past women in modern times have achieved a lot but in reality they have to still travel a long way. Their path is full of roadblocks. The women have left the secured domain of their home and are now in the battlefield of life, fully armored with their talent. They had proven themselves. But in India they are yet to get their dues. The sex ratio of India shows that the Indian society is still prejudiced against female. There are 933 females per thousand males in India according to the census of 2001, which is much below the world average of 990 females. There are many problems which women in India have to go through daily. These problems have become the part and parcel of life of Indian women and some of them have accepted them as their fate.

First Woman of India

Women had played an important role in the Modern World. Here are some of the most successful & first women of the world, who lead a Nation, a Party, a State, etc.

- First woman President of Indian National Congress — Annie Besant (1917)
- First Indian woman President of Indian National Congress — Sarojini Naidu (1925)
- First woman Ambassador from India — Vijay Lakshmi Pandit (to USSR from1947-49)
- First woman Governor of an Indian State — Sarojini Naidu (UP from 1947-48)
- First woman Minister of an Indian State — Vijay Lakshmi Pandit (UP)
- First Mayor of Delhi — Aruna Asif Ali (1958)
- First woman Central Minister — Rajkumari Amrit Kaur
- First woman Film star to be a member of Rajya Sabha — Nargis Dutt
- First woman Chief Minister of an Indian State — Sucheta Kriplani (UP from 1963-67)
- First woman Prime Minister of India — Indira Gandhi (1966-77 & 1980-84)
- First woman Speaker of an Indian State — Shano Devi
- First woman winner of the Bharat Ratna — Indira Ghandi (1971)
- First woman Judge of the Supreme Court — Justice M Fatima Bevi (1989)
- First woman Chief Justice of a High Court — Leila Seth (CJ of Himachal Pradesh 1991)
- India's officially recognized billionth citizen — Aastha (Born on May 11, 2000 at ND)

Conclusions

Indian women have mastered anything and everything which a woman can dream of. But she still has to go a long way to achieve equal status in the minds of Indian men. The desire of Indian women can be best summed up in the following lines of 'Song of an African Women':

I have only one request.
I do not ask for money
Although I have need of it,
I do not ask for meat . . .
I have only one request,
And all I ask is
That you remove
The road block
From my path.

Educate all the children in the family. Education is the most powerful instrument for the development of women and children in the society.8th March is observed as *International Women's Day.* It is necessary to celebrate International Women's Day every year in a grand manner. Our present president Pratibha Patil is also a woman. It is the power and credit of woman. It is also very important to celebrate Children's Day on November 14th and Mother's day.

Reference

1. Census of India, (2001), Government of India, New Delhi.
2. Child and Women Development Report, (2006), Ministry of Women and Child
3. Development, Government of India, New Delhi.
4. Heilbroner, R. L. (1995) Visions of the future: the distant past, yesterday, today, and tomorrow (New York: Oxford University Press).
5. National Crime Records Bureau, (2007), Government of India, New Delhi.

6. National Family Health Survey, (2006), Government of India, New Delhi.

7. National Institute of Child Health and Human Development. (2001). The National Reading Panel: Reports of the Subgroups.

21

Impact of Education on Ethno-medicine And Health care Practices Among the Tribal People of India

We must protect the forests for our children, grandchildren and children yet to be born. We must protect the forests for those who can't speak for themselves such as the birds, animals, fish and trees.

Introduction

Anthropology as an integrated science of man deals with biological and cultural aspects of man. Presently anthropologists are more involved in applying their knowledge and techniques for human welfare.

Ethno-medicine is a sub-field of medical anthropology and deals with the study of traditional medicines: not only those that have relevant written sources (e.g. Traditional Chinese Medicine, Ayurveda), but especially those, whose knowledge and practices have been orally transmitted over the centuries. In the scientific arena, ethno-medical studies are generally characterized by a strong anthropological approach, more than a bio-medical one. The focus of these studies is then the perception and context of use of traditional medicines, and not their bio-evaluation.

Tribes in India

The Indian sub-continent is inhabited by 88.2 million tribal populations belonging to over 577 tribal communities that come under 227 linguistic groups. They inhibit varied geographic and climatic Zones of the country. Their vocation ranges from hunting, gathering, cave dwelling nomadic to societies with settled culture living incomplete harmony with nature.

Forests have been their dear home and totally submitted themselves to forest settings. Their relationship with the forest was symbolic in nature. They have been utilizing the resources without disturbing the delicate balance of the eco-system. Tribal thus mostly remained as stable societies and were unaffected by the social, cultural, material and economic evolutions that were taking place with the so called civilized societies. But this peaceful co-existence of the tribal has been disturbed in recent years by the interference in their habitats. Traditional communities living close to nature have, over the years acquired unique knowledge about the use of living biological resources. Modernisation, especially industrialization and urbanization has endangered the rich heritage of knowledge and expertise of age old wisdom of the traditional communities.

A study on the utilization of local tribal revealed that they hold precious knowledge on the specific use of a large number of agents of wild plant and animal origins, the use of many are hitherto unknown to the outside world.

Herbal History and Tradition in Indian Context

The Rigveda, the oldest document of human knowledge mentions the use of medicinal plants in the treatment of man and animals. Ayurveda gives the account of actual beginning of the ancient medical science of India, which according to western scholars was written between 2500 to 600 B.C. Charaka and Susruta wrote around 1000 B.C. Charaka concentrates more on medicine while Susruta deals with surgery in details along with therapeutics.

Tribes and Ethno-Medicine

Ethno-medicine refers to "those beliefs and practices relating to disease which are the products of indigenous cultural development and are not explicitly derived from the conceptual frame work of modern medicine" (Hughes, 1968, cited from Misra et al, 2003). Various institutions are now concerned with the traditional health care system and means of traditional treatment.

The tribal people are the real custodians of the medicinal plants. Out of 45,000 species of wild plants, 7500 species are used for medicinal purposes. The World Health Organization (WHO) has been promoting a movement for 'Saving plants for saving lives'. This is because of the growing understanding of the pivotal role medicinal plants play in providing herbal remedies to health maladies.

India is the home of several important traditional system of health care like Ayurveda. This system depends heavily on herbal products. Several millions of Indian households have been using through the ages nearly 8000 species of medicinal plants for their health care needs. Over one and half million traditional healers use a wide range of medicinal plants for treating ailments of both humans and livestock across the length and breadth of the country. Over 800 medicinal plant species are currently in use by the Indian herbal industry.

In recent times with the increased knowledge of life and culture of the tribal communities, the social scientists are taking interest in ethno-medicinal studies. Many works have been reported especially from among the rural and tribal communities of India (Choudhury, 1986; Bhadra and Tirkey, 1997; Sharma Thakur, 1997).Ray and Sharma (2005) have given a description of ethno-medicinal beliefs and practices prevalent among the Savaras, a tribal community of Andhra Pradesh.

Kumari (2006) gave an account on the concept of illness and disease and the application of folk medicine among the Saureas of Jharkhand. However, ethno-medicinal studies are relatively less in Northeast India. Guha (1986) has reported from among the Boro-Kachari tribe of Assam. A glimpse of indigenous health practices among the plain tribes of Assam is given by Sharma Thakur (1999). The socio-economic condition of some of the tribes of Arunachal Pradesh and their problems of health and indigenous methods of treatment has been reported by Choudhury (2000), Duarah and Pathak (1997), Kohli (1999), Bhasin (1997, 1999,2002, 2003, 2005).

Ethno-Medicine and Health Care Practices among Sonowal Kacharis in Assam (India)

The Sonowal Kacharis is an endogamous group of Kachari tribe and a popular plain scheduled tribe population of Assam. Various types of locally available herbs and leaves of wild plants are used by them as medicine. Like many other communities of the region, there are few herbal specialists among the Sonowal Kachari. These specialists or medicine-men have considerable knowledge about the herbs and its medicinal use. Normally they learn about these medicinal plants and its uses from their ancestor. These medicine-men are referred by different term according to the cultural norms. Among the Sonowal Kachari's they are called as Bez (Barua and Phukan, 1958: 334). Of course in rural Assam, they are mainly known by this term.

It has been observed in the villages that use of herbal medicine for curing certain diseases are quite known to the people and besides medicine-men, many elderly persons known about the use of herbal medicines. Some of the diseases and their indigenous methods of treatment are given below:

(1) Fever: Lime (Citrus auran tifolia) juice mixed with sugar is applied on the forehead of the patient to get relief from fever.

(2) Diarrhoea: Dry goose berry (Emblica officinalis) powder and black salt mixed with cold water is taken. Bark of Long Pepper (Pipoli tree) mixed with Misiri water is also used to cure the disease.

(3) Dysentery: Lime (Citrus auran tifolia) juicewith hot water and little salt are used in dysentery. The juice of black Tulsi leaves (Ocimum sanctum) and Sirata (Swertiachirata) is also used for the purpose. The juice of tender leaves (three numbers) of mango (Mangifera indica), black berry (S.cuminii) and goose berry (Emblica officinalis) (equal proportions) together with honey are mixed with goat milk and is taken to cure blood dysentery. Honey together with the juice of Dubari grass (Family-Gramineae) can cure blood dysentery and need to be taken for three/ four days. They also use a kind of wild herb, locally called Manimuni (Centila Asiatic).The juice of this herb mixed with sugar or honey should be taken continuously for a month to cure the disease. They also use limewater (Chun pani) mixed with juice of turmeric (Purcuma domestic) leave to get relief from blood dysentery and mucous.

(4) Blood Vomiting: A table spoon of carrot (Dancus carota) juice mixed with honey can cure blood vomiting.

(5) Liver Disease: Two to three raw or ripe Papayas (Carica papaya) daily can cure liver disease. A curry prepared from the bud of banana (Musa paradisiaca) and the meat of pigeon is also used as a medicine for the purpose.

(6) Jaundice: The medicine is prepared by pounding five or six number of Silikha (Myroballum) mixing with jaggery and it can cure jaundice. A glass of sugarcane (Saccharum officinarum) juice twice daily prescribed for the purpose. Boiled raw papaya (Carica papaya) is said to be good for curing the disease. Kardoi (Averrhoa carambola), Goose Berry (Emblica officinalis), Sugar cane (Saccharun officinarum), Neem leave (Azadirachta indica), a wild herb known as Duran ban (Lecas aspera), Brahmi sak (Herpestis monnieria), Purakol (Musa sapientum) are prescribed edibles for the patient.

(7) Nose Bleeding: Flower of Pomegranate (Punica granatum Linn) is crushed and 3-4 drops of juice is poured inside the nose to give immediate relief.

(8) Tonsilities: Juice is prepared by mixing one Amara seed (Sponolias mangifera), one Silikha seed (Mysoballum) and a piece of Turmeric (Purcuma domestica) and advice the patient gargles for a week regularly.

(9) Worms: Paste of five lemon seeds (Citrus aurantifolia) mixed with water and is prescribed to eat in empty stomach for a few days. The twigs of Chirata (Swertia chirata) are soaked in the water overnight and the water is prescribed to drink in empty stomach in the morning for one week regularly.

(10) Scabies: Lemon juice (Citrus aurantifolia) mixed with coconut oil is massaged for curing scabies. To remove scabies they take bath with hot water in which leaves of Neem (Azadirachta officinarum) were boiled. Twigs of Chirata (Swertia chirata) are crushed into paste with water to be used as an ointment and applied on the skin. Chirata water is prescribed to drink in the morning in empty stomach.

(11) Pain in the Ear: Juice of Tulsi (Ocimum sanctum) is boiled and put it in the ears to heal earache.

The patient is treated with available herbs, flora and minerals. Some of these are home remedies and some are specially prescribed by herbalist or folk medicine man available in the community. The practice of ethno-medicine is a complex multi-disciplinary system constituting the use of plants, spirituality and the natural environment and has been the source of healing for people for millennia. The spiritual aspects of health and sickness have been an integral component of the ethno-medicinal practice for centuries.

Disease due to wrath of the supernatural

Disease	Supernatural agencies	Pujas (Rituals)
Dysentery, mental diseases, cancer	Deo	Propitiated by sacrificing two red cocks, one red hen, and one egg, besides other items of feast. Arrangement is made in the forest.
Asthama, Mental Disease, cancer	Lord of water	Jalkhai puja, worshipped by sacrificing one white duck and other items of feast, rice, salt vegetables, etc.
Accident, sudden illness	Burah-dangoria	No sacrifice. Only raw items, e.g. gram, rice, powdered rice, etc. are offered to propitiate Burah-dangoria.
Gastritis	Ancestral spirits	Ai puja, no sacrifice is made except offering of raw articles, powdered rice, gram with betel nut and leaves.
Epidemic and natural calamities	Mother goddess	Community level worship by arranging bhur-utuwa puja. One pair of betel nut and leaf is offered from each family. One red duck is offered on behalf of the villagers. All the offered articles are placed in a boat.
Epidemic and large scale death of men and animals	Mother goddesses of forest.	A white goat is a must for the Puja besides other offering.

Present Position of Tribes

The tribal health care practices and system of treating diseases are based on their deep observation and belief in nature. But with the development of education and their awareness towards importance of health and health care and also with the advent of modern health care facilities, Government health measures these people are becoming more interested in taking modern medicine instead of traditional herbal medicine.

Saving the Plant is Saving the Life

According to the text of Vishnu Samhita, causing any harm to the plants/animals is a sin. Even purloining of parts/ products of any of these living beings is a crime. The sinner/ criminals are liable to chastisement in this life and also after death. The punishments are of diverse nature:-pecuniary, corporal, expiatory and donation of specific articles to Brahmins.

Conclusions

The growing disinterest in the use of the ethno-medicinal plants and its significance among the younger generation of the tribes will lead to the disappearance of this practice. Educated younger generation of the tribes should be encouraged by the Government to protect and cultivate these valuable herbal plants before they get lost due to the impact of modernization and urbanization and also due to deforestation.

The role of Anthropology is also very important in the field of saving herbal plants. By educating tribal people we can preserve all these things for future generation. It is the Government duty to take necessary steps to preserve all these things.

References

1. Barua, I. and R. Phukan. 1990. "Socio-religious aspects of Health among Sonowal Kachari". The Eastern Anthropologist, 55: 4.
2. Bhasin, Veena. 1997. "Medical Pluralism and Health Services in Ladakh." J. Soc. Sci., 1: 43-69.
3. Bhasin, Veena. 1997. "The Human Settlements and Health Status of People of Sikkim", (Pp. 153-187), in K.C. Mahanta

(ed.), People of the Himalayas:Ecology, Culture, Development and Change. Delhi:Kamla-Raj Enterprises.

4. Bhasin, Veena. 1999. Tribals of Ladakh: Ecology, Human Settlements and Health. Delhi: Kamla-Raj Enterprises.

5. Bhasin, Veena. 2002. “Traditional Medicine among Tribals of Rajasthan.” J. Soc Sci., 6(3): 153-172.Bhasin, Veena. 2003.”Sickness and Therapy among Tribals of Rajasthan.” Stud. Tribes and Tribals, 1(1): 77 -83.

6. Choudhury, S. 2000. “Indigenous beliefs and Practices of herbal Medicine among the few Arunachalis”.Resarun, 26. 72-81, Govt. of Arunachal Pradesh,Department of Cultural Affairs.

7. Das, B. M. 2007. “Sonowal Kachari Nigostiya parichya”, (Pp. 1-3) in M. Sonowal (ed.), Sonowal Saurav Smarak Granth. Assam: Sonowal Kachari SanskriticMahotsava.

8. Duarah, D. K. and S. D. Pathak. 1997. “A short note on the health care practices among the Nishis of Arunachal Pradesh. (Pp. 73-78) in F. Ahmed Dasand R. K. Kar (eds.), Health Studies in Anthropology. Department of Anthropology, Dibrugarh University, Dibrugarh.

9. Kumari, P. 2006. “Etiology and Healing Practices: A study in primitive societies of Jharkhand”, (Pp. 487-499) P. Dash Sharma (ed.), Anthropology of Primitive Tribes in India. New Delhi: Serial Publications.

10. Guha, A. 1986. “Folk medicines of the Boro-Kacharis –A Plain Tribe of Assam”, (Pp. 191-199) B. Choudhuri(ed.), Tribal Health. New Delhi: Inter-India Publications.

22

Poverty, Illiteracy & Alcoholism in India and Solutions Through Education

Introduction

The development of any nation depends mainly on the standards of its educational institutions. Education is the most powerful and effective instrument for inducing radical changes in the behaviour of students. Education is a powerful instrument of national development-social, economic and cultural. The teacher occupies pivotal position in the system of education. Teaching has been one of the oldest and most respected professions in the world.

Education is the process of instruction aimed at the all round development of boys and girls. Education dispels ignorance. It is the only wealth that cannot be robbed. Learning includes the moral values and the improvement of character and the methods to increase the strength of mind.

Now India is facing so many problems like Terrorism, Poverty, High-population, Alcoholism and Illiteracy. With the help of Science and Technology India have developed in all the fields. Different types of religions and castes people are living in India. The greatness of India is 'Unity in Diversity'.

Poverty in India

Poverty in India can be defined as a situation only when a section of peoples are unable to satisfy the basic needs of life. The definition and methods of measuring poverty differs from country to country. According to an expert group of Planning Commission, poverty lines in rural areas are drawn with an intake of 2400 calories in rural areas and 2100 calories in urban areas. If the person is unable to get that minimum level of calories is considered as being below poverty line.

The Planning Commission made a survey for finding out the number of persons below poverty line and estimated that 18.96% of the total peoples live below poverty line as of the year 1993-94.

The poverty in India can be defined on the basis of rural poverty as well as urban poverty.

Rural Poverty in India

India is a more rural based country highly dependent on agricultural sector. There is higher concentration of poverty in the rural India as to the given statistics. Government's plans and procedures have failed in many times. The important reasons for country's poverty are as follows:

- Alarming population Growth
- Lack of Investment
- Lower Literacy Rate
- Regional inequalities
- Failure of PDS system

The Government of India has taken various steps from time to time to reduce Rural poverty in India. The recent steps are as follows:

- Small Farmers Development Programme
- Draught Area Development Programme
- Food For Work Programme
- Minimum Needs Programme
- Integrated Rural Development Programme
- National Rural Employment Programme

- Rural Labour Employment Guaranty Programme
- Assurance on Employment

Urban Poverty in India

India is stepping forward for becoming a country with more urbanized. The recent experiences tell that the urban areas are facing the same problem of poverty as of the rural areas. The reasons behind urban poverty are as follows:

- Improper Training
- Growing population
- Slower job Growth
- Failure of PDS System

Government's policy initiatives for eradicating the problem of urban poverty are as follows:

- Nehru Rozgar Yojana
- Prime Minister Rozgar Yojana
- National Social Assistance Programme
- Urban Basic Services for the Poor Programme

The following table shows the overall poverty in India over various years given by Tenth Five Year Plan.

Year	Poverty Ratio (Per cent)			Number of Poor (Millions)		
	Rural	**Urban**	**Combined**	**Rural**	**Urban**	**Combined**
1977-78	53.1	45.2	51.3	264.3	64.4	328.9
1983	45.7	40.8	44.5	252.0	70.9	322.9
1987-88	39.1	38.2	38.9	231.9	75.2	307.1
1993-94	37.3	32.4	36.0	244.0	76.3	320.3
1999-00	27.1	23.6	26.1	193.2	67.1	260.3
2007*	21.1	15.1	19.3	170.5	49.6	220.1

Steps to minimize poverty ratio through Education

We know through education we get strength of mind and knowledge. Strength of mind and knowledge gives solutions for different problems. Through education we can motivate any type of person in the society.

- Take proper steps to use advanced technology for caste based occupation people in the society.
- Good training for formers to use advanced technology and hybrid seeds.
- Conduct good programmes for all type of people to proper utilization of natural sources.
- Take care about health and clean & green.

Illiteracy in India

The Constitution of India advocates free and compulsory education of children below the age of 14. There are so many commissions and committees to increase literacy rate in India. But we failed to improve literacy rate when compared to other countries in the world.

Adult literacy rate is 61.3% for the age group 15 years and above. Youth literacy rate is 76.4% (2000-2004) for the age group 15-24 years. Overall literacy rate of India is 61 %. (73% male and 48% female literacy) according to 2000 report. There are 268.42 million illiterates in India (2000).

Life in India or in that case in any part of the world is easy if you have resources (money and infrastructure). Moreover, a social and economic factor slows you down. While driving back home you must have seen children selling books or flowers. Estimates cite figures of between 60 and 110 million working children in India. Child labor is a source of income for poor families. Is it poverty responsible for child labor or is it the inadequacy of school system in India?

Because of poverty and illiteracy some people participating in the anti-social activities. These activities can't help national development. Rural illiteracy rate is very high when compared to urban illiteracy rate.

A high illiteracy rate in rural parts of India is an area of the Indian education system that cannot be overlooked. Hampered by the government and by other factors the quality of education in rural districts has been quite poor. High dropout rates and low enrollment by the children have contributed to the large illiteracy rate. Kerala, a rural state of India boasts many areas of progress and serves as a model for other rural areas and many of the wealthier parts of India. Without drastic changes by the government and by its citizens, India is well on its way to becoming the world's most illiterate nation.

Steps to minimize illiteracy rate in India

The following steps are necessary to minimize illiteracy rate in India.

- Minimize wastage and stagnation in the schools.
- Increase teacher-student ratio in the class (1:20).
- Give quality education for both rural and urban students.
- Continue mid-day food programme in all the schools and extent this programme to higher classes also.
- Give free books and clothes for all types of students in the rural area.
- Motive the parents to send their children to school regularly.
- Arrange Parent, Teacher and Student (PTA) meetings at least twice in every three months.
- Increase school numbers.
- Use advanced technology in the school at the time of teaching and learning.
- o Continue adult education programmes perfectly.

Alcoholism in India

Prevalence of alcohol use India is generally regarded as a traditional 'dry' or 'abstaining' culture. A recent National Household Survey of Drug Use in the country, the only systematic effort to document the nation-wide prevalence of drug use, recorded alcohol use in only 21% of adult males. Expectedly, this figure cannot accurately mirror the wide variation that obtains in a large and complex country like India. The prevalence of current use of alcohol ranged from a low of 7% in the western state of Gujarat (officially under Prohibition) to 75% in the Northeastern state of Arunachal Pradesh. There is also an extreme gender difference. Prevalence among women has consistently been estimated at less than 5 per cent but is much higher in the Northeastern states. Significantly higher use has been recorded among tribal, rural and lower socioeconomic urban sections.

Indian society is currently undergoing another tectonic shift in its socio-economic fabric. The impact of globalization and economic liberalization (exposure to satellite television, rapid socioeconomic transition and growing disposable incomes) appears to have influenced a widespread attitudinal shift to greater normalization of alcohol use.

The social welfare system and the criminal justice system, often the first to come into contact with alcohol related problems, can be sensitized in identifying and assisting individuals and families at risk from heavy drinking and acting as early referral systems. Extensive opportunities exist to lessen alcohol problems through community education and the prevention of drunk driving, domestic violence, public disorder, unintentional injuries and criminal damage.

Community programmes supporting healthier lifestyles, mass media campaigns that present the advantages of reduced consumption rather than the dangers of heavy alcohol and community development in general, (job creation, skills development and upgrading infrastructure or recreational facilities in communities with high levels of alcohol abuse) should be utilized to encourage alternatives to drinking among the young and disadvantaged. Community action can also serve to shape attitudes, values and norms about drinking. Recently, several effective temperance campaigns have been led by heads of certain Hindu religious orders, though the impact has been limited to their immediate followers.

The official response to the alcohol problem

Unfortunately, the official response remains focused on the visible tip of the alcohol problem, – persons with alcohol dependence (around 4% of the adult male population) instead of on the emerging crisis due to hazardous drinking in more than 20% of the adult population. This is reflected in the approach to alcohol control policies at federal and state levels. The focus is exclusively on supply reduction (prohibition-centric) and tertiary prevention.

Steps to minimize alcohol use through education

Through education it is easy to minimize alcohol users and heavy alcohol users in India. The following steps are necessary.

- Lessons about good health are provided in the curriculum at both school and college levels.
- Number of counselling centers should increased for heavy alcohol users both in rural and urban areas.
- Tell disadvantages of alcohol with the help of print and electronic media and use technology.
- Write good quotations in the campus of schools, colleges, bus and railway stations and other heavy movable places.

References

1. *Economic Survey 2004-05*, Economic Division, Ministry of Finance, Government of India, quoting UNDP Human Development Report 2004.
2. National Institute of Child Health and Human Development. (2000). The National Reading Panel: Reports of the Subgroups.
3. National Institute of Child Health and Human Development. (2001). The National Reading Panel: Reports of the Subgroups.
4. UNESCO Institute for Statistics: Literacy rates, youth (15-24) and adult (15+), by region and gender (September 2006 Assessment).

23

Privatization of Professional Education

Introduction

The development of any nation depends mainly on the standards of its educational institutions. Education is the most powerful and effective instrument for inducing radical changes in the behaviour of students. Education is a powerful instrument of national development-social, economic and cultural. The teacher occupies pivotal position in the system of education. Teaching has been one of the oldest and most respected professions in the world.

Importance of Education

Education is the process of instruction aimed at the all round development of boys and girls. Education dispels ignorance. It is the only wealth that cannot be robbed. Learning includes the moral values and the improvement of character and the methods to increase the strength of mind.

Higher and Professional Education in India

Higher education in India is gasping for breath, at a time when India is aiming to be an important player in the emerging knowledge economy. With about 300 universities and deemed universities, over 15,000 colleges and hundreds of national and regional research institutes, Indian higher education and research sector is the third largest in the world, in terms of the number of students it caters to. However, not a single Indian university finds even a mention in a recent international ranking of the top 200 universities of the world, except an IIT Kharagpur ranked at 41, whereas there were three universities each from China, Hong Kong and South Korea and one from Taiwan.

On the other hand, it is also true that there is no company or institute in the world that has not benefited by graduates, post-graduates or Ph.D.s from India be it NASA, IBM, Microsoft, Intel, Bell, Sun, Harvard, MIT, Caltech, Cambridge or Oxford, and not all those students are products of our IITs, IIMs, IISc/TIFR or central universities, which cater to barely one per cent of the Indian student population. This is not to suggest that we should pat our backs for the achievements of our students abroad, but to point out that Indian higher educational institutions have not been able to achieve the same status for themselves as their students seem to achieve elsewhere with their education from here.

While many reasons can be cited for this situation, they all boil down to decades of feudally managed, colonially modeled institutions run with inadequate funding and excessive political interference. Only about 10 per cent of the total student population enters higher education in India, as compared to over 15 per cent in China and 50 per cent in the major industrialised countries. Higher education is largely funded by the state and central governments so far, but the situation is changing fast. Barring a few newly established private universities, the government funds most of the universities, whereas at the college level, the balance is increasingly being reversed.

The Privatization Experience

The experience over the last few decades has clearly shown that unlike school education, privatisation has not led to any major improvements in the standards of higher and professional education. Yet, in the run up to the economic reforms in 1991, the IMF, World Bank and the countries that control them have been crying hoarse over the alleged pampering of higher education in India at the cost of school education. The fact of the matter was that school education was already privatised to the extent that government schools became an option only to those who cannot afford private schools mushrooming in every street corner, even in small towns and villages. On the other hand, in higher education and professional courses, relatively better quality teaching and infrastructure has been available only in government colleges and universities, while private institutions of higher education in India capitalised on fashionable courses with minimum infrastructure.

Nevertheless, successive governments over the last two decades have only pursued a path of privatisation and deregulation of higher education, regardless of which political party ran the government. From the Punnaiah committee on reforms in higher education set up by the Narasimha Rao government to the Birla-Ambani committee set up by the Vajpayee government, the only difference is in their degree of alignment to the market forces and not in the fundamentals of their recommendations.

With the result, the last decade has witnessed many sweeping changes in higher and professional education: For example, thousands of private colleges and institutes offering IT courses appeared all across the country by the late 1990s and disappeared in less than a decade, with devastating consequences for the students and teachers who depended on them for their careers. This situation is now repeating itself in management, biotechnology, bioinformatics and other emerging areas. No one asked any questions about opening or closing such institutions, or bothered about whether there were qualified teachers at all, much less worry about teacher-student ratio, floor area ratio, class rooms, labs, libraries etc. All these regulations that existed at one time (though not always enforced strictly as long as there were bribes to collect) have now been deregulated or softened under the self-financing scheme of higher and professional education adopted by the UGC in the 9th five-year plan and enthusiastically followed by the central and state governments.

This situation reached its extreme recently in the new state of Chattisgarh, where over 150 private universities and colleges came up within a couple of years, till the scam got exposed by a public interest litigation and the courts ordered the state government in

2004 to derecognise and close most of these universities or merge them with the remaining recognized ones. A whole generation of students and teachers are suffering irreparable damage to their careers due to these trends, for no fault of theirs. Even government-funded colleges and universities in most states started many "self-financing" courses in IT, biotechnology etc., without qualified teachers, labs or infrastructure and charging huge fees from the students and are liberally giving them marks and degrees to hide their inadequacies.

It is not that the other well established departments and courses in government funded colleges and universities are doing any better. Decades of government neglect, poor funding, frequent ban on faculty recruitments and promotions, reduction in library budgets, lack of investments in modernization leading to obsolescence of equipment and infrastructure, and the tendency to start new universities on political grounds without consolidating the existing ones today threatens the entire higher education system.

Another corollary of this trend is that an educational institution recognized in a particular state need not limit its operations to that state. This meant that universities approved by the governments of Chattisgarh or Himachal Pradesh can set up campuses in Delhi or Noida, where they are more likely to get students from well off families who can afford their astronomical fees. What is more, they are not even accountable to the local governments, since their recognition comes from a far away state. Add to this a new culture of well-branded private educational institutions allowing franchisees at far away locations to run their courses, without being responsible to the students or teachers in any other way. This is increasingly becoming a trend with foreign universities, especially among those who do not want to set up their own shop here, but would like to benefit from the degree-purchasing power of the growing upwardly mobile economic class of India. Soon we might see private educational institutions getting them listed in the stock market and soliciting investments in the education business on the slogan that its demand will never see the sunset.

The economics of imparting higher education are such that, barring a few courses in arts and humanities, imparting quality education in science, technology, engineering, medicine etc. requires huge investments in infrastructure, all of which cannot be recovered through student fees, without making higher education inaccessible to a large section of students. Unlike many better-known private educational institutions in Western countries that operate in the charity mode with tuition waivers and fellowships (which is one reason why our students go there), most private colleges and universities in India are pursuing a profit motive. This is the basic reason for charging huge tuition fees, apart from forced donations, capitation fees and other charges. Despite huge public discontent, media interventions and many court cases, the governments have not been able to regulate the fee structure and donations in these institutions. Even the courts have only played with the terms such as payment seats, management quotas etc., without addressing the basic issue of fee structure.

Privatization of Teacher Education

"The destiny of India is now being shaped in her class rooms". This is the opening sentence of the Kothari Education Commission report (1964-66). What kind of destiny has been actually shaped during the last sixty years? There are thousands of schools without primary needs. The position of teacher's economic condition is also poor when compared to USA teachers. Majority of teacher educational institutions are under the control of private sector. The main aim of private organizations is to get profit.

It is not only students but also teachers who are at the receiving end of the ongoing transformation in higher and professional education. The nation today witnesses the declining popularity of teaching as a profession, not only among the students that we produce, but also among parents, scientists, society and the government. The teaching profession today attracts only those who have missed all other "better" opportunities in life, and is increasingly mired in bureaucratic controls and anti-education concepts such as "hours" of teaching "load", "paid-by-the-hour", "contractual" teachers etc. With privatisation reducing education to a commodity, teachers are reduced to tutors and teaching is reduced to coaching. The consumerist boom and the growing salary differentials between teachers and other professionals and the value systems of the emerging free market economy have made teaching one of the least attractive professions that demands more work for less pay. Yet, the society expects teachers not only to be inspired but also to do an inspiring job!

Present Status of Teacher Education

Permission is granted by the NCTE regional centers to number of teacher education institutions/colleges especially in the private unaided sector. Take for example, in Andhra Pradesh, there are more than 300 B.Ed Colleges in the private unaided sector and there are less than 20 B.Ed colleges in Government and aided sector. Is there any kind of supervision either by the university authorities or by the government officials or by the officers of NCTE with regard to availability of the staff during college days, proper attendance of the students, proper organization and running of different programmes of B.Ed Course? It is a doubtful validity. The first and foremost supervising authority for running B.Ed programme is the concerned University. The concerned officials of the university have to make frequent surprise visits to the B.Ed Colleges under its Jurisdiction. If any loopholes identified, necessary steps may be taken for rectifying them at the earliest possible time; then only the quality of B.Ed programmes can be improved.

In the most of the private B.Ed. colleges in the state of Andhra Pradesh, there is two or three teaching staff only. In some of the universities, there are no selection committees for these colleges. The managements will run the colleges according to their whims and fancies. In majority of the situations, they are charging Rs.6000/- for a set of B.Ed. records which cost about Rs.300/- in the market. They will pay less than Rs. 5000/- to the teaching staff. They are collecting huge amounts from the students under the heads; 'practical examinations', 'study tours', etc. they allow less than 20% attendance students to the examinations by collecting huge amounts from them. Some private management resort to all types of fraud activities. Then, who will set right these things? The first and foremost is the concerned affiliating university, then the state government and NCTE at the regional level and national level. Honesty persons with surprise visits can make the situation better.

Conclusion

India is a developing country. Different types of religious people are living in the country. We have thousand years of tradition and culture. Now we are living in the technological and modern world. Because of globalization a lot of change occurring. Education is a primary need for all in the society. It is the duty of government to provide free education for all up to 14 years. All people have no opportunity to study higher and professional education. Now majority of professional educational institutions are under the control of private organizations. Especially all teacher educational institutions are in the private sector. The main aim of private sector is to get profit. How it is possible to expect quality education? It is not possible to study Medicine or Engineering course for a poor student in the society. It is necessary to establish more and more professional and higher educational institutions in the country. Teacher is a national builder. He has a capacity to change the world. There are some benefits and losses due to privatization of professional education. But India is a developing country. It is better to establish all professional educational institutions under the government sector. Then only it is possible to study all type of courses for poor section children and India will become developed country in the world.

24

Role of Information Technology in Teacher Education

Education is the learning of human souls to what is best, and making what is best out of them? – John Ruskin.

Now we are living in the modern world. A lot of change is occurring in every day. With the help of science and technology we have developed in all the fields. With the help of technology now it is easy to know any type of information within seconds throughout the world.

Radio, Television, Phone, Mobile, Computer and Internet have changed the human life. Through education we can learn anything easily with the help of these instruments. According to Mahatma Gandhi, the father of Indian Nation, by giving good education to each and every one we can remove poverty and develop good character. India is a developing country. Now we have very much demand in the IT filed. The development of IT is a wonder. Now lacks of student are entering in to the IT filed. Our central and state governments are also giving more importance for Information Technology. There is a separate department for Information Technology under the Ministry of Communication and Information Technology.

Definition of Information Technology

Information technology (IT): The science and activity of using computers and other electronic equipment to store and send information.

Information Technology is also defined as, "The technology involved with the transmission and storage of information, especially the development, installation, implementation, and management of computer systems within companies, universities" and other organizations".

Goals and Objectives

1. To provide in-service training to teachers and teacher educators on computers and IT.
2. To incorporate all the IT facilities into teacher education model.
3. To extend internet, e-mail facilities to all teachers and students in teacher education.
4. To provide network how to operate computers and internet to all the student teachers.
5. To provide network to teacher education centers all over India.
6. To extend distance mode of teacher education online and also include a live interactive practical teaching.
7. To restructure teacher education curriculum.
8. To incorporate use of IT in special education.
9. To use IT in teacher education research.
10. To create a virtual teacher education centre.
11. To incorporate good hidden curriculum strategies to restore the humanistic tendencies required for a teacher.
12. Ensure the protection and security of data.
13. Minimize duplication of effort, services and resources.
14. Eliminate inefficient and costly redundancies.
15. Define what services, if any, should be restructured or eliminated.
16. Eliminate non-compatible standards and architectures.

17. Identify obstacles for departments wanting to move computing operations to the Division of Information Technology.
18. Recommend a strategy for evaluating the university-wide impacts of major information technology purchases including analysis of total cost of ownership.
19. Evaluate the complexity and risks of managing a complex distributed computing environment, including system security, exposure to data loss and virus protection.
20. Identify issues and trends in technology that may affect the university's technology infrastructure and long-term architecture.
21. Recommend the most effective balance of central and distributed technology services, staffing and resources. Detail any logical alternatives. Recommendations will include background, advice and alternatives that address the following:

- Create a cost efficient blend of centralization and decentralization of information technology resources - properly aligning the university's information technology infrastructure to best meet the needs of its teaching, research and outreach missions.
- Create a coherent campus-wide information technology computing architecture and a solid foundation for the university's information technology infrastructure.
- Develop a long-term organizational process and structure to ensure the best utilization of the university's information technology resources for the future.
- Estimate the costs of infrastructure and support, including personnel and training, in the current distributed environment and to estimate the same costs for the alternatives proposed.

Need of Information Technology in Teacher Education

It is well known fact that IT and Cyber age have brought a revolutionary transformation and drifted the whole life style of people. No area left untouched with it. We have arrived at global village concept with all virtual realities on our desktops. But is it the teacher education, which has remained untouched in this direction.

We have a lot of educational institutions in the field of Information Technology like ‘Indian Institute of Information Technology (IIIT), ‘International Institute of Information Technology, ‘Tata Institute of Information Technology’ and ‘Deerubai Ambani Institute of Information Technology’. There are so many Information Technology departments in the universities at both state and central level. The effect of Information Technology in our daily life is very much. It is very necessary to take Information Technology help for teacher education. There is a separate subject for trainee teacher ‘Educational Technology’. With the help of Information Technology it is possible to give quality and effective education for trainee teachers.

A nation’s development potential depends upon its ability to continuously educate its population and its ability to create armies of skilled manpower. In particular, use of Information Technology (IT) in acquiring knowledge and skill has become an essential element in education and training. These IT elements in the educational process have magical effects.

Higher education without the support of IT makes the lives of learner and teachers equally difficult. A nation’s intellectual strength depends on IT support. The use of computing and communication technology to enhance the efficacy of transaction and productivity is the driving force in this new era of social and economic transformation in the new society called Information Society.

A strong IT infrastructure can give an institution a competitive advantage for the best students and faculty and an advantage in competition for absorbing external research grants to execute studies, research etc. in a short time and with great resolution. The quality of an institution’s environment for digital information storage and retrieval has, for any disciplines, become more important than the institution’s conventional, library resources in print media.

Virtually every economic sector that is labour intensive has managed to improve productivity through the use of technology except education. Faculty/student ratios in higher education have changed significantly in more than 50 years. The most advanced technology in common use in the classroom today in our country is the overhead projector, and it took nearly three decades to migrate from the national level training institute to the classroom. Institutions like

UGC, IGNOU, and CIET have begun to transact curriculum on DD 1 but the ETV programmes are mostly of enrichment type and not as per the demand of the students. It is unlikely that IT will have a major impact on teaching and learning if the current paradigm for instruction changes.

Generally majority trainee teachers have no knowledge about usage of technology. Because their lower classes curriculum is separate. It is necessary to change curriculum at school level and implement Information Technology at school level also. 'Today's children are tomorrow's citizens', so it is necessary to take care about school curriculum. It is government duty to provide Information Technology labs for all type of Educational Institutions in the country.

Uses of Information Technology

Now we are using Information Technology in all the fields like education agriculture, banking, transport, medicine, research and manufacturing and in social service mode.

Specific Uses of Information Technology

- Animation for simulation of urban environments and video for assembling and disseminating results of the analysis and design work.
- Graphic Information System (GIS) for the study of housing and development patterns.
- Computer Aided Design (CAD) for geometric modeling: Digital image archival systems for compiling data about the built environment.

Role of Information Technology in Teacher Education

In-service Training

There is a need to provide in-service training to all the teachers and teacher educators with updated computer operation skills and provide with IT know how. To utilize the facilities to access updated information and solutions to their problems in their areas of specialization, it can be provide on-line.

Teacher Education Training Programmes through IT facilities

A virtual teacher education centre can be created. All the necessary skills and training can be provided in different modes on the network. It should incorporate all the available facilities like, tele-education, teleconferencing, floppy diskettes and CD-ROMs in teacher education. Networks like ERNET, INTERNET and futuristic concept of bringing satellite channels directly to homes by DTS (Direct to Home) service and expert talks through virtual classrooms can also be made available.

Distance Mode of Education

The present practice of TV and other media in distance mode of education can be substituted by multimedia systems which have an extra advantage of intractability through GUI (Graphics User Interface) which controls the response of information transfer process according to the learners pace. It helps in using screen as an instructor for self-learning.

IT in special Education

IT is providing solutions for the education of physically challenged people as well. As reported by BBC web-site (web-site at BBC news, science), the Germans have developed a technology and associated software for which people, where computer will sense the signals from the head of a paralyzed person through two attached electrodes, and thereby, allow him to surf the net like a normal person. These facilities will transform the lives of the physically challenged and IT can be used even for diagnosing.

Research and INTERNET

Internet facilities should be made available to research students, teacher educators. All the departments should have internet connectivity. It helps in accessing information about the ongoing research in their respective fields and it also avoids overlapping.

Restructuring Curricula of Teacher Education

1. Teacher education curriculum needs drastic changes by incorporating all facilities available through IT. Primarily IT can be used to keep on par with the existing knowledge

structure. It can be thoroughly incorporated into methodologies of teacher education.

2. There should not be exclusive theoretical orientation in curriculum. It shall have more practically demonstrable skill and strategies in the curriculum.
3. All possible attempts should be made to train teachers apart from virtual classrooms, to incorporate the necessary live interactive experiences to understand the significance of physical interaction with the child in the classroom.
4. Humanistic and affective hidden curriculum and an effective training to acquire all traits and qualities required in teacher to handle human society should also be included in the curriculum.

Conclusion

Information Technology has a prominent role in the field of teacher education. With the help of information technology it is easy to know any type of information within seconds throughout the world. The advanced knowledge of information technology is much helpful for research in all the fields of education. With the help of Information Technology it is easy to educate trainee teachers. By knowing the usage of technology they have a change to share their opinions with other teacher throughout the world. Information Technology motivates the teacher to learn lot of things in their subject area.

Now we are happy that our State and Central Governments have taking good steps to introduce online education in the educational institutions. There are separate subjects in D.Ed., and B.Ed., like Computer Education and Educational Technology. Now teachers are using computers and internet in the educational institutions. But the percentage is very less. It is more important to give equal importance to theory and practical in the computer education and educational technology subjects. It is the duty of the Government to provide Computer and Educational technology labs for each and every teacher education institution in the country.

Now NCTE, CIET, NIEPA, NCERT, SCERT and other educational departments have recognized the advantages of Information Technology in the field of education. They motivate the students to use IT. They are conducting national seminars, workshops, and conferences about Information Technology. Teachers must be given excellent training in setting, grading papers and preparing assignment, etc. These can be used in teacher training network. Excellent stimulated models can be made available to access on network.

References

1. Promotion of Quality of Teacher Education for 21st Century, Dr. N. Ramanath Kishan, Editor, Ashoka Krishna Offset Printers, Warangal.
2. http://www.ciet.nic.in/
3. http://www.aponline.gov.in/

25

Some Reflections on Public Transportation for Disabled Persons in Academic Institution

Introduction

- Look first at my strengths and not at my weaknesses.
- Great pleasure in life is doing what people say you cannot do.
- Open your arms to change, but don't let go of your values.
- The most pathetic person in the world is someone who has sight but has no vision.
- The tragedy of life is what dies inside a man while he lives.
- I am always doing that which I cannot do, in order that I may learn how to do it.

The Universe is so beautiful. Human being is the greatest animal in the animal kingdom. Because of Education and Science & Technology he became a greatest and strongest animal in the world. All persons in the world are good at the time of birth. But, they will become different types of criminals because of society. Man and Woman are parts in the society. If the society takes care about each and every person in the community then there will be no place for cruel, theft, corruption, non-violence, harassment and inequality. We want that type of society. We want such people which have full kindness, co-operation, co-ordination, helping nature and sensitiveness.

Disabled Persons

The Disability Discrimination Act (DDA) of United Kingdom defines a disabled person as someone who has a physical or mental impairment that has a substantial and long-term adverse effect on his or her ability to carry out normal day-to-day activities.

The Constitution of India ensures equality, freedom, justice and dignity of all individuals and implicitly mandates an inclusive society for all including persons with disabilities. In the recent years, there have been vast and positive changes in the perception of the society towards persons with disabilities. It has been realized that a majority of persons with disabilities can lead a better quality of life if they have equal opportunities and effective access to rehabilitation measures.

Facts and Figures

The World Health Organization estimates that there are 600 million disabled people worldwide, about 10% of the world population. It is also estimated that about 80% of all disabled people worldwide live in developing countries.

According to the Census 2001, there are 2.19 crore persons with disabilities in India who constitute 2.13 percent of the total population. This includes persons with visual, hearing, speech, locomotors and mental disabilities. Seventy five per cent of persons with disabilities live in rural areas, 49 per cent of disabled population is literate and only 34 per cent are employed. The earlier emphasis on medical rehabilitation has now been replaced by an emphasis on social rehabilitation. There has been an increasing recognition of abilities of persons with disabilities and emphasis on mainstreaming them in the society based on their capabilities.

More and more, disability is seen as a social issue which is not only based on medical reasons. The organization "Disabled Peoples'

International" defines disability as the interaction between the person with impairment and environmental and attitudinal barriers he or she may face. Therefore the reasons for disability are always complex and can only be understood within the context of societies and cultures.

Types of Disability

According to Government of India, there are five types of disabilities in our society.

- Mental Retardation
- Visual Disability
- Speech Disability
- Hearing Disability
- Locomotors Disabilities

Causes of Disability

According to WHO there are so many causes for disability. The main causes are given bellow.

Causes of Disability	In millions
Non-contagious somatic illnesses	100
Injuries/wounds	78
Malnutrition	100
Functional psychiatric disorders	40
Chronic alcoholism and drug abuse	100
Congenital diseases	100
Contagious diseases	56

Programmes and Policies for the Development of Disabled Persons

The Government of India has enacted three legislations for persons with disabilities viz.

(i) Persons with Disability (Equal Opportunities, Protection of Rights and Full Participation) Act, 1995, which provides for education, employment, creation of barrier free environment, social security, etc.

(ii) National Trust for Welfare of Persons with Autism, Cerebral Palsy, Mental Retardation and Multiple Disability Act, 1999 has provisions for legal guardianship of the four categories and creation of enabling environment for as much independent living as possible.

(iii) Rehabilitation Council of India Act, 1992 deals with the development of manpower for providing rehabilitation services.

In addition to the legal framework, extensive infrastructure has been developed. The following seven national Institutes are working for development of manpower in different areas, namely:

- Institute for the Physically Handicapped, New Delhi.
- National Institute of Visually Handicapped, Dehradun
- National Institute for Orthopaedically Handicapped, Kolkata
- National Institute for Mentally Handicapped, Secunderabad.
- National Institute for Hearing Handicapped, Mumbai
- National Institute of Rehabilitation Training & Research, Cuttack.
- National Institute for Empowerment of Persons with Multiple Disabilities, Chennai.

There are five Composite Rehabilitation Centres, four Regional Rehabilitation Centres and 120 District Disability Rehabilitation Centres (DDRCs) providing various kinds of rehabilitation services to persons with disabilities. There are also several national institutions under the Ministry of Health & Family Welfare working in the field of rehabilitation, like National Institute of Mental Health and Neuro Sciences, Bangalore; All India Institute of Physical Medicine and Rehabilitation, Mumbai; All India Institute of Speech and Hearing, Mysore; Central Institute of Psychiatry, Ranchi, etc. In addition, certain State Government institutions also provide rehabilitation services. Besides, 250 private institutions conduct training courses for rehabilitation professionals.

National Handicapped and Finance Development Corporation (NHFDC) has been providing loans on concessional terms for undertaking self-employment ventures by the persons with disabilities through State Channelizing Agencies.

Panchayati Raj Institutions at Village level, Intermediary level and District level have been entrusted with the welfare of persons with disabilities.

India is a signatory to the Declaration on the Full Participation and Equality of People with Disabilities in the Asia Pacific Region. India is also a signatory to the Biwako Millennium Framework for action towards an inclusive, barrier free and rights based society. India is currently participating in the negotiations on the UN Convention on Protection and promotion of the Rights and Dignity of Persons with Disabilities.

National Policy Statement

The National Policy recognizes that Persons with Disabilities are valuable human resource for the country and seeks to create an environment that provides those equal opportunities, protection of their rights and full participation in society. The focus of the policy shall be on the following:

Prevention of Disabilities

Since disability, in a large number of cases, is preventable, there will be strong emphasis on prevention of disabilities. Programme for prevention of diseases, which result in disability and the creation of awareness regarding measures to be taken for prevention of disabilities during the period of pregnancy and thereafter will be intensified and their coverage expanded.

Rehabilitation Measures

Rehabilitation measures can be classified into three distinct groups: (i) physical rehabilitation, which includes early detection and intervention, counseling & medical interventions and provision of aids & appliances. It will also include the development of rehabilitation professionals. (ii) Educational rehabilitation including vocational education and (iii) economic rehabilitation for a dignified life in society.

Education and Disabled Persons

Persons with disabilities have a right to lead a life of dignity and self-respect, this is not a favour given to them. This can be possible only if they get adequate opportunities to pursue their education and thereafter, get gainful employment and status in society. The goal of inclusive and universal education is being pursued under the Sarva Shiksha Abhiyan.

In fact, families of the disabled have a leading role in being a source of strength and encouragement. In cases, when the family neglects the disabled person on account of either poverty or lack of resources or sometimes apathy, the disabled person is confronted with a difficult situation. Education and awareness can correct negative perceptions. NGOs can play an important part in making society and families aware of the needs of the disabled and to make them face the world with confidence. I would urge NGOs to undertake projects for disabled people, particularly in rural areas and urban slums.

According to Swami Vivekanada "We want that education by which character is formed, strength of mind is increased, and the intellect is expanded and by which one can stand on one's own feet". If we give this type of education for disabled persons, they live happily. Education is the solution for all types of problems in the society. Through education it is possible to change any type of person in the society. Education changes the life style of the disabled persons.

Persons with Disability (Equal Opportunities, Protection of Rights and Full Participation) Act, 1995, which provides for education, employment, creation of barrier free environment, social security, etc.

Education for Persons with Disabilities

Education is the most effective vehicle of social and economic empowerment. In keeping with the spirit of the Article 21A of the Constitution guaranteeing education as a fundamental right and Section 26 of the Persons with Disabilities Act, 1995, free and compulsory education has to be provided to all children with disabilities up to the minimum age of 18 years. According to the Census, 2001, fifty-one percent persons with disabilities are illiterate. This is a very large percentage. There is a need for mainstreaming of the persons with disabilities in the general education system through Inclusive education.

Sarva Shiksha Abhiyan (SSA) launched by the Government has the goal of eight years of elementary schooling for all children including children with disabilities in the age group of 6-14 years by 2010. Children with disabilities in the age group of 15-18 years are provided free education under Integrated Education for Disabled Children (IEDC) Scheme.

Under SSA, a continuum of educational options, learning aids and tools, mobility assistance, support services etc. are being made available to students with disabilities. This includes education through an open learning system and open schools, alternative schooling, distance education, special schools, wherever necessary home based education, itinerant teacher model, remedial teaching, part time classes, Community Based Rehabilitation (CBR) and vocational education.

IEDC Scheme implemented through the State Governments, Autonomous Bodies and Voluntary Organizations provides hundred percent financial assistance for various facilities like special teachers, books and stationery, uniform, transport, readers allowance for the visually handicapped, hostel allowance, equipment cost, removal/ modification of architectural barriers, financial assistance for purchase/production of instructional material, training of general teachers and equipment for resource rooms.

There will be concerted effort on the part of the Government to improve identification of children with disabilities through regular surveys, their enrollment in appropriate schools and their continuation till they successfully complete their education. The Government will endeavor to provide right kind of learning material and books to the children with disabilities, suitably trained and sensitized teachers and schools which are accessible and disabled friendly.

Government of India is providing scholarships to students with disabilities for pursuing studies at post school level. Government will continue to support the scholarships and expand its coverage.

Facilities for technical and vocational education designed to inculcate and bolster skill development suited to various types of productive activities by adaptation of the existing institutes or accelerated setting up of institutes in un-served/underserved areas will be encouraged. NGOs will also be encouraged to provide vocational training.

Persons with disabilities will be provided access to the Universities, technical institutions and other institutions of higher learning to pursue higher and professional courses.

International Day of Disabled People

"Nothing about us without us" is the motto of 2007 year's International Day of the Disabled People. Proclaimed by the General Assembly in October 1992, this day aims to raise awareness on disabled people's rights at national and international levels.

On the 3rd December 1982, the UN General Assembly decided on the World Programme of Action for Disabled People. The United Nations committed itself and its members to promote the full participation of disabled people in social life and development as well as prevention and rehabilitation measures.

Disabled people are not yet fully considered within international development issues. They are still excluded from society in many countries of the world. Even where effective disability legislation is in place, the implementation lacks ideas and is hindered by negative attitudes towards disabled people.

The United Nations (UN) has set up an international human rights convention on the rights of disabled people.

Public Transportation for Disabled People

Every individual including people with disabilities have an equal right to travel and use public transportation with dignity and independence. It should be regarded as a fundamental right of all citizens, since travel is usually a daily necessity for education, employment, medical attention, entertainment etc. Transport is important in facilitating human communication and face-to-face meetings. It plays a significant role in economic development of the nation.

People with diverse disabilities (sensory or physical) and reduced mobility (people with health problems for example respiratory, cardio-vascular, joint problems or temporary ailments; senior citizens; pregnant women; families with young children and people with heavy luggage, etc.,) constitute sizeable number of the population.

Since majority of this segment belong to lower and middle-income group, it is beyond their economic capacity to use private taxis/ three-wheeled auto rickshaws or purchase their own vehicle and are, therefore, dependent on public transport.

Existing transportation system, i.e., vehicles, terminals, and operations are either full of obstacles or impossible to use. It induces fatigue, restricts educational and employment opportunities, causing frustration. It hinders right to freedom of movement, equal participation and access to health and other social services.

Move towards Accessible Transportation

The Persons with Disability (Equal Opportunities, Protection of Rights and Full Participation) Act 1995, states non-discrimination in built environment and transportation Delhi has set the lead in accessible transportation. The best example is Delhi Metro Rail Corporation (DMRC), a joint venture of Government of India and Government of National Capital Territory of Delhi.

Access Provisions for Public Transport

Transport facilities and means of transport include land, water and air transport systems.

(a) Road transport

Public buses are common man's transport but it is not fully used by people with reduced mobility and people with disabilities.

i. Regulations should specify that new vehicles bought by public and private transport companies be accessible for people with disabilities. Studies indicate that buying a bus with lifts adds only 5 per cent to its cost.

ii. Access regulations should specify modifications required for public buses, which are already in use.

iii. A minimum of four seats in all buses should be designated for persons with disabilities. Those seats should be near entrance/exit doors.

iv. Adequate space for one wheelchair should be provided in all buses.

v. Parallel transport services for persons with disabilities who cannot use mainline systems are recommended.

vi. Access regulations should be adapted to meet the needs of rural communities.

Note: Concessions are provided for persons with physical impairments and visually handicaps. Student concessions are provided to all children. Mostly each state has its own policy.

(b) Rail transport (including local trains, under and over ground trains and inter-city trains)

i. Access regulations should stipulate that new rail transport facilities must be accessible for persons with disabilities.

ii. All mainline train stations must be modified to become accessible.

iii. One car per existing train should be modified to incorporate access features.

iv. A minimum of two seats per car should be designated for persons with disabilities. Those seats should be near entrance/exit doors.

v. A minimum of one accessible toilet should be available near the above-mentioned seats.

Note: Railways allow disabled persons to travel at concession fares up to 75% in the first and second classes. Escorts accompanying blind, orthopedically and mentally handicapped persons are also eligible to 75% concession in the basic fare.

(c) Sea and river transport (including ferries, as well as domestic and international passenger ships)

i. Access regulations should stipulate that new sea/river transportation must be barrier-free.

ii. A minimum of one deck in ferries and domestic and international passenger ships should be modified to incorporate access features.

iii. Ramps, passageways, gangways, safety equipment and at least two berths or cabins must be modified to incorporate access features.

(d) Air transport (including domestic and international passenger aircrafts)

i. Access regulations should stipulate that new air transport facilities must be barrier-free.

ii. A minimum of two seats near the entrance/exit doors in all domestic passenger aircraft should be available for persons with disabilities.

iii. A minimum of one accessible toilet should be near the above-mentioned seats.

Note: The Indian Airlines Corporation allows 50% concessional fare to disabled persons.

Transport allowance

Disabled persons are entitled to double the normal transport allowance to other similarly placed employees. However, disabled persons who are provided with government transport are not entitled to transport allowance. Transport allowance is allowed at normal rates if the disabled person has been provided with government accommodation.

Conclusions

Today we are living in the Scientific and Techological Modern world. With the help of science and techology the disabled people are also participating and entering into all types of jobs by fulfilling the government rules. It is necessary to take care about them. The literacy rate of disabled persons is very low. Necessary programmes are important to raise the literacy rate. Education gives strength and power. Give priority and importance for disabled persons in the public transportation. Teachers and NGOs role are very important for the development of disabled persons. Celebrate 'International Day for Disabled Persons' in a grand manner. Talk lovely with disabled persons. If you like, encourage them but don't discourage. Try to see their strengths but not their weaknesses.

References

1. "Disability India Journal", Volume III, Issue XXXXV, December 2007.

2. “National Policy for Persons with Disabilities”, Ministry of Social Justice and Empowerment, Government of India, New Delhi, December, 2006.

3. “Research study on Accessibility of Buses and Bus Shelter”, 2006.

4. “Research study on Accessibility of Indian Railways”, 2005.

5. http://www.samarthyaindia.com/researchrailways.html.

6. http://www.google.com

7. http://www.yahoosearch.com

26

Strategies to Create Awareness on Domestic Violence Through Educational Institutions

Introduction

The development of any nation depends mainly on the standards of its educational institutions. Education is the most powerful and effective instrument for inducing radical changes in the behaviour of students. Education is a powerful instrument of national development-social, economic and cultural. The teacher occupies pivotal position in the system of education. Teaching has been one of the oldest and most respected professions in the world.

Once the first Prime Minister of India, Jawaharlal Nehru said, "you can tell the condition of a nation by looking at the status of its women". This is absolutely true. Woman of any nation is the mirror to its civilization. If women enjoy good status it shows that the society has reached a level of maturity and sense of responsibility while a decadent image conjures up if the opposite is true. The story of Indian women is as old as the history of Indian civilization.

Domestic Violence

Across cultures, the family, whether natal or marital, is often associated with love, support, and bonding among members. Though these characteristics are often present, it has become evident through recent research that the home is also frequently the site of violent human relationships. Eight recent studies coordinated by the International Center for Research on Women (ICRW) document the pervasiveness of domestic violence among women in India regardless of age, education level, class, length of marriage, and family living arrangement. For example, in a multi-site study of nearly 10,000 households, 40 percent of the women reported experiencing at least one form of physical abuse and 26 percent reported severe physical abuse, including being hit, kicked, or beaten. Fifty percent of the women experiencing severe physical abuse reported being beaten three or more times in their lifetime and at least once during pregnancy (INCLEN 2000, Visaria 1999)

What is Domestic Violence?

"Nonviolence is not a garment to be put on and off at will. Its seat is in the heart, and it must be an inseparable part of our being" - Mahatma Gandhi.

Domestic violence is controlling behaviour and includes all kinds of physical, sexual, economic, psychological and emotional abuse within all kinds of intimate relationships. The perpetrators of domestic violence or abuse are usually men and the victims or survivors are usually women and children that they know. It includes:

- Punching and slapping.
- Kicking and hair pulling.
- Biting and pinching.
- Pushing and shoving.
- Being forced to have sex.
- Being beaten or cut with other objects.
- Disrespect, neglect and emotional blackmail.
- Verbal abuse and swearing.
- Being prevented from going out or seeing people – being isolated.

Forms of Domestic Violence

The following are the forms of Domestic Violence:

1. Physical Abuse
2. Sexual Abuse
3. Psychological Abuse
4. Emotional Abuse
5. Financial Abuse

Education and Employment of Indian Women

Women constitute almost half of the population in the world. But the hegemonic masculine ideology made them suffer a lot as they were denied equal opportunities in different parts of the world. The rise of feminist ideas has, however, led to the tremendous improvement of women's condition throughout the world in recent times. Access to education has been one of the most pressing demands of theses women's rights movements. Women's education in India has also been a major preoccupation of both the government and civil society as educated women can play a very important role in the development of the country.

According to last census held in 2001, the percentage of female literacy in the country is 54.16%. The literacy rate in the country has increased from 18.33% in 1951 to 65.38% as per 2001 census. The female literacy rate has also increased from 8.86% in 1951 to 54.16%. It is noticed that the female literacy rate during the period 1991-2001 increased by 14.87% whereas male literacy rate rose by 11.72%. Hence the female literacy rate actually increased by 3.15% more compared to male literacy rate.

Kumud Sharma of the Centre for Women's Development Studies in New Delhi traced the correlation between education and domestic violence to patriarchal attitudes. "Educated women are aware of their rights," she said. "They are no longer willing to follow commands blindly. When they ask questions, it causes conflicts, which, in turn, leads to violence. In many Indian states, working women are asked to hand over their paycheck to the husband and have no control over their finances. So, if they stop doing so or start asserting their right, there is bound to be friction."

Women Universities in India

The Government of India and State Governments established separate universities for women for the development of women in India.

- **Andhra Pradesh**-Sri Padmavati University, Tirupati
- **Delhi**- Lady Shri Ram College for Women, Lajpat Nagar
- **Maharashtra**- SNDT Women's University, Mumbai
- **Rajasthan**- Banasthali Vidyapith, Banasthali

After living in the shadows, women in India have entered the workplace with a vengeance, snapping up a larger chunk of jobs whereas the employment figures for men have declined. Indian women have outshone their male counterparts with a 3.35 per cent rise in the employment growth rate for the period of seven years from 1998 to 2004 as against a dip of 8 per cent in case of men in the country, an Assocham survey reveals. The chamber's study on 'women employment growth rate and gender budgeting' shows that the total number of women employed in the public and private sector has increased to 49.34 lakh in 2004 from 47.74 lakh in 1998, while the number of men employed has fallen to 215.09 lakh in 2004 from 233.92 lakh in 1998.

"The public sector has been hiring women much more aggressively than the private sector. The number of women employed in the public sector has risen from 27.63 lakh in 1998 to 28.9 lakh in 2004, witnessing a growth of close to 4.6 per cent. The private sector added 0.33 lakh women staff with a growth of 1.64 per cent over 1998, taking the total number to 20.44 lakh," the study said.

Minimizing the Dangers of Domestic Violence

A victim does not want to willingly continue living in an abusive relationship. However, until circumstances improve, she may have no choice but to continue living with her abuser. In this situation, there are a few things she can do to try to prevent serious injury to members of her family.

Avoid certain areas: A victim cannot control where her abuser is going to attack her. However, she and her children can take a few precautions. If the abuser confronts her or the children and starts arguing with them, be prepared to be attacked. Avoid being attacked in an area like the kitchen or bathroom. These are small enclosed spaces with only a single entry or exit point. If any member of the family is in either of these places when the abuser confronts her, she should back away slowly and try to exit the room. This should be done discreetly, so as not to trigger the violent instincts of the abuser. A victim must never appear as if she is trying to run away.

Not only are areas like the kitchen and bathroom small, they are also filled with potential weapons. These include knives, razors, plates, etc. Similarly, keep potential weapons out of reach or not easily accessible to your abuser. Objects like heavy bowls, knives, rolling pins, etc. should be kept inside cabinets so that the abuser is less likely to use them.

Keep children informed: Children are living in the same home and are definitely going to be affected by the violence. Explain to them what is happening, in a calm and rational manner. Make sure that they know it is not their fault. Children are very sensitive and often perceive situations as being caused due to their behaviour. Make sure that children do not harbor any guilt over the situation.

Make sure that children do not get involved in any of the violence. If they hear a fight, they should stay out of sight or retreat to their room. At no time should they attempt to interfere. Children will naturally want to try to protect the abused parent. However noble the gesture, it is one of the main reasons why children get hurt. An abuser might turn on the children in a fit of rage and strike them. At the same time, the abused partner may not be in a position to attempt to step in and shield the children. For an abused parent, her first priority should still be to protect her children at all costs.

A victim of domestic violence cannot be blamed for her situation. Although she may not be able to leave her home, there are ways in which she can seek help. The police are duty bound to register a complaint and investigate the situation if a victim approaches them. In addition, there are a number of non-governmental organizations, which provide legal and financial aid to victims of domestic violence.

Safety Plans against Domestic Violence

The National Coalition against Domestic Violence (US) urges women in abusive relationships to create a safety plan. The following plan may help woman in difficult situations:

1. Find a safe place to go in your home if an argument begins. Avoid rooms without an exit and rooms with potential dangers such as a kitchen.
2. Know who to contact in a crisis and establish a code word or sign among trusted family or friends to let them know you need help.
3. Memorize all important phone numbers.
4. Always keep money and change with you.
5. Keep important papers and documents in a place you can easily access if necessary, including: social security cards, birth certificates, marriage license, checkbook, charge cards, bank statements, health insurance cards, and any records of past abuse including photographs and police reports.

Strategies to Create Awareness on Domestic Violence through Education

According to Swami Vivekananda "We want that education by which character is formed, strength of mind is increased, and the intellect is expanded, and by which one can stand one's own feet". So this type of education is necessary for all type of persons mainly children and women in the society. Education gives strength, power, knowledge, courage and creativity. We can solve any type of problem in the society through education. Today the world is suffering from so many problems like terrorism, poverty, illiteracy and high population. Domestic violence is also a world problem. Because in each and every county domestic violence is happening. The following steps are necessary to create awareness on domestic violence through education.

- Educate all type of women and children in the society.
- Establish some more schools, colleges and universities for girls and women respectively.
- Introduce lessons about domestic violence in the curriculum.

- Conduct awareness programmes about domestic violence every month in the selected area.
- Introduce Value Education in the curriculum.
- Tell the women; domestic violence is crime. You are not alone. A helping hand is always is ready for you.
- Tell the women about 'Women Protection Act'.
- Tell the women about 'Safety Plans against Domestic Violence'.
- Tell the women about Government and Non-Government organizations working against domestic violence.
- Conduct awareness program for men about gender equality.
- Tell the women about constitutional rights about women.
- Establish some more women police stations for better protection of women.
- Establish separate women special courts.
- Create awareness about domestic violence with the help of print and electronic media.
- Educate all type of parents in the family and create awareness about domestic violence and rights of women.
- Write good articles against domestic violence in the news paper.
- Create awareness about domestic violence with the help of documentary. Mass media is more effective than others.
- Create awareness about domestic violence through speeches of great persons like cine stars, sports men and women, writers, poets and models in the society. Because they are role models.
- Create awareness about domestic violence through simple advertisements.
- Create awareness about domestic violence with the help of SGHs (Self Help Groups).
- Celebrate 'Women's Day' and 'Mother's Day' in a grand manner to tell the importance and power of women in the society.
- Establish some more research institutes to study about women development in the society. And create awareness about domestic violence through these institutions.

Conclusions

We know mother is the first teacher. Respect of women is respect of God. Domestic violence is cruel and unsocial thing. We can't encourage this thing. Education is the instrument for the development of women in the society. Through education we can solve any type of problem in the society. Education gives strength, power, creativity and courage for the individual. Give preference for women education in the society. Establish some more schools, colleges, universities and research centers for the benefits of women. Create awareness about domestic violence through schools, colleges, universities, research centers, prints media, mass media, electronic media and great persons in the society. Celebrate 'Women's Day' and 'Mother's Day' in a grand manner every year.

Reference

1. Child and Women Development Report, (2006), Ministry of Women and Child Development, Government of India, New Delhi.
2. Heilbroner, R. L. (1995) Visions of the future: the distant past, yesterday, today, and tomorrow (New York: Oxford University Press).
3. National Crime Records Bureau, (2007), Government of India, New Delhi.
4. National Family Health Survey, (2006), Government of India, New Delhi.
5. National Institute of Child Health and Human Development. (2001). The National Reading Panel: Reports of the Subgroups.
6. UNESCO Institute for Statistics: Literacy rates, youth (15-24) and adult (15+), by region and gender (September 2006 Assessment).

27

Values in Teacher Education

Introduction

The development of any nation depends mainly on the standards of its educational institutions. Education is the most powerful and effective instrument for inducing radical changes in the behaviour of students. Education is a powerful instrument of national development-social, economic and cultural. The teacher occupies pivotal position in the system of education. Teaching has been one of the oldest and most respected professions in the world.

According to Indians Teacher is the third god. Today we are living in the technological world. India developed in the fields of Science and Technology. It is possible to know each and everything within seconds throughout the world. Today's children are tomorrow's citizens. It is necessary to give quality and value based education to each and every student in the society. Then only all children will become good citizens in the future.

Values

Values are the guiding principles, decisive in day to day behaviours as also in critical life situations. Values are a set of principles or standards of behaviour. Values are regarded desirable, important and held in high esteem by a particular society in which a person lives. Thus values give meaning and strength to a person with character by occupying a central place in his life. Values reflect one's personal attitudes and judgments, decisions and choices, behaviour and relationships, dreams and vision. They influence our thoughts, feelings and actions. They guide us to do the right things.

Values are the guiding principles of life which are conductive to all round development. They give direction and firmness to life and bring joy, satisfaction and peace of life. Values are like the rails that keep a train on the track and help it move smoothly, quickly and with direction. They bring qualities to life.

Value Education

Value education means inculcating in the children a sense of humanism, a deep concern for the well being of others and the nation. This can be accomplished only when we instill in the children a deep feeling of commitment to values that would build this country and bring back to the people pride in work that brings order, security and assured progress.

Through value education, we like to develop the social, moral, aesthetic and spiritual sides of a person which are often undermined in formal education. Value education teaches us to preserve whatever is good and worthwhile in what we have inherited from our culture. It helps us to respect the attitude and behaviour of those who differ from us. Value education does not mean value imposition or indoctrination.

Value education has the capacity to transform a diseased mind into a very young, fresh, healthy, natural and attentive mind. The transformed mind is capable of higher sensitivity and a heightened level of perception this leads to fulfillment of the evolutionary role in man and in life. Values in general, could be classified broadly under five headings personal, social, moral, spiritual and behavioural.

Education in general and value education in particular occupies a prestigious place in the modern context of the contemporary society. The problem of value education of the young has assumed increasing prominence in educational discussions during recent times. Parents, teachers, administrators and society at large are concerned of about values and value education of children.

"The destiny of India is now being shaped in her class rooms". This is the opening sentence of the Kothari Education Commission report (1964-66). What kind of destiny has been actually shaped during the last sixty years? There are thousands of schools without primary needs. The position of teacher's economic condition is also poor when compared to USA teachers.

Nature of Values

- Values relate to the aims of human life. For the achievement of aims man frames certain notions and these notions are called values.
- Our conduct is motivated by our values.
- Value is the act of cherishing something. A person who values justice will spend a lot of energy in search for it.
- Values are masterminds which give direction to one's strivings. Values represent feelings, wants, interests, attitudes, preferences and opinions about what is right, just fair or desirable.

Classification of Values

There are so many classifications of values. According to Plato's classification, there are three types of values: (1) Truth, (2) Beauty and (3) Goodness.

Gandhi's Classification:

In order to create new social order Gandhiji introduced Nai Talim in the year 1937, which is popularly known as Basic Education.

1. Truth
2. Non-violence
3. Freedom
4. Democracy
5. Sarva Dharma Samabhava
6. Equality

7. Self-realisation
8. Purity of ends and means
9. Self-discipline
10. Suddhi

The numbers of values are unlimited. The NCERT listed 83 values. It is unmanageable to deal with so many values in schools. Under the Sathya Sai Organization, these 83 values are classified and grouped under the five well known prime values. These five are: Sathya (Truth), Dharma (righteousness), Prema (Love in its broadest Sense), Shanti (Peace) and Ahimsa (Non-violence in various forms and actions, thoughts, feelings etc).

We have the constitution of India which we are bound to follow: major values embedded there in are (1) Justice, Equality, liberty and Fraternity and (2) Democracy, Secularism, and Social Justice. Next we have individual and personal values: Cleanliness, Neatness, Punctuality, Regularity, Industriousness, Health care, honesty, Self respect, Self reliance etc. We must add values necessary for Peace and Harmony. These are concern and compassion for others, co-operation, self-sacrifice, national integrity and unity and world/ universal brotherhood. For all values, the approach has to be through a spirit of enquiry, persuit of truth, logical thinking, open mindedness, sharing and a scientific bent of mind.

Characteristics of a Real Teacher

Teacher is a national builder. He has a power to change the society. In the 13th chapter of the "Bhagavad-Gita" the characteristics of a real teacher are laid down as follows: absence of pride, free from hypocrisy, non-violence, forgiving nature, straight forwardness, service of the preceptor, purity of mind and body, steadfastness and self-control. Centuries ago in this land of Vedas the teacher devoted all his time for the upliftment of his pupils in all directions-knowledge, morals, values etc. He was called the 'Guru or Acharya'.

According to V.S.Mathews "No system of education, no syllabus, no methodology, no text book can rise above the level of its teachers. If a country wants to have quality education it must have quality teachers". So, it is necessary to give importance for values in the teacher education.

Teacher Education

"Values are to be caught and not taught', is a very old saying. It was perhaps true in days gone by when parents at home and leaders in community in various walks of life were all value-based people. Therefore younger children and growing adolescents could catch values of elderly people and either by imitation or by special efforts developed appropriate values accepted and respected in society. Much water has flowed under the bridge since then and there is a grave deterioration both among parents and community leaders in terms of their being value models for the younger generation. We cannot therefore expect values to be caught from undesirable situations and persons in society. In today's world, therefore values have got to be taught in addition to being caught from selected situations and personalities.

According to V.S.Mathews "No system of education, no syllabus, no methodology, no text book can rise above the level of its teachers. If a country wants to have quality education it must have quality teachers". So, it is necessary to give importance for values in the teacher education. Let we observe the teacher education system in the state of Andhra Pradesh, India. There are 24 Government D.Ed. colleges for the academic year 2006-07 with 2565 students, 324 B.Ed. colleges with 36009 students, 3B.Ed. institution in distance mode with 1500 students, 17 Telugu Pandit colleges with 1700 students, 10 Urdu Pandit Colleges with 480 students, 35 Hindi Pandit colleges with 2090 students, 5 D.P.Ed.colleges with 400 students, 7 B.P.Ed. colleges with 435 students and 20 M.Ed. colleges with 457 students both in Government and Private sectors.

It is necessary to take care in the framing of teacher education curriculum. Teacher is a national builder. So, it is important to give good quality and value based education to the teacher in teacher education. It is necessary to provide all types of labs and library facilities to improve quality education in teacher education.

Need for value based Teacher Education

Today we are in a technological world where things are happening fast. Parents and teachers would like to be getting results fast. India has kept pace in science and technology with forward nations but we have shown slower pace in our value system even when we have a strong heritage of human values. India was quoted by great visionaries and saints as a punya bhumi. Swami Vivekananda reiterated in his powerful words: " *If there is any land on this earth that can lay claim to be the blessed punya bhumi, to be land to which souls on this earth must come to account for karma, the land to which every soul is wending its way Godward must come to attain its lost home, the land where humanity has attained its highest towards gentleness, towards generosity, towards purity, towards calmness, above all, the land of introspection and of spirituality-It is India.*" Thus value Education has been elucidated by swamiji. From such a state, we are in the Pythonic Grip of deepening Value crisis. How unfortunate it is!!!

How can we overcome this? When can we become capable of training the young citizens to be the carriers of the noble human resources? What value, value has changed to? Present scenario and surroundings looms large with terroristic acts, violence, negative thoughts, anti-social acts, many an immoral qualities are all seen everywhere and the world looks a big booming , buzzing confusion . Such is the case in all fields, braving such conditions the wise men of our country has been trying to put forth issues like a national system of education and a national policy of education which should focus & bridge the gaps that are widening .

The NPE (*1986) and subsequently the POA's have been emphasising the faith in *vidya dadati vinayam, vinayat yati patratam, patratwat dhanamapnoti, dhanat dharmam tataha sukham-* it is learning and knowledge that gives capability to earn, and earning the ability to do dharma for a noble cause and this results in gaining peace. The analysts and educationists of our country have consciously changed the curriculum and prioritized universalisation of primary education, the girl child education, and inculcating value-based education in their recent policy recommendations like –the Eshwarbhai Patel's; Ramamurthy commission; Prof .Yashpal's commission and the present focus on the same issues through the national curriculum framework.

All these commissions, reports and recommendations have one thing in common and that is, changing curriculum at different levels for capacity building among teachers. Further, recent studies and analysis of evaluation of achievements at different levels have clearly shown the quality concerns and that teacher factor and his /her performance is poor but his responsibilities are more and there is need to train teachers in several of the new techniques & bring him to the frontline in this task of building a national system of education with a focus on value education. Thus educating the whole child and developing values assumed importance in recent years.

Implementation Process

The following points may be considered for implementing the value education in in-service and pre-service teacher training programmes and at different stage of educational institutions.

In-service Teacher Training

As a first step, three training camps may be arranged for teachers- (1) coaching camp, (2) evaluation camps and (3) refresher courses. A minimum of two teachers from each school must be covered by this programme. The above programmes for the teachers should be in such a way that it kindles the vast potentialities lying dormant in a teacher resulting in the teacher developing his/her own ways of imparting VE. These courses should enable the teacher to have his perspective in all the activities of school viz. classes on subjects, sports and games, cultural activities, youth festivals and all other extra-curricular activities. **In other words, moral education will not get confined to one moral class only.**

A teacher's manual of guidelines may be prepared, based on the values listed above, containing portions from the existing textbooks that deal with values, to help them give a special thrust to values while teaching the students.

Progammes

- Conduct periodically essay writing, elocution, storytelling, poems recital, quiz on value-based subjects.
- Teach life stories of eminent characters in the epics and history, poems that would spur national favour and devotion, patriotic songs, environmental hygiene etc.

- Motivate children to write short notes on value-based topics from the school library books. This will also encourage the development of reading habit.
- Organize special programmes on value-based subjects on every January 26, August 15 and October 2, and give awards to all the participants in the form of leaflets/pamphlets/books containing value-oriented articles and stories.
- Conduct a class exclusively for moral instruction, based on Gandhian lines, in every school once a week to focus the student's attention on the observance of a proper code of conduct and good behaviour at home, in school, in public places, and while moving about in the society.
- Begin the classes every day with a universal peace prayer.
- Display every day, messages and sayings of Mahastmas and great thinkers related to values at a prominent place in the schools under the caption 'Thought for the Day'. Such sayings may be read out and explained in the morning school assembly.
- Invite distinguished persons to talk to the students and parents on the need for importance of leading a value-based life.
- Organize occasionally common gatherings of students of government, aided and unaided schools to bridge the gap in the level of their awareness and absorption capacity.
- Institute recognition and bravery awards for those students whose assimilation of values outshines that of their fellow-students.
- Observe once a year a Parents' Day; to enable the children to express their abiding love, reverence and gratitude for all that their parents have been doing for them.
- Celebrate Teachers' Day in the true spirit to enable children to remember with great reverence and abiding gratitude what their teachers have done for them.
- Arrange debates, speeches and skits on the life and teachings of outstanding national leaders, who can be considered as role models for the young generation.

Outdoor camps

- Conduct periodical outdoor camps for selected children from a group of schools. This is an easy way to enable the children to understand the gifts of nature and to study the infallible laws of nature.
- In this context, it may be most appropriate to arrange for at least one outdoor self-contained campsite in each of the approximately 50 districts in the country. This site may also provide facilities for nature cure, organic farming and yoga as it is felt that there is growing importance given to this in many countries and therefore, students may be trained in this at an early age itself. Such a facility would basis in the outdoor camps that may be conducted every weekend in each district.

Conclusion

According to Sarvepalli Radhakrishnan teacher is a national builder. He has a power to change the society. It is government duty to provide quality education for prospective and in-service teachers. Teacher is a back bone for national development. Through education we can change the world. Teacher is a good resource to develop values in the society. Without teacher the education have no meaning. Value oriented education is necessary for today's situation.

References

1. Achievement of B.Ed. Students, Dr. C. Manchala, Discovery Publishing House, New Delhi - 110002.
2. http://www.ncte-in.org.
3. Value Education in India, Usha Rai Negi, Editor, Published by association of Indian Universities, AIU House, 16 Kotla Mark, New Delhi - 110 002, 2000.
4. Value Education, Dr. Venkataiah, Editor, APH Publishing Corporation, 5, Ansari Road, Daryaganji, New Delhi - 110 002, First Edition, 1998.

28

Base of Teacher Education Through the Ncte, Ncert, Ciet, Scert

We have thousands of years of tradition and culture. In Vedas the teacher was called 'Guru'. According to Indians teacher is third god. National Council for Teacher Education, National Council of Educational Research and Training, Central Institute of Educational Technology, State Council of Educational Research and Training etc. are the institutions for the strengthening the teacher education in India. The main objective of the NCTE is to achieve planned and coordinated development of the teacher education system throughout the country, the regulation and proper maintenance of Norms and Standards in the teacher education system and for matters connected therewith. The broad mandate given to the NCTE is to achieve planned and co-ordinated development of the teacher education system throughout the country, the regulation and proper maintenance of norms and standards in the teacher education system and for matters connected therewith. The objective of NCERT is to assist and advise the Ministry of Education and Social Welfare in the implementation of its policies and major programmes in the field of education, particularly school education. The teacher has a power to change the world. It is necessary to take care about teacher education. NCTE, NCERT, CIET and SCERT have to play prominent role in the development of quality in teacher education. NCTE has major role in framing of teacher education curriculum and establishment of teacher education institutions.

According to Sri *Sarvepalli Radha Krishnan,* Teacher is a national builder. Education is a powerful instrument of national development. Education is a solution of all types of problems in the society. Through education we get knowledge, good habits, character, morals and values. We have thousands of years of tradition and culture. In Vedas the teacher was called 'Guru'. According to Indians teacher is third god. We give more respect to teacher after mother and father in the society.

Teacher is a national builder. It is necessary to give importance to teacher education. Today's children are tomorrow's citizens. By taking good steps in the framing of teacher education curriculum, we can give good quality and value based education to the teachers.

National Council for Teacher Education, National Council of Educational Research and Training, Central Institute of Educational Technology, State Council of Educational Research and Training etc. are the institutions for the strengthening the teacher education in India.

National Council for Teacher Education (NCTE)

The National Council for Teacher Education, in its previous status since 1973, was an advisory body for the Central and State Governments on all matters pertaining to teacher education, with its Secretariat in the Department of Teacher Education of the National Council of Educational Research and Training (NCERT). Despite its commendable work in the academic fields, it could not perform essential regulatory functions, to ensure maintenance of standards in teacher education and preventing proliferation of substandard teacher education institutions. The National Policy on Education (NPE), 1986 and the Programme of Action there under, envisaged a National Council for Teacher Education with statutory status and necessary resources as a first step for overhauling the system of teacher education. The National Council for Teacher Education as a statutory body came into existence in pursuance of the National Council for Teacher Education Act, 1993 (No. 73 of 1993) on the 17th August,1995.

Objective of NCTE

The main objective of the NCTE is to achieve planned and coordinated development of the teacher education system throughout the country, the regulation and proper maintenance of Norms and Standards in the teacher education system and for matters connected therewith. The mandate given to the NCTE is very broad and covers the whole gamut of teacher education programmes including research and training of persons for equipping them to teach at pre-primary, primary, secondary and senior secondary stages in schools, and non-formal education, part-time education, adult education and distance (correspondence) education courses.

Organizational Structure of NCTE

NCTE has its head quarter at New Delhi and four Regional Committees at Banglore, Bhopal, Bhubaneshwar and Jaipur to look after its statutory responsibilities. In order to enable the NCTE to perform the assigned functions including planned and co-ordinated development and initiating innovations in teacher education, the NCTE in Delhi as well as its four Regional Committees have administrative and academic wings to deal respectively with finance, establishment and legal matters and with research, policy planning, monitoring, curriculum, innovations, co-ordination, library and documentation, in-service programmes. The NCTE Headquarters is headed by the Chairperson, while each Regional Committee is headed by a Regional Director.

The Parliament appreciated the role of quality teacher education in providing quality teachers for quality school education and passed an Act in 1993 for setting up of the National Council for Teacher Education (NCTE) as a statutory body. The broad mandate given to the NCTE is to achieve planned and co-ordinated development of the teacher education system throughout the country, the regulation and proper maintenance of norms and standards in the teacher education system and for matters connected therewith.

The NCTE has been conducting orientation programmes on education in human values for teacher educators and repackaging electronically the contributions of the experts and those of the participants. The outcomes of its programmes are distributed to each of its recognized institutions on multimedia CD-ROMs and through the World Wide Web of the Internet. Full texts of publications on value education in easily downloadable form have been made available on the NCTE web site (http://www.ncte-in.org). Titles related to value education available from the NCTE web site are: Education for Character Development; Education for Tomorrow; Report of the Working Group to Review Teachers' Training Programme; Role and Responsibility of Teachers in Building up Modern India; Gandhi on Education; Sri Aurobindo on Education; and Tilak on Education. The titles of the NCTE CD-ROMs on value education are New Education for New India - Integral Education of Sri Aurobindo, Jeevan Vigyan and Teachers as Transformers. A CD-ROM based on the workshop that was organised by the NCTE jointly with the Chinmaya World Centre will be released shortly. Recently, in December 2001 two workshops on value orientation in teacher education for teacher educators of the Southern States were organised by the RIMSE (Ramakrishna Institute for Moral and Spiritual Education). It may be appreciated that the role of the NCTE in bringing any curricular change in teacher education programme, even providing facilitation in integration of education in human values in it, at best, is that of a catalytic agent. What NCTE is trying is to make available a basketful of resource materials on education in human values to teacher education institutions.

National Counsel of Educational Research and Training (NCERT)

The National Council of Educational Research and Training (NCERT) is an apex resource organisation set up by the Government of India, with headquarters at New Delhi, to assist and advise the Central and State Governments on academic matters related to school education. NCERT doing so many researches to improve the quality of teacher education. The objective of NCERT is to assist and advise the Ministry of Education and Social Welfare in the implementation of its policies and major programmes in the field of education, particularly school education. The NCERT provides academic and technical support for improvement of school education through its various constituents, which are:

- National Institute of Education, New Delhi
- Central Institute of Education Technology, New Delhi

- Pandit Sunderlal Sharma Central Institute of Vocational Education, Bhopal
- Regional Institute of Education, Ajmer
- Regional Institute of Education, Bhopal
- Regional Institute of Education, Bhubaneswar
- Regional Institute of Education, Mysore.
- North Eastern-Regional Institute of Education, Shillong

Priorities

Among the top priorities of NCERT are:

- Implementation of National Curriculum framework
- Universalization of Elementary Education (UEE)
- Vocational education
- Education of groups with special needs
- Early childhood education
- Evaluation and examination reform information technology (IT) education
- Value Education
- Educational Technology
- Development of exemplary textbooks/workbooks/teacher's guide/supplementary reading materials
- Production of the girl child
- Identification and nurturing of talent
- Guidance and counselling
- Improvement in teacher education
- International relations

By conducting national seminars, workshops and conferences NCERT gives valuable recommendations to teacher education. Now we are living in the technological world.

Programmes and Activities

The NCERT undertakes the following programmes and activities.

Research

Being an apex national body for research in school education, the NCERT performs the important functions of conducting and supporting research and offering training in educational research methodology. The different Departments of the National Institute of Education (NIE), Regional Institutes of Education (RIEs), Central Institute of Educational Technology (CIET) and Pandit Sunderlal Sharma Central Institute of Vocational Education (PSSCIVE) undertake programmes of research related to different aspects of school education, including teacher education.

Besides conducting in-house research, the NCERT supports research programmes of other institutions/organizations by providing financial assistance and academic guidance. Assistance is given to scholars for publication of their Ph.D. theses. Research fellowships are offered to encourage studies in school education to create a research base for developmental, training and extension programmes and to create a pool of competent research workers. It also organizes courses for educational research workers. The NCERT also organizes educational research in the country. It has computer facilities for storing, processing and retrieval of data. It collaborates with international agencies in inter-country research projects.

Development

Developmental activities in school education constitute an important function of the NCERT. The major developmental activities include development and renewal of curricula and instructional materials for various levels of school education and making them relevant to changing needs of children and society. The innovative developmental activities include development of curricula and instructional materials in school education in the area of pre-school education, formal and non-formal education, vocationalisation of education and teacher education. Developmental activities are also undertaken in the domains of educational technology, population education, and education of the disabled and other special groups.

Training

Another important dimension of NCERT's activities is the pre-service and in-service training of teachers at various levels; pre-primary, elementary, secondary and higher secondary, and also in such areas as vocational education, educational technology, guidance and counseling, and special education. The pre-service teacher education programmes at the Regional Institutes of Education (RIEs) incorporate innovative features such as integration of content and methodology of teaching, long-term internship of teacher trainees in the actual classroom setting, and participation of students in community work. The RIEs also undertake the training of key personnel of the states and of state level institutions and training of teacher educators and in-service teachers.

Extension

The NCERT has comprehensive extension programmes in which various Departments of the NIE, RIEs, CIET, PSSCIVE and the offices of the Field Advisers in the states are engaged in various ways. It works in close collaboration with various agencies and institutions in the states and also works extensively with Extension Service Departments and Centres in teacher training colleges and schools with the purpose of providing assistance to various categories of personnel, including teachers, teacher educators, educational administrators, question-paper setters, textbook writers, etc. Conferences, seminars, workshops and competitions are organized *as* regular on-going programmes as a part of the extension activities. Several programmes are organized in rural and backward areas in order to reach out to the functionaries in these areas where special problems exist and where special efforts are needed. Special programmes are organized for the education of the disadvantaged sections of the society. The extension programmes cover all States and Union Territories of the country.

Publication and Dissemination

The NCERT publishes textbooks for different school subjects for Classes I to XII. It also brings out workbooks, teachers guides, supplementary readers, research reports, etc. In addition, it publishes instructional materials for the use of teacher educators, teacher trainees and in-service teachers. These instructional materials, produced through research and developmental work, serve as models to various agencies in States and Union Territories. These are made available to state level agencies for adoption and/or adaptation. The textbooks are published in English, Hindi and Urdu.

For dissemination of educational information, or the NCERT publishes six journals: *The Primary Teacher* is published both in English and Hindi and aims at giving meaningful and relevant educational inputs to primary school teachers for direct use in the classroom; *School Science* serves as an open forum for discussion on various aspects of science education; *Journal of Indian Education* provides a forum for encouraging original and critical thinking in education through discussion on current educational issues; *Indian Educational Review* contains research articles and provides a forum for researchers in education; and *Bharatiya Adhunik Shiksha,* published in Hindi, provides a forum for encouraging critical thinking in education on contemporary issues and for dissemination of educational problems and practices. Besides these, a house journal called *NCERT Newsletter* is also published in English and Hindi. The title of the Hindi version of the newsletter is *Shaikshik Darpan.*

Exchange Programmes

The NCERT interacts with international organisations such as UNESCO, UNICEF, UNDP (United Nations Development Progammes), NFPA (National Federation of Paralegal Associations) and the World Bank to study specific educational problems and to arrange training programmes for personnel from developing countries. It is one of the Associated Centres of APEID (Asia-Pacific Programme of Educational Innovation for Development). It also acts as the Secretariat of the National Development Group (NDG) for Educational Innovations. The NCERT has been offering training facilities, usually through attachment programmes and participation in workshops, to educational workers of other countries. The NCERT also acts as a major agency for implementing the Bilateral Cultural Exchange Programmes entered into by the Government of India with the governments of other countries in the fields of school education and teacher education by sending delegations to study specific educational problems relevant to Indian requirements and by arranging training and study visits for scholars from other countries. Educational materials are exchanged with other countries. On request, the faculty members are deputed to participate in international conferences, seminars, workshops, symposia, etc.

Central Institute of Educational Technology (CIET) - India

Central Institute of Educational Technology (CIET) is a constituent unit of the National Council of Educational Research and Training (NCERT), an autonomous organisation under the Ministry of Human Resources Development, Government of India. Established in 1984 with the merger of the Centre of Educational Technology and Department of Teaching Aids. Its chief aim is to promote Educational Technology especially mass media singly or in combinations (multimedia packages) to extend educational opportunities and improve quality of educational processes at the school level.

As a premier institute of Educational Technology at the apex level, major functions of the CIET are

- To design, develop, try out and disseminate alternative learning systems to achieve the national goal of universalisation of primary education and
- To address various educational problems at micro and macro levels. The broad areas of activities of the CIET are as given below:
- To design and produce media software materials viz., television/ radio (for both broadcast as well as non-broadcast use) film, graphics and other programmes for strengthening the transaction of curricular and co-curricular activities at the school level.
- To create competencies in development and use of educational software materials mentioned above through training in areas such as script development, media production, media communication, media research, technical operations, setting up studios, repair and maintenance of equipment.
- To train the faculty of Institutes of Advanced Study in Education/Colleges of Teacher Education and District Institutes of Education and Training in the use of Educational Technology in their teacher education programmes.

- To undertake research evaluation and monitoring of the systems, programmes and materials with a view to improving the materials and increasing their effectiveness.
- To document and disseminate information, materials and media programmes for better utilization and to function as a clearing house / agency in the field of Educational Technology.
- To advise and coordinate the academic and technical programmes and activities of the SIET set up by the MHRD in six states of India.
- To ensure a continuous progress in the quality of production, various evaluation studies are carried out on a regular basis. Some of the important research programmes undertaken during the year 1997-98 are:

Monitoring? and evaluation of Training

Analysis of? viewer's mail

Field-testing? of media programmes

Review of? research with implications for media production

A need? assessment for media programmes for the middle schools.

Sate Counsel of Educational Research and Training

The State Council of Educational Research and Training (SCERT) Andhra Pradesh was established on 27-07-1967, amalgamating the following institutions:

The State Institute of Education.

The State Bureau of Education and Vocational Guidance.

The State Science Education Unit and

The State Evaluation Unit

Objectives

- To organize in – service training for teacher educators and to teachers of Primary, Upper Primary and Secondary Schools.
- To Act as a clearing house for ideas and information to keep the teacher educators and teachers abreast of the latest developments in the field of Education

- To provide academic guidance to the schools through extension services.
- To undertake studies, investigations and surveys relating to educational matters on the appraisal of educational programmes.
- To Undertake and co – ordinate action research projects on instructional practices, Educational problems etc.
- To undertake publication of books, periodicals and other literature necessary for furtherance of knowledge for teachers.
- To undertake evaluation and research studies to find out the impact of educational programmes in the state.

Functions

Based on its objectives as the academic wing of the Department of School Education. The following are the functions of SCERT.

- Preparation of curricula, syllabi, instructional material for Primary, Upper Primary, Secondary and alternative systems of education.
- Department of evaluation procedures and material which are helpful to the practicing teachers.
- Bridging gaps between the methods and techniques advocated in training and the actual classroom practices.
- Dissemination of knowledge to improved methods and techniques to be followed by educational institutions.
- Co-ordination with national and international organizations in academic programmes.
- Organization of orientation programmes for the professional growth of teachers, teacher – education, supervisor's etc.
- Publication of journals, periodicals, books etc. ,
- Resource support to implement the academic policies lay down by the Government.

Services

Constituent Units

SCERT has some constituent units spread over the entire state. They are:-

- Institutes or Advances Study in Education (IASEs) Colleges of Teacher Education. (CTEs)
- District institutes of Education and Training (DIETs) / Teacher Training institutes (T. T. I. s)
- Extension Service Departments.
- Science Teacher's Centres.

Professional Growth

For the professional growth of teachers, SCERT takes up in-service training courses for Primary, Upper – Primary, Secondary teachers and teacher–educators, besides providing sources material like hand books, manuals and other publications.

SCERT also organizes seminars. Workshops, conferences involving teachers, teacher - educators, supervisors and administrators.

Research and Evaluation

SCERT undertakes action research, studies, experimental research and evaluation of the programmes implemented by it. It also promotes research and evaluation studies by teacher educators and action research by the practicing teachers.

Co–ordinate Efforts

SCERT co-ordinates various academic programmes of IASE's CTE's. DIETs. TTIs and the Extention Services Departments functioning in IASE, CTEs and DIETs.

Future Vision of the Department

National Policy of Education 1986 and Programme of action lay a lot of stress on the qualitative improvement of education. The Govt. of India has made the State Councils of Education Research and

Training as nodal agencies to look into the task of qualitative improvement of Elementary Education at Elementary and Secondary Education levels. Teacher Education Institution like DIETs, IASEs, CTEs etc., co-ordinate and implement UNICEF projects like UGC, EFA (Education For All) and other projects like MLL (Minimum Level of Learning), Distance Education. The institution's major responsibility is to ensure quality in teacher education.

SCERT organizes seminars, workshops, conferences with the help of NCERT, NCTE AND NIEPA to give quality education for teachers.

Conclusion

We know teacher is a national builder. He has a power to change the world. It is necessary to take care about teacher education. NCTE, NCERT, CIET and SCERT have to play prominent role in the development of quality in teacher education. NCTE has major role in framing of teacher education curriculum and establishment of teacher education institutions. We are living in the modern world. It is necessary to use technology. It is necessary to provide computer and technology labs and other type of labs.

29

Spiritual Development Through Education -swami Vivekananda

Keep your thoughts positive because your thoughts become your words. Keep your words positive because your words become your behaviors. Keep your behaviors positive because your behaviors become your habits. Keep your habits positive because your habits become your values. Keep your values positive because your values become your destiny. ...M.K. Gandhi

Introduction

Swami Vivekananda (1863 – 1902), a great thinker and reformer of India, embraces education, which for him signifies 'man-making', as the very mission of his life. Vivekananda realizes that mankind is passing through a crisis. The tremendous emphasis on the scientific and mechanical ways of life is fast reducing man to the status of a machine. Moral and religious values are being undermined. The fundamental principles of civilization are being ignored. Conflicts of ideals, manners and habits are pervading the atmosphere. Disregard for everything old is the fashion of the day. Vivekananda seeks the solutions of all these social and global evils through education. With this end in view, he feels the dire need of awakening man to his spiritual self wherein, he thinks, lies the very purpose of education.

Goal of Education

Vivekananda points out that the defect of the present-day education is that it has no definite goal to pursue. A sculptor has a clear idea about what he wants to shape out of the marble block; similarly, a painter knows what he is going to paint. But a teacher, he says, has no clear idea about the goal of his teaching. Swamiji attempts to establish, through his words and deeds, that the end of all education is man making. He prepares the scheme of this man-making education in the light of his over-all philosophy of Vedanta. According to Vedanta, the essence of man lies in his soul, which he possesses in addition to his body and mind. In true with this philosophy, Swamiji defines education as 'the manifestation of the perfection already in man.' The aim of education is to manifest in our lives the perfection, which is the very nature of our inner self. This perfection is the realization of the infinite power which resides in everything and every-where-existence, consciousness and bliss (satchidananda). After understanding the essential nature of this perfection, we should identify it with our inner self. For achieving this, one will have to eliminate one's ego, ignorance and all other false identification, which stand in the way. Meditation, fortified by moral purity and passion for truth, helps man to leave behind the body, the senses, the ego and all other non-self elements, which are perishable. He thus realizes his immortal divine self, which is of the nature of infinite existence, infinite knowledge and infinite bliss.

At this stage, man becomes aware of his self as identical with all other selves of the universe, i.e. different selves as manifestations of the same self. Hence education, in Vivekananda's sense, enables one to comprehend one's self within as the self everywhere. The essential unity of the entire universe is realized through education. Accordingly, man making for Swamiji stands for rousing mans to the awareness of his true self. However, education thus signified does not point towards the development of the soul in isolation from body and mind. We have to remember that basis of Swamiji's philosophy is Advaita which preaches unity in diversity. Therefore, man making for him means a harmonious development of the body, mind and soul. Education for him means that process by which character is formed, strength of mind is increased, and intellect is sharpened, as a result of which one can stand on one's own feet.

Education of the Masses

According to Swami Vivekananda a nation's progress is depending on the spread of education among the masses. The bane of India's progress is that the whole education and intelligence of the land became the monopoly of a handful of men. Unless and until we care for the spread of education among the masses^ no progress will be achieved in this country. Priest power and foreign rule have exploited the poor people to such an extent that they don't even think they are human beings. In a sad situation like this we have to open their eyes and make them see what is happening in the world around. "Our duty is to put the ideas into their heads, they will do the rest." He contended.

Swami blamed 'the cruel society which is interested to shower blows upon the poor man instead of coming to his help in this terrible situation. Next he takes to task the educated of our country. "So long as the millions live in hunger and ignorance I hold every man a traitor who, having been educated at their expense, pays not the least heed to them', said Vivekananda. He regarded the neglect of the masses as a great national sin.

Vivekananda was fully convinced that only through education the lot of the poor can be improved here. Through education we should develop in them their lost individuality, once they become conscious of their human dignity, they would naturally try to rise up from their miserable state. But he was very much disappointed to see that nothing substantial has been done for educating the people. The germs of spirituality stored in our sacred books have to be brought to the common man. This can be done by spreading education among the masses through the medium of mother tongue. Ideas can easily be understood and assimilated even by the common-eat man if they are taught through their own mother-tongue. Our duty is to give those ideas and culture. "Without giving them culture, there can be no permanence in the raised condition of the masses", Vivekananda warned. Besides, they must be instructed in simple words about the necessities of -life and in trade, commerce, agriculture etc.

Once the poor man is made conscious of his strength, that he is the 'Omnipotent' and the 'Omniscient', the rest of the work becomes easy. The moment a fisherman thinks that he is spirit; he will be a better fisherman. Likewise a student becomes a better student, too. But so long as the novelty of the people is not banished, the hope of mass education remains a pious wish. For, even if free schools are opened in villages, the children would rather so to help their parents in their work or try to make a living than going to the school, if the poor bony cannot come to school for education, education must go to him.

Spiritual Development through Education

There are different types of education for spiritual development viz., Religious Education, Yoga Education, Moral Education...etc.

Religious Education – Spiritual Development

Hinduism is the world's oldest religious tradition; it goes back to the very dawn of history. The hymns composed some 5,000 years ago are still recited today.

Hinduism is the third largest of the world's religions, after Christianity and Islam. Nearly one-seventh of humanity calls Hinduism their spiritual home. Millions more in South and Southeast Asia and in the Far East trace their spiritual roots to Hinduism.

Hinduism is also the world's largest pluralistic tradition. A multiplicity of spiritual paths and ways are recognized as valid in Hinduism. Hinduism is not based on the teachings of a single Prophet or a single Book. The teachings of many different sages and saints find home within Hinduism. God may be worshiped both in male and female forms. Hinduism has much in common with the earth based religious traditions of the world.

Hinduism is not a creedal religion, based on dogma. Its emphasis is not on correct belief but on search for the Truth. The scripture describes several paths to spiritual development. The mountain peak may be reached by taking any of the several paths.

Sri Aurobindo (1872-1950), the great Indian seer of the first half of the twentieth century declared that Hinduism (also known as *Sanatan Dharma* or the eternal tradition) was rising not for India alone but for the world. Arnold Toynbee in his *A Study of History* was of the view that Hinduism will gain the status of a world religion in the new century.

Hindus believe that Reality is One – Ekam Sat. This Reality is everywhere, in everything, in every being. It is one and many at the same time and it also transcends them both. At the popular level, the One Reality is worshipped as the Trinity: Brahma the creator, Vishnu the preserver and Shiva the dissolver. Brahma, Vishnu and Shiva are not different gods, but they represent different faces of the One Supreme. Brahma, Vishnu and Shiva have their respective female consorts: Saraswati, Lakshmi and Durga. Even though God is One, Hindus worship God in a number of both male and female forms. Ram Swarup puts the matter this way:

Spiritual life is one but it is vast and rich in expression. The human mind conceives it differently. If the human mind was uniform without different depths, heights and levels of subtlety; or if all men had the same mind, the same psyche, the same imagination, the same needs, in short, if all men were the same, then perhaps One God would do. But a man's mind is not a fixed quantity and men and their powers and needs are different. So only some form of polytheism alone can do justice to this variety and richness. - **The Word As Revelation: Names of Gods, 1980.**

FOUR PATHS: Hinduism prescribes four ways of spiritual salvation, depending on the personality of the seeker.

1. For the active person, there is Karma yoga, the path of selfless works.
2. For the contemplative and intellectual person, there is Jnana Yoga, the path of Knowledge.
3. For the emotional person, there is Bhakti yoga, the path of love and surrender. Bhakti yoga is said to be similar to the Christian path of love.
4. Finally, Raja yoga is the path of meditative exercises including concentration and one-pointedness. This path focusing on meditation has become popular in the West

Yoga Education – Spiritual Development

The Eight Limbs (Ashtanga) of Raja Yoga

The eight "limbs" or steps prescribed in the second pada of the Yoga Sutras are: Yama, Niyama, Asana, Pranayama, Pratyahara, Dharana, Dhyana and Samadhi.

Ashtanga yoga consists of the following steps: The first five are called external aids to Yoga (bahiranga sadhana)

- **Yama** refers to the five abstentions. These are the same as the five vows of Jainism.
- **Ahimsa**: non-violence, inflicting no injury or harm to others or even to one's own self, it goes as far as nonviolence in thought, word and deed.
- **Satya**: truth in word & thought.
- **Asteya**: non-covetousness, to the extent that one should not even desire something that is not his own.
- **Brahmacharya**: abstain from sexual intercourse; celibacy in case of unmarried people and monogamy in case of married people. Even this to the extent that one should not possess any sexual thoughts towards any other man or woman except one's own spouse. It's common to associate Brahmacharya with celibacy.
- **Aparigraha**: non-possessiveness
- **Niyama** refers to the five observances
- **Shaucha**: cleanliness of body & mind.
- **Santosha**: satisfaction; satisfied with what one has.
- **Tapas**: austerity and associated observances for body discipline & thereby mental control.
- **Svadhyaya**: study of the Vedic scriptures to know about God and the soul, which leads to introspection on a greater awakening to the soul and God within,
- **Ishvarapranidhana**: surrender to (or worship of) God.
- **Asana**: Discipline of the body: rules and postures to keep it disease-free and for preserving vital energy. Correct postures are a physical aid to meditation, for they control the limbs

and nervous system and prevent them from producing disturbances.

- **Pranayama**: control of breath. Beneficial to health, steadies the body and is highly conducive to the concentration of the mind.
- **Pratyahara**: withdrawal of senses from their external objects.

The last three levels are called internal aids to Yoga (antaranga sadhana)

- **Dharana**: concentration of the citta upon a physical object, such as a flame of a lamp, the midpoint of the eyebrows, or the image of a deity.
- **Dhyana**: steadfast meditation. Undisturbed flow of thought around the object of meditation (pratyayaikatanata). The act of meditation and the object of meditation remain distinct and separate.
- **Samadhi**: oneness with the object of meditation. There is no distinction between act of meditation and the object of meditation. Samadhi is of two kinds:

Samprajnata Samadhi conscious samadhi. The mind remains concentrated (ekagra) on the object of meditation, therefore the consciousness of the object of meditation persists. Mental modifications arise only in respect of this object of meditation. This state is of four kinds:

- Savitarka: the Citta is concentrated upon a gross object of meditation such as a flame of a lamp, the tip of the nose, or the image of a deity.
- Savichara: the Citta is concentrated upon a subtle object of meditation , such as the tanmatras
- Sananda: the Citta is concentrated upon a still subtler object of meditation, like the senses.
- Sasmita: the Citta is concentrated upon the ego-substance with which the self is generally identified.

Asamprajnata Samadhi supraconscious. The citta and the object of meditation are fused together. The consciousness of the object of meditation is transcended. All mental modifications are checked (niruddha), although latent impressions may continue.

Combined simultaneous practice of Dhâranâ, Dhyâna & Samâdhi is referred to as Samyama and is considered a tool of achieving various perfections, or Siddhis.

Yoga and Religion

Yoga is not a religion. It has no creed or fixed set of beliefs, nor is there a prescribed godlike figure to be worshipped in a particular manner. Religions for the most part seem to be based upon the belief in and worship of things (God or godlike figures) that exist outside one-self. The core of Yoga's philosophy is that everything is supplied from within the individual. Thus, there is no dependence on an external figure, either in the sense of a person or god figure, or a religious organization.

The common belief that Yoga derives from Hinduism is a misconception. Yoga actually predates Hinduism by many centuries. Ancient seals unearthed in the Indus Valley provide clear evidence of widespread Yoga practice earlier than 3,000 B.C.E. The techniques of Yoga have been adopted by Hinduism as well as by other world religions. Yoga is a system of techniques that can be used for a number of goals, from simply managing stress better, learning to relax, and increasing limberness all the way to becoming more self-aware and acquiring the deepest knowledge of one's own self.

The practice of Yoga will not interfere with any religion. Many American Yoga Association students who have practiced Yoga intensively for many years continue to follow the religious traditions they have grown up in or adopted without conflict.

Swami Vivekananda Spiritual Quotes

1. Anything that brings spiritual, mental or physical weakness, touch it not with the toes of your feet.
2. Be brave! Be strong! Be fearless! Once you have taken up the spiritual life, fight as long as there is any life in you. Even though you know you are going to be killed, fight till you "are killed." Don't die of fright. Die fighting. Don't go down till you are knocked down.

3. BY the study of different RELIGIONS we find that in essence they are one.
4. By the Vedas no books are meant. They mean the accumulated treasury of spiritual laws discovered by different persons in different times. Just as the law of gravitation existed before its discovery, and would exist if all humanity forgot it, so is it with the laws that govern the spiritual world
5. External nature is only internal nature writ large.
6. Give up all desire for enjoyment in earth or heaven. Control the organs of the senses and control the mind. Bear every misery without even knowing that you are miserable. Think of nothing but spiritual freedom.
7. GOD is to be worshipped as the one beloved, dearer than everything in this and next life.
8. God is very merciful to those whom He sees struggling heart and soul for spiritual realization. But remain idle, without any struggle, and you will see that His grace will never come.
9. GOD of truth, be Thou alone my guide...
10. Let us put forth all our energies to acquire that which never fails—our spiritual perfection. If we have true yearning for realization, we must struggle, and through struggle growth will come. We shall make mistakes, but they may be angels unawares.
11. Never think there is anything impossible for the soul. It is the greatest heresy to think so. If there is sin, this is the only sin? To say that you are weak, or others are weak.
12. Our supreme duty is to advance toward freedom—physical, mental, and spiritual—and help others to do so.
13. Records of great spiritual men of the past do us no good whatever except that they urge us onward to do the same, to experience religion ourselves.
14. Renunciation is the background of all religious thought wherever it is, and you will always find that as this idea of renunciation lessens, the more will the senses creep into the field of religion, and spirituality will decrease in the same ratio.

15. Salvation is not achieved by inactivity but by spiritual activities.

16. Save the spiritual store in your body by observing continence.

17. "Seek ye first the kingdom of God, and everything shall be added unto you". This is the one great duty, this is renunciation. Live for an ideal, and leave no place in the mind for anything else. Let us put forth all our energies to acquire that which never fails—our spiritual perfection. If we have true yearning for realization, we must struggle, and through struggle growth will come. We shall make mistakes, but they may be angels unawares.

18. Take up one idea. Make that one idea your life - think of it, dream of it, live on that idea. Let the brain, muscles, nerves, every part of your body, be full of that idea, and just leave every other idea alone. This is the way to success that is way great spiritual giants are produced.

19. The animal has its happiness in the senses, the human beings in their intellect, and the gods in spiritual contemplation. It is only to the soul that has attained to this contemplative state that the world really becomes beautiful.

20. The first sign of your becoming religious is that you are becoming cheerful

21. The greatest help to spiritual life is meditation. In meditation we divest ourselves of all material conditions and feel our divine nature. We do not depend upon any external help in meditation. The touch of the soul can paint the brightest color even in the dingiest places; it can cast a fragrance over the vilest thing; it can make the wicked divine—and all enmity, all selfishness is effaced.

22. The more we come out and do good to others, the more our hearts will be purified, and God will be in them.

23. This is the great lesson that we are here to learn through myriads of births and heavens and hells—that there is nothing to be asked for, desired for, beyond one's spiritual Self (atman).

24. Tremendous purity, tremendous renunciation, is the one secret of spirituality. "Neither through wealth, nor through progeny, but through renunciation alone is immortality to be reached," say the Vedas. "Sell all that thou hast and give to poor, and follow me," says the Christ. So all great saints and prophets have expressed it, and have carried it out in their lives. How can great spirituality come without renunciation?

25. We are what our thoughts have made us; so take care about what you think. Words are secondary. Thoughts live; they travel far.

26. What is material and what is not material? When the world is the end and God the means to attain that end, then that is material. When God is the end and the world is only the means to attain that end, spirituality has begun.

27. Where can we go to find God if we cannot see Him in our own hearts and in every living being.

28. You cannot believe in God until you believe in yourself.

29. You have to grow from the inside out. None can teach you, none can make you spiritual. There is no other teacher but your own soul.

Conclusions

Inculcation of Spiritual values in each and every student is important. Today we are facing so many problems like terrorism, poverty, corruption, illiteracy, alcoholism and teenage pregnancy. Terrorism is the most dangerous problem in the modern world. The only cause for all these problems is lack of spiritual knowledge. We are giving priority or importance for external world. "*Brahma Satyam, Jagat Mithya, and Jivo Brahmaiva naparah*"... according this the ultimate reality is Brahman. There is no difference between self and Brahman. If anyone loves God, definitely he loves fellow human beings. Love and affection towards fellow human beings, animals and plants is more important. Spiritual knowledge gives discriminative power- what is right? What is wrong? Which is good? Which is bad? What is right way? Etc. It is the duty of parents and teacher to develop spiritual values in the students. Education is power. Through Education it is easy to inculcate spiritual knowledge in the students. According to swami Vivekananda education means that character is formed, strength of mind is increased, and intellect is sharpened, as a result of which one can stand on one's own feet. It is the fore most duty of government to provide such type of education for all.

30

Quality Enhancement of Distance Education

Introduction

Distance Education as the phrase indicates, is the education at a distance, which means there is a distance between teacher/ education provider and the student. In formal education, the teaching learning process is time-bounded and space bounded. A student has to attend classes in a particular place (Academic Institution) where the teacher imparts education. That means the teacher and the student should be in the same place for the teaching-learning process to take place. Similarly, the students have to be there in the school or college during specified periods. On the other hand distance learners need not go to an educational institution. They need not go to their institution at a particular time. Here the teaching-learning process is not time-bounded and space-bounded. These students can take up any kind of employment to support their families financially. Obviously distance Education is the best alternative for these students who also have to fulfill family commitments, a regular feature of all developing countries.

Distance Education became an alternative route for the process of democratization of education and developing countries could read the writing on the wall. Several Asian and African Countries have adopted Distance Education mode for educating masses. These Programmes are yielding encouraging results. However, we are yet to exploit the fullest potential of Distance Education. We have established that Distance Education can act as a social catalyst for the development of developing nations. In this regard, we have to assure that there is improvement in the present status of education so that Distance Education can reach more and more Un-reached. Especially, in the Indian context, the importance of distance Education has been increasing day by day. The increasing number of students, Universities, institutions, and study centers indicates the growing importance of Distance Education.

Concept of Distance Education

Distance Education is an Expression, Generally used to indicate correspondence studies, open learning, open Education, Extra studies, off-campus studies etc. Distance Education is a non-formal form of teaching-learning process in which teaching learning take place not in the class room, but in distant places and the role of teacher is carried out by print and non-print media, with a provision for frequent counseling sessions and supplemented by educational broadcast. The whole teaching-learning process is under the supervision and control of the distance-teaching institution/ university. The subject experts prepare study materials and these are sent to the students by post or distributed through study centers. A study center is the basic functional unit of an open university where counseling sessions are held.

The study centers are located in most accessible places and they are supervised by Regional centers of an open university. Open universities establish study centers even in rural areas remote areas, islands etc.

OBJECTIVES FOR OPEN SCHOOL SYSTEM

- To provide education to all these who are employed and completed 16 years of age, even if they have no formal education, by making them qualified to continue education through a system of foundation courses.

- Democratizing education by expanding educational opportunities to all.
- Raising the Educational qualifications of People.
- Eradicating illiteracy by joining hands with non-formal education.
- Continuing education for those who are employed.
- Reaching out education to the door steps of individual learners.
- Raising the productivity and performance level of working force in the country.

DEVELOPMENT IN DISTANCE EDUCATION IN INDIA

Educational history of India can be traced back to the days of Vedic Aryan society, which was characterized by the Guru Kula system. In India correspondence education started in 1962 when the university of Delhi offered correspondence courses. In 1982, the Andhra Pradesh Government established Andhra Pradesh Open University (now BRAOU) and in 1985 Indira Gandhi National Open University was established In New Delhi.

In India several commissions recommended open education system as an alternative to the conventional education. The Kothari Commission, the Parthasarathy commission, and state Education Ministers Conference, New Delhi have recommended the establishment of correspondence schools/open Universities with a view to provide Distance Education.

The System of Distance Education was first set up in 1962 at the Delhi University for undergraduate courses. The success of this experiment Prompted many such institutes at different places in the country. The upper Level Distance Education is channelized through open school set up at the union Level and in some of the states. Open Universities and Distance Education Institutes, besides running traditional courses are also engaged in providing professional courses in all the areas. We can thus say that Distance Education has crossed the take off stage. The Education policy 1986 has given and Important Place to the system of Distance Education in fulfilling the educational objectives.

Distance Education systems stands on six prominent pillars which are categorized as,

- Study material popularly known as lecture scripts.
- Teaching for short duration to maintain personal contacts. i.e., Personal Contact Programme.
- Student Assignment. i.e., Response sheets.
- Electronic media: Broadcasts on selected topics through radio; video, tele conferencing, computer etc.,
- Study centers.
- Personal guidance: Casual visit by the students to meet the faculty.

IMPORTANCE OF DISTANCE EDUCATION

1. The student Population is increasing at a fast rate. Distance Education has gone up in the galaxy of the education system.
2. There are many people who cannot pursue higher education due to poor socioeconomic backgrounds and other limitations. These persons were denied the benefits of higher education. The Distance Education System offers them a second chance of updating and acquiring higher education.
3. The traditional system provides education within the timeframe. Scientific and technological changes are occurring at a fast rate. The Distance Education system can meet the needs through fresh courses specially designed for the purpose.
4. Education through Distance Education can be beautifully synthesized with family life and work environment. In this way, the students can learn while working as well as living in home environment.
5. The Distance Education system has a great potential for providing in- service training especially for technical personal.
6. Distance Education being a flexible system can meet the requirements of a large number of people as per their needs.
7. Development and expansion of Distance Education is a worldwide phenomenon and its popularity is due to its

openers, flexibility, wider access, multimedia teaching and the wide range of course openings relevant to the social needs.

8. Distance Education has not only ushered in an era of globalization but is emerging as an effective tool to overcome the evils of Privatization and in providing wider access to higher education.
9. Distance Education system has the potentiality, capability and expertise to promote higher Education in diverse fields. However, there is a need to be more careful in ensuring quality and effectiveness from the institutions engaged in Distance Education System. The distance Education systems all over the world have become increasingly popular on account of their flexible admission requirements, curriculum and pacing of learning taking education to the very door steps of the learner.

CONCLUSION

Distance Education became an alternative route for the process of democratization of education and developing countries could read the writing on the wall. Several Asian and African Countries have adopted Distance Education mode for educating masses. These Programmes are yielding encouraging results. However, we are yet to exploit the fullest potential of Distance Education. We have established that Distance Education can act as a social catalyst for the development of developing nations. In this regard, we have to assure that there is improvement in the present status of education so that Distance Education can reach more and more Un-reached. Especially, in the Indian context, the importance of distance Education has been increasing day by day. The increasing number of students, Universities, institutions, and study centers indicates the growing importance of Distance Education.

31

Value Based Instructional Strategies and Approaches for Distance Education Learners

Introduction

The term distance education means the type of education that is liable to be organized and imparted in keeping cognition of the distance factor, who imparts such education and who receives it, both are separated by a common factor known as distance. The word 'distance' has multiple meanings –the term distance education has been applied to a tremendous variety of programs serving numerous audiences via a wide variety of media. Axiology is a branch of philosophy deals with values. Ethics (moral behavior) and aesthetics (appreciation of beauty) are two sub branches of axiology in philosophy. Philosophy, education and values are intimately related to the branches of knowledge. Further, education and values seem to be the reciprocal planes of each other. To be more specific and precise in this regard, it is said that "Education is Value Enterprise". Since education is a means of value development, the end product is development of moral character, personality and good human being. The whole thrust of education is the development of values in human behavior.

Instructional Strategy may stand for plans, means and specific ways especially devised and employed by the teachers for guiding, directing and showing path to the learners for the realization of the set instructional objectives. All forms of teaching and learning cannot be provided through single source or teacher should draw form a variety of learning resources either independently or in combination. With this analysis and understanding background, the following strategies and techniques like classroom learning activities, practical activities, socialized techniques, incidental learning strategy and few approaches like evocation approach, inculcation approach, value clarification approach, commitment approach, simulating and moralizing, for inculcating values among distance education learners.

Values are the pillars of life, they are part of education. Values differ from place to place, culture to culture and time to time. Indian view with regard to values is different because of difference in perspective of life. The educative process for value based instruction will be effective and efficacious only through multipronged teaching strategies and approaches. The prevailing formal system alone will not do. All the three strategies – formal, non formal and informal channels working simultaneously will bring rich dividends.

Distance education mode is now being recognized globally as an effective supplement for even substitute for the regular classroom instruction. More and more universities and school education boards are coming with some or the other advanced network of the distance education. It has necessitated on the part of the prospective as well as in-service teachers to become acquainted with the nature and functioning of the distance education mode not only for helping the cause of distance education, but also to make its proper utilization for professional growth.

Distance education

The term distance education means the type of education that is liable to be organized and imparted in keeping cognition of the distance factor, who imparts such education and who receives it, both are separated by a common factor known as distance. The word 'distance' has multiple meanings –the term distance education has been applied to a tremendous variety of programs serving numerous audiences via a wide variety of media.

Value based Instruction

Axiology is a branch of philosophy deals with values. Ethics (moral behavior) and aesthetics (appreciation of beauty) are two sub branches of axiology in philosophy. Philosophy, education and values are intimately related to the branches of knowledge. Further, education and values seem to be the reciprocal planes of each other. To be more specific and precise in this regard, it is said that "Education is Value Enterprise". Since education is a means of value development, the end product is development of moral character, personality and good human being. The whole thrust of education is the development of values in human behavior.

Instructional Strategies

Instructional Strategy may stand for plans, means and specific ways especially devised and employed by the teachers for guiding, directing and showing path to the learners for the realization of the set instructional objectives. All forms of teaching and learning cannot be provided through single source or teacher should draw form a variety of learning resources either independently or in combination. With this analysis and understanding background, the following strategies and techniques may be suggested.

1. Classroom learning activities
2. Practical activities
3. Socialized techniques and activities
4. Incidental learning Strategy

Classroom Learning Activities

A very basic purpose of value based strategy is to develop the moral autonomy of the learner and also sensitive's of value content of school and classroom activities. This may include reading, listening, discussions, narration, direct presentation of ideas by the teacher and other strategies. These strategies should be used with any of the following sources of value based education.

Biographies and Stories

A biography is a written document on the life history of an eminent personality. Biographies of scientist, social reformers and spiritual leaders acquaint one with their life, thoughts, and actions and various forces which molded their lives as depicted by biographer. Stories of various kinds are attractive to students of varied age groups. Stories may be presented by the teacher, presented by students themselves, followed by discussions and on questioning and analysis. The teacher should use his direction in selecting the story appropriate to the developmental level of the learner. Simple and short stories such as fairy tales and fables are better suited to elementary level of students.

Extracts From Essays, Articles, Classics and News Paper

Non fictional writings dealing with value themes, such as essays, articles and news paper reports may be used for value based education purpose. These may be scholarly writings on issues of social and national concern appearing in books and journals. Students may be asked to collect articles and writings from various sources, encouraged to write articles on a chosen value theme. Teachers can frame questions that provoke in the learner to think and reflect on many issues of the values covered.

Value/Moral Dilemmas

Value or moral dilemma may be used as important instructional strategies in value based education. They present very effective situations for learners to think, to reason and to make moral judgment and arrive at a decision after considering all issues involved in the moral dilemma. The dilemmas constructed may be on issues like environmental conservation, scientific temper, social justice and equality. A teacher can prepare a lesion or initiate discussion on a dilemma indicating all the essential steps involved.

Practical Activities

Value based instruction merely by cognitive precept is not enough even though it is essential. Children should engage themselves in life related practical activities which will promote the application of principles and values in daily life. The essence of practical approach is that they provide the learners with suitable opportunities to practice and live their lives according to the principles and values they have perceived and understood, such an activities like...

- Institutional campus/classroom maintenance activities
- Social forestry/ community development activities
- Work experience related activities
- Organizing campaigns on community sanitation, literacy, environmental awareness, AIDS prevention awareness
- Yoga , meditation and prayer sessions
- Eradication of social evils campaign activities (gender inequality, dowry, alcoholism........)
- Co-curricular/self government activities

Socialised Techniques and Activities

The socialized technique is involved in activities and experience which best represent functions and problems of agents of socialisation. The experience the learner gets here is not the same type of experience deriving from direct encounters with reality, nor it is completely indirect and abstract as in the case of cognitive area. They are the simplified versions of real social experiences and one necessary and useful when the reality is too abstract and obscured. These include social role playing enacting and modeling.

Modeling is a strategy in which qualities of an individual who is considered to posses desirable or ideal values worth emulating are presented to the learners as a model a broad indication of the kinds of activities possible under the heads of socialised strategies for inculcating value is listed below.

- o Dramatization activities like staging play, dramas, both of traditional folk and modern on value themes.
- o Enacting opportunities to take up and practice the role of different kinds, taking the role from epics/ scriptures.
- o Modeling exercise, the ideal persons and group on themes such as
  a) Gender inequality
  b) Problems pertaining to women's role and education

c) Caring animals and human beings
d) Problems related to environmental protection
e) Consequences of air water pollution.

Incidental Strategy

An incident is an episode or experience in the life of an individual or group. The incidental strategy has a very good point in its favour in that it can used both inside as well as outside the classroom for value education purposes. It consists in identifying the wrong or right actions of an individual or group, either preplanned to occur or observed by accident, and reprimanding or rewarding those concerned. This strategy is psychologically effective since it is like striking the iron while it is hot. Episodes or incidents centered around experience of everyday occurrence in the life of children can help children identify themselves with them and understand their own thought powers and feelings. Incidents are to be recorded properly and discussed to promote better insight into human problems.

Values based Approaches:

1.Evocation Approach: the students are encouraged to make spontaneously free, non-rational choices, without thought or hesitation. It provides an environment which allows maximum freedom for students, and provides a provocation situation for which spontaneous reaction are elicited.

2.Inculcation approach: students are forced to act according to specific desired values. A positive and negative reinforcement by the teacher helps value inculcation. This can be done by a teacher's natural actions and responses. This time honoured method has been notably unsuccessful.

3.Awareness approach: This approach helps students to become aware and identify their own values. The students are encouraged to share their experiences. The teacher presents value laden situations or dilemmas through readings, films, role playing, small group discussions and simulation.

4.Analysis approach: The group or individuals are encouraged to study social value problems. They are asked to clarify value questions, and identify values in conflict. They are encouraged to determine the truth and evidence of facts, and arrive at value decision, applying analogues cases, inferring and testing value principles underlying the decision.

5.Value clarification approach: It helps students to use both rational thinking and emotional awareness to examine personal behaviour patterns and classify and actualise values.

6.Commitment approach: it enables the students to perceive themselves not merely as passive reactors or as free individuals but as inner-relative members of a social group and system. The action project helps to clarify and restructure one's value system and to ascertain the depth of commitment of one's values.

7.Role playing: acting out the true feelings of the actor by taking the role of another person but without the risk of reprisals.

8.Simulating: a strategy in which the learners are asked to pretend to be in a certain situation called for by the lesson and then to portray the events and also by imitating the character's personality.

9.Problem solving: an approach where in a dilemma is presented to the learners asking them what decisions they are going to take.

10.Moralising: The process of working out a sense of morality through active structuring and restructuring of one's social experience;(e.g. moral reasoning and analysis)

Conclusion

Values are the pillars of life, they are part of education. Values differ from place to place, culture to culture and time to time. Indian view with regard to values is different because of difference in perspective of life. The educative process for value based instruction will be effective and cfficacious only through multipronged teaching strategies and approaches. The prevailing formal system alone will not do. All the three strategies – formal, non formal and informal channels working simultaneously will bring rich dividends.

References

1 Naqi Mohammad., 'Modern Value Education' Ammol Publications Pvt Ltd, New Delhi, 2005.

2 Shrimali.K.L., 'A Search for Values in Indian Education' Vikas Publishers, Delhi, 1974.

3 Shukla.P.D., 'Towards the New Pattern of Education in India', Sterling Publishers Pvt Ltd, New Delhi,1976.

4 Ruhela.S.P. 'Human Values And Education', Sterling Publishers Pvt Ltd, New Delhi, 1986.

5 Sing.M.S., 'Values Education' , Adhyayan Publishers & distributors, New Delhi,2007.

6 Venkataiah.S., 'Quality Education', Ammol Publications Pvt Ltd, New Delhi,2007.

7 Mangal.S.K and Uma mangal., 'Essentials of educational technology', PHI Learning private Ltd, New Delhi,2009.

32

Problems and Prospectus of Distance Education

Introduction

Distance learning is an excellent method of reaching the adult learner. Because of the competing priorities of work, home, and school, adult learners desire a high degree of flexibility. The structure of distance learning gives adults the greatest possible control over the time, place and pace of education; however, it is not without problems. Loss of student motivation due to the lack of face-to-face contact with teachers and peers, potentially prohibitive startup costs, and lack of faculty support are all barriers to successful distance learning. This paper explores distance learning and its barriers and how to overcome those barriers.

Distance education, or **distance learning**, is a field of education that focuses on the pedagogy, technology, and instructional system designs that aim to deliver education to students who are not physically "on site" in a traditional classroom or campus. It has been described as "a process to create and provide access to learning when the source of information and the learners are separated by time and distance, or both." In other words, distance learning is the process of creating an educational experience of equal quality for the learner to best suit their outside the classroom.

History of Distance Learning

Before any discussion of distance learning, we need to look at the way the term has been defined in the past and how it is currently defined in the literature. The term can be used to describe any of a number of instructional situations. Although it is thought of as a new term, distance learning has been around for well over 100 years. One of the earlier forms of distance learning was done through correspondence courses started in Europe. This stayed the primary means of distance learning until the middle of this century when instructional radio and television became more popular (Imel, 1996). As technology has changed, so has the definition of distance learning. Videotaped lectures have been a standard in university and professional courses for the last two decades (Moore & Lockee, 1998). Audiotapes and lessons sent through the mail have been used in correspondence courses to teach subjects such as foreign language for quite some time (Teaster & Blieszner, 1999). Today, the Internet and compressed video have taken distance learning in new directions, allowing distance learning to occur in real time. Live video instruction is the most popular and fastest growing delivery mode in the United States (Ostendorf, 1997).

Importance of distance education

As the world continues to move forward, adults must maintain pace with all the latest advances in knowledge and job skills for their careers. These same adults are also constrained with full time employment, meeting family commitments, and trying to maintain some semblance of a social life.

To meet the needs of adults desiring to continue their education, distance education provides the answers to their professional and personal commitments. Distance education is often referred to as distance learning and online education. Regardless of the terminology used, distance education is designed for adults with busy schedules and need flexibility for completing continuing education courses.

Because the 21st century job market is increasing specialized and complex, distance education provides many advantages for adults who need to continue their education for career sustainability. Adults who do not take advantage of distance education opportunities will be left behind by those adults who have recognized the potential.

PROs of Distance Learning

- Require no or little commuting which saves time and money. Less time in car means less gas burned and less car maintenance.
- Allow you to complete course work when it is convenient for you. Do work where and when you want to.
- Taken from home means savings in child care costs.
- Are learner centered. Pacing, sequencing, style of the learning experience are left up to you.
- Offer easy access to learning resources. The teacher, other students, library are only a click away.
- Allow learners to access enrichment content of personal interest.
- Lead to an advanced degree that will result in increased career salaries.
- Directly address physical accessibility issues such as access to buildings, sitting in uncomfortable chairs.
- Are great equalizers. You will work with fellow class members without regard for appearance, race, sex, ethnicity, or other common prejudices.
- Allows a broader perspective by interacting with people from other parts of the world.
- Will teach you project management along with distance collaboration skills. These skills will help you work on virtual teams on your jobs.

Problems of Distance Learning

Despite the promises and obvious advantages to distance learning, there are problems that need to be resolved. These problems include the quality of instruction, hidden costs, misuse of technology, and the attitudes of instructors, students, and administrators. Each one of these has an effect on the overall quality of distance learning as a product. In many ways, each of these issues relates to the others.

7 Success Strategies for Distance Learners

Distance learning has special challenges. You will probably never see or meet the teacher. You won't have classmates. You don't have a campus full of people studying the same thing. But you can succeed! Plan on it! Follow the simple tips below, and you'll do better in your learning. They may seem pretty basic, but they'll help keep you focused and on track.

1. Set Goals

- Goal #1: "I will succeed in this course."
- At the beginning of a new course, look through the materials. Break the lessons/assignments into manageable chunks. You might not have time to do a full lesson in one night, so plan for how much you can do, and then stick to it until you're done.

2. Establish a Regular Study/Learning Schedule

- Keep a calendar or journal with your study goals and important dates clearly marked-and look at it every day (a calendar can't help you if it's closed!)
- Determine what time is best for you to study. Is it after dinner on Wednesdays when your partner is at bowling? Is it Saturday mornings when the kids are at soccer?
- Take breaks-walk around and stretch. Drink some water or have a light snack. If you're studying nutrition or health topics, you know how important this is!
- If possible, have a dedicated study place with all the supplies you might need (computer, paper, pens, calculator, etc.)
- Pace yourself. Don't over extend yourself. There's a reason it takes several years to graduate from traditional university. You're in this to learn, not just to get a certificate, so make sure you're learning, not just racing through the materials.

3. Talk about It

- Tell people what you're doing. You're more likely to stick to a course if your co-worker knows you're doing it. If you are studying high-tech or internet development, the person might just know a programmer he can hook you up with for tutoring.
- Ask a friend to check up on you.
- Ask someone to proof your work before you submit it.

4. Join a Study Group-This doesn't have to be Stuffy!

- Join a club. Aspiring financial planners could join a local investing club.
- If you're studying a language like Spanish or Japanese, ask the owners of a local restaurant if they know anyone who might like to do language exchange with you.
- Get a mentor. If you're taking a course related to health or medicine, ask a nurse or pharmacist if you can take them for coffee once a month.
- Search the Internet for bulletin boards or chat rooms related to your topic.

5. Know Your Learning Style and Use It

- Look for real-world situations and examples of what you're learning about. If you're studying about civil engineering, pay attention to bridges.
- You'll be much more interested if you're involved, not just reading about a topic.
- Put things into practice as early as possible.
- If you're studying accounting, practice by balancing your checkbook.

6. Celebrate Successes

- Reward yourself with whatever works for you, along the way. Remember, you chose to do this. Be proud of your accomplishments!

7. Ask Questions

- If you don't understand something, ASK. It's been said a zillion times: the only dumb question is the one you don't ask.

It's not about memorizing - it's about learning material that will help you in your hobbies, career, and life. Memorization isn't a bad thing, but make sure you're memorizing because you are really interested in the information, and figure out a way to use the memorized information several times within a few days of learning it. It'll stick if it has real-world meaning.

Conclusion

Despite the challenges distance education presents to our traditional conceptions of education and instructional delivery, distance education enrollment at community colleges has increased greatly over the last decade, suggesting that distance education offers an alternative to the traditional classroom experience that accommodates many students' individual circumstances and educational needs. Although the goals and outcomes of distance education are still somewhat unclear, it is generally agreed upon, however, that the marriage of technology and higher education will be a lasting one, and by the year 2000 more students will be instructed via more media than was ever thought possible.

Today, we are living in the information technology world. Here, lot of resources is available for learning at sitting home. So distance learning is getting ease because of ICT revolution and advancement. We can easily destroy the difficulties by using advanced technology for learning purpose and so on.

To succeed in distance education, students must be willing to learn on their own with little guidance. It is important to stay with the class or ahead, not behind. Finding the appropriate environment for studying and setting aside time for studying are essential for online students: since there is no physical time in class, in fact, students need to respect deadlines to do the required reading and complete assignments as well as actively participate to online discussions, ask questions, and make replies weekly.

Distance education also requires an extra effort from teachers who need to be available for e-questions throughout the day and need to provide a clear course syllabus or outline to guide students through the course.

References

1. Basom, M., & Sherritt, C. (1992). *Higher education problems in the twenty-first century: A survey of higher education administrators and politicians.* Paper presented at the Annual Conference for International Higher Education Administrators, Nice, France.
2. Bates, T. (1995). *Technology: Open learning and distance education.* New York: Routledge.
3. Bollag, B., & Overland M.A. (2001). Developing countries turn to distance education. *Chronicle of Higher Education, 47* (40), 29-31.
4. Caffarella, E., et al. (1992). *An analysis of the cost effectiveness of various electronic alternatives for delivering distance education compared to the travel costs for live instruction.* Greeley, Colorado: University of Northern Colorado, Western Institution for Higher Learning. (ERIC Document Reproduction Service No. ED 380 127).
5. Carr, S. (2001). Union publishes guide citing high cost of distance education. *Chronicle of Higher Education, 47* (35), 39-41.
6. Carter, A. (2001). Interactive distance education: Implications for the adult learner. *International Journal of Instructional Media, 28* (3), 249-261.
7. Christensen, E. et al. (2001). Receptivity to distance learning: The effect of technology, reputation, constraints, and learning preferences. *Journal of Research on Computing in Education, 33* (3), 263-276.
8. Clark, T. (1993). Attitudes of higher education faculty toward distance education: A national survey. *The American Journal of Distance Education, 7,* 19-33.
9. Dervarics, C. (2001). Support builds for distance learning. *Community College Week,* 14 (1), 3-5.

10. Dibiase, D. (2000). Is distance education a Faustian bargain? *Journal of Geography in Higher Education, 24* (1), 130-136.

11. Ferguson, L., & Wijekumar, K. (2000). Effective design and use of web-based distance learning environments. *Professional Safety, 45* (12), 28-33.

12. Gober, P. (1998). Distance learning and geography's soul. *AAG Newsletter, 33* (5), 1-2.

13. Greenberg, G. (1998). Distance education technologies: Best practices for K-12 settings. *IEEE Technology and Society Magazine,* (Winter) 36-40.

14. Harner, M., et al. (2000). Measuring the effect of distance education on the learning experience: Teaching accounting via Picturetel. *International Journal of Instructional Media, 27* (1), 37-50.

15. Hiltz, S.R., & Wellman, B. (1997). A synchronous learning network as a virtual classroom. *Communications of the ACM, 40* (9), 44-49.

16. Holmberg, B. (1989). The concept, basic character, and development potentials of distance education. *Distance Education, 10* (1), 127-135.

17. Horgan, B. (1998). Transforming higher education using information technology: first steps. (On-Line). Available: http://microsoft.com/education/hed/vision.html

33

Evolution of Distance Education

Introduction

Distance education, also called distance learning, has existed for centuries. It involves obtaining knowledge outside of the traditional avenues of attendance at learned institutions. Some recent definitions have focused on it as a new development, involving advanced technology. A few have even sought to define it in terms of a single technology ¯ usually the one they are reviewing or marketing. Others have viewed it simply as a recent extension of the classroom environment into a remote location. Such definitions have proven too restrictive and fail to recognize the actual needs of distance education users or providers.

A simpler definition, more open to expanded possibilities, would be that distance education should provide whatever educational opportunities are needed by anyone, anywhere, at any time. Whatever words are finally settled on, the end result will be increased educational opportunities for broader segments of the population, accommodating different situations and needs.

Adult learning

In the past, most distance education focused on adult learners, especially in rural districts. The largest use was for "short courses to help farmers and small businesses adapt to new technologies". This remains the most common usage worldwide. Estimates of the number of distance learners in China range from one to two million. Other adult-oriented programs include the entire Open University in the UK, and extensive programs from Norway to South Africa. In recent years, complete post-secondary degree programs have begun to appear.

K-12 Education

The most rapidly-growing distance learning sector is the pre-university age group - what in the U.S. is referred to as K-12. This is usually in the "form of curriculum enrichment modules and ongoing telecommunications projects" This is an exploding market, and Universities are increasingly providing advanced course programs for middle school students ¯ courses for which there is not enough demand at their local school to allocate the resources, but which can prove profitable when made available to students at all of the area K-12 schools.

Disabled and Homebound

Individuals who cannot easily travel, including senior citizens and the disabled, are natural candidates for distance education. Some people also may not be able to physically manipulate the technologies required ¯ a situation which will worsen as technologies evolve, unless specific action is taken to reduce the problems. Devices exist to alleviate physical barriers, and need to be incorporated in instructional designs.

Non-Native Language Speakers

Increasing population migration has led to a growth in the numbers of people in all areas who are non-native language speakers, and who are unable to comprehend the classes normally on offer.

Changing Needs

http://sqzm14.ust.hk/distance/04.gifThe changes in demographics of distance learners are tightly interrelated to the changes being experienced by education providers. These are changes which are expected to dramatically increase in intensity.

Increasing Rate of Technological Change The rapidity of technological development has an enormous impact on distance education, and educational needs are providing much of the direction for end products. Tools for distance learning must be flexible and adaptable for a variety of different needs and situations ¯ including their own obsolescence, where possible.

Most importantly from an institutional viewpoint, the expectation has developed that expanding technology will enable expanding service, and that distance education will prove more effective and less expensive than constructing new campuses.

Decreasing Geographic Barriers Decreasing barriers of distance and communication are leading to the expansion of institutional boundaries and involvements. An "increased catchment area" beyond regional/national boundaries is developing, and many educational institutions are starting to move into overseas markets ¯ often in direction competition with local educational suppliers.

This is causing increasing competition between education providers for 'market share.' New paradigms are required concerning institutional boundaries. While this is not a new development, the increasingly real 'global village' is accelerating the pace, and these issues must be addressed.

Growth of the Service Industry Whole economies are transforming from an industrial to a service foundation. To maintain competitiveness institutions need to be innovative. One idea is to offer courses for which there is not enough local demand to justify the expense of program creation. Local course offerings can also be improved by planning programs which would not be possible without distance education, such as pulling together part-time instructors who are geographically disparate experts in their fields. One of the most interesting points raised is that by involving off-campus participants in course programs which included local students, "adding this networked community to the discussion has sharply increased the quality of the course for [local] students."

At the same time, programs of marginal quality will need to be eliminated and their resources redirected to strengthen mid-range programs. Competitiveness will become increasingly important, and the potential learner will go to whoever can provide training tailored to their needs. We will continue to see Universities scrambling to experiment with different instructional paradigms.

What very few researchers mention is the strategic importance of providing improved support services to distance learners, from Library systems to remote course registration. These 'add-ons' may make the difference for a number of institutions.

Changing Institutional Contexts The California State educational system expects to as much as double its student population from 326,000 in the next ten years. To do this in the traditional manner would require building a new campus during each of those years — a clear impossibility. While some doubt these sorts of figures, for now administrators are looking for options

The ever-expanding directive to educate more people with limited or declining resources, without lowering standards — to do more with less — will lead to increased competitiveness in the distance education market along with demands for increasing faculty, staff, and student productivity. There are increasing expectations that technological development will lead to market expansion through non-traditional educational institutions and methodologies.

There is an increasing need for institutional collaboration and resource sharing. This is coupled with a rising ability to pool human resources, share experts in different fields, and reduce duplication as technology develops.

Another driving force will be the need to develop new markets by offering unique educational experiences. One example is a collaborative exploration of the performing arts using a two-way video link between New York's Lincoln Centre and schoolrooms around the U.S.

Providers of distance education will need to carefully explore these changes, and make decision which match their local resources, target audience, and institutional philosophy. Institutions offering distance education programs need to focus on what best fits their particular mission, goals, and circumstances.

Tools Available for Distance Education

The past 100 years have seen phenomenal growth in avenues of information development and dissemination. The earliest form of distance education simply involved people reading what scholars had written on a variety of topics, and was almost exclusively the province of the upper classes, who could afford both the time away from survival-oriented tasks, and the cost of individually hand-crafted manuscripts.

Gutenberg's invention of the printing press was perhaps the earliest example of technology revolutionizing distance education. The written word could now be mass-produced with relative efficiency. Coupled with the emergence of international postal services, correspondence courses began to appear. Through the latter half of the nineteenth century and up to the middle of the twentieth century this was distance education. A much larger segment of society had access to the thoughts and ideas of their fellow men (as opposed to women, who have remained marginalized throughout much of recorded history).

The next great advance was radio. In the space of a few decades programs and materials were available which greatly reduced the barrier of distance. Much more revolutionary was the advent of instructional television. Technology seemed to have provided a mechanism to duplicate the classroom setting, in a medium which could be sent right into the learner's home.

But both of these technologies had significant drawbacks. First, they were one-way mediums of communication. The learner remained essentially enrolled in a correspondence course, but with some useful supplemental materials. Second, the broadcasts were only available 'live.'

With the development of phonographs, audio and video tapes, and xerographic equipment, all of these course materials could be duplicated with relative ease. Production costs declined, more varied course schedules could be accommodated, and review of materials became commonplace. In addition, with the widespread availability of telephone communications in some parts of the world, distance learners and educators finally began to be able to provide fairly rapid feedback and communication.

The development of microwave and satellite technologies greatly expanded radio and television coverage. Signals could be broadcast farther, to more locations, at reduced cost compared to terrestrial systems. In the past 10-20 years, as the cost of reception equipment has declined, and the variety of programs available has increased, there has been a significant increase in television-based distance education courses. But this remained a one-way means of communication. Critics complained that distance education programs “should be more than a passive transmission of academic information.”

The big change needed was interaction ¯ starting with two-way communication between the learner and the instructor. Joan Fulton put forth five fundamentals of an effective program:

1. contact between the student and the instructor
2. active learning through writing out answers
3. timely feedback to the instructor on students’ comprehension
4. timely feedback to students on work done
5. opportunity for students to make revisions to work done and learn from their mistakes

Four of these require timely bidirectional communication. Communicating by mail was increasingly unsatisfactory. Telephone and conference calls helped a great deal, but remained awkward and expensive. It is also not feasible for the instructor to communicate with every learner in this manner. Fax machines took up some of the burden, especially easing administrative tasks. As computer networks expand, electronic mail is beginning to take hold as the principal alternative for non-real-time communication between learners and instructors, and among learners themselves. This is a rapid and inexpensive method of communication, and it is flexible enough to accommodate both individual and group communication.

One of the biggest movements currently is the provision and expansion of two-way video communication, whether through satellites or communication networks. Most of these are an expansion from the one-many to include the many-one paradigm. The instructor can see the students, and the students can see and respond to the instructor. This sort of 'full presence' system is becoming the minimum standard required for such distance education programs. The past year has even brought technologies such as auto-tracking cameras, zoom lenses, and other devices which permit the instructor to move around during the class.

Satellites continue to be the favored medium, but as coaxial and fiber-optic cables spread to more locations this is starting to change. Fiber, especially, has the capacity to handle multi-directional full-motion video. A contributing factor recently has been the sharp rise in satellite costs. The problem is here now, but the cable system alternatives have been installed in only limited areas. Institutions are also finding it increasingly difficult to maintain awareness of the changing technological fields, and to make long-term purchasing decisions.

As an example, many providers have failed to update their satellite technology and find themselves unable to incorporate new advances ‾ from signal compression to analog-to-digital conversion. The need for the latter is increasingly apparent, as new technologies evolving with the computer age permit the encoding and transmission of a variety of data formats through everything from telephone lines to satellite links.

One probable future direction will be the leasing of cable services from local service suppliers such as telephone or cable television corporations. This will reduce the burden on the institution for making market decisions, and for handling maintenance and upgrades. It will also position them more effectively for the emerging global electronic information environment.

The Internet - Changes in Tools and Tool making

One of the limitations on satellite technology is its continuing emphasis on geographic dependence. Satellite classrooms are constructed, to which learners must travel. While the distributed nature of the system permits a much wider instructional provision, it is not well suited to providing educational programs and resources to more remote users; or to those who are unable to attend at the specified time-slots set by the instructional facility.

The Internet, or Information Superhighway, is providing mechanisms for fundamental changes in the way people learn. A summary of computer networking advantages over other distance education technologies includes: http://sqzm14.ust.hk/distance/09.gif

- standardized cross-platform tools for multi-media and hypertext access, notably World-Wide Web browsers
- rapid revision and dissemination of instructional programs
- increased freedom of time and location for learners
- world-wide network expansion
- increased instructor-student interaction and feedback
- network-capable desktop videoconferencing
- much lower transmission and delivery costs
- completely digital environment, with few limitations on transmission of data in any form

Fundamentally, the Internet expands service provision to the desktop level. Tools developed for the Internet can be utilized from any location, so that learners can be freed from the requirement of travelling to a specific location for instruction. The idea is not new, but the tools being developed make its implementation much more viable. Successive waves of support tools will be increasingly simple to use, moving towards transparency of computing technology. This will be aided by the growing technological literacy of the user populations' ¯ a literacy which is not a foregone conclusion for all users.

While some users are attempting to run completely Internet-based distance education programs, most of those involved are using the Web to supplement classroom instruction. One user praised the dynamic nature of Web information, as data (e.g. syllabi) can be rapidly modified as the circumstances change. However, this capability implies that learners will need to have full Internet access from hand-held units so that they do not rely on printouts for accuracy! The field is already looking beyond what had been anticipated (desktop access), and calling for a more comprehensive version of the anyone, anytime, anywhere education provision model.

Problems and Challenges of Distance Education

The acceleration in distance education brought on by the development of sophisticated computer network tools is pushing discussion and action on a variety of challenges faced by distance educators. Answers need to be worked out before the field is swamped in a morass of conflicting instructional and institutional directions.

Technological Literacy - Including Computer Literacy The target population will require training in the use of the tools, and so will the providers. Instructors will need focused training in order to make effective use of the technologies involved.

Program Evaluation and Accreditation Care must be taken to ensure that distance education programs are as well developed as their in-house counterparts. Mechanisms need to be developed for faculty evaluation of programs originating at their institutions. There need to be standards for course evaluation and program accreditation. Successful programs need to be reevaluated before implementing them in a different cultural environment in this increasingly global village.

Losing the Content in the Technology There is a need to avoid simply providing information, rather than instruction; or of simply transmitting lectures through this new medium. This would be a disservice to the learners, and a *reduction* in content and functionality over the intended result. Avoid focusing on the technology rather than the instructional design and support

Alienating Instructors Faculty should be involved in the whole process, and should understand that while one goal may be to reduce costs, this will not be at the expense of faculty jobs. Distance education technologies are not alternatives to teaching. Failing to address these issues can lead to significant faculty rejection of the proposals, and may include Union confrontation

Non-Native Language Instruction Many of the tools available, whether on the Internet or not, have severe limitations in their ability to accommodate non-native language instruction. 2-byte character systems like Chinese are especially problematic. This is slowly becoming less of an issue on the Internet as standards begin to coalesce. http://sqzm14.ust.hk/distance/11.gif

Institutional Support for Distance Learners Academic institutions must remember that course content is just one element of the education they provide. If distance learners are being sought, they will need to be provided with similar support to that received by on-campus users. This includes everything from *full* library support to academic counselling – in addition to more mundane administrative assistance.

Increasing Regional Focus It is not credible to expect that learners who are a dozen time zones apart will be interested in participating in live programs when they would normally be asleep. As interactive programs develop, we may see an increase in two alternatives. First, institutions seeking to market their educational products beyond their shores will offer sessions tailored to the needs of students in specific areas. Second, regional consortia or education hubs may begin to form. There is a danger of becoming isolated from the more global learning environment. In most cases there will be benefit in designing programs which include challenge and stimulation, and which involve the learner in discussion and collaboration with those outside their immediate circle of fellow 'classmates'.

Copyright Issues While few researchers raise the issue explicitly, all are aware that many questions of copyright in an electronic environment remain unanswered. It is important to examine the goals and intentions of the program, and make sure that the necessary clearances have been obtained as needed.

Conclusion

The growth of the Internet is bringing many changes to distance education, and forcing providers and instructors to consider a number of difficult issues. The Internet may be on its way to replacing almost all other mediums of communication utilized by distance education programs worldwide. It should be kept in mind, however, that little of this is new. The way education is viewed continues to evolve, as do the tools available for shaping its growth and development. What may be emerging is a more social view of education, focusing on collaborative learning.

34

The Role of Information and Communication Technologies (ICTs) In Distance Education

Introduction

Education is the backbone of a nation. Despite knowing this, a huge number of people of least developed countries are far beyond the reach of higher education. One of the key reasons may be the poor economic condition of those countries. Perhaps this is the crucial challenge to be addressed by those nations for overall development where education may be on the top list. Information, Knowledge, and Communication Technology also play vital role in the growth as well as producing and offering goods and services at relatively reduced costs. Smart use of ICTs can process information, create knowledgebase and make them available wherever and whenever necessary. But despite having relatively poor economic condition, Information and Communication. Technologies (ICTs) in most cases have tremendous success in providing services at reduced costs to the people's door steps. ICTs have the same to do for making the higher education available to all classes of people throughout the country at a lower cost. As a result, on one hand people will have the access right on higher education and on the other hand will gain the necessary knowledge, skills, and experiences to serve the nation and prosper accordingly.

In 21st century, one can hardly find a country where higher education through distance mode is not available. In fact it has been practiced since long before. But at present days, having revolution of ICTs, the higher education through distance mode has been more practical and well accepted by the all people around the globe. It is now being called Virtual learning. In developed country, people are getting more interested in learning through Virtual Campus than that of a Brick-and-Mortar Campus. Virtual Campus is nothing but ICT enabled campus, where students are attending their classes, discussing with teachers, accessing learning resources, seating exams, joining forums/clubs, submitting assignments etc virtually having the facility of real-time interactions between teacher and students.

Practically, from records and researches into it plans of last two decades (the mid 80s to the millennium), evolving rolling plans are consistently observed and reviewed to accommodate changes in the ambit of standardisation, upgradeability, compatibility and operate ability both cost effective synchronous and asynchronous systems of delivering education contents. Hence the ICT department is always faced a dynamic and rolling plan that will consistently and integrated rolled into the overall goal of the distance learning institution which is to provide and deliver quality education contents removing the distance barrier.

The planning process involves a conducted wide systems analysis and consultation with the various units on their operations in order to have a system design for the distance learning institution. Events such as admission and registration exercises that involve collation of forms, processing and the collaborations that evolved from such exercises will give the it department the necessary logic and defined procedures to adopt.

According to Everett Rogers (2003) the perceived attributes of innovations are

- Relative advantage (how the innovation is perceived to be an improvement),

- compatibility (consistency with existing experience, values and needs),
- complexity (perceived difficulty in understanding and using an innovation),
- trial ability (the degree to which an innovation can be experimented with),
- observability (how visible the results of an innovation are to others).

Each of these five very useful concepts can be seen to have an "external" dimension that can be measured and quantified, and an "internal" dimension, the perception, that is relative to the individual. In order to distinguish clearly between these two dimensions as well as to bring out the complexity of introducing ICT solutions in a learning environment, we have chosen to combine diffusion theory of analysis of the observability on how these new information technologies are effectively used by the end users.

Despite this new trend a very few research has been done on the impact this new change has brought in meeting student's learning needs and expectations, and learner's ability to use these technology effectively, during their study. This research will focus on the types of types of Physical learning environments or resources learners use for online studying. Here a physical learning environment is defined as the place or physical surroundings where a student can gain knowledge or skills either by themselves, or by interaction with a teacher or other students.

Objectives of the study

Following broad based objectives were derived for his study.

- To identify the types of physical learning environments and resources used by the students.
- To analyze the theory and practice on the use of online teaching and learning.
- To inform the course designers and teachers to apply appropriate teaching strategies and students support systems to meet the needs and demands of students.

- To inform the appropriateness of the physical learning environment as an important component in the design of course materials and support systems to meet the needs and demands of students.

Methodology

The main aim of the study is to assess the place or physical surroundings where a student can gain knowledge either by themselves or by interaction with teachers and fellow students. How the students use the internet resources for their learning purpose. The research is done by using a survey technique. The survey is divided into two sections.

- The first section asked the participant (Both distance education/Regular) questions relating to the types of information gathering techniques used for their study. How often they have participated in different learning environments? The types of resources they have used in their previous study. Responses are collected on a four point likert-type scale ranging from –Never, Sometimes, Often and Always.
- The second section sought students demographic information including the number of courses the participants had undertaken previously an online component and their previous level of education etc. These were used as variables such gender, age, income, education, occupation, personal access, frequency of computer use were included in the questionnaires

Components of survey questionnaires

Questions relating to the types of information gathering techniques used

1. How often they have participated in different physical learning environments
2. Types of resources they have used in their learning process.

Student demographic information

The course the participant is undergoing, e.g. Distance mode or regular mode.

Study sample

A particular cohort of participants was selected who were pursuing various courses offered in distance mode where online component is mandatory and students who were doing their course in regular mode. The data is collected from the students who have online component mandatory for their study. The study sample is collected from selected students who have some prior knowledge of ICTs and computer literacy.

The study was conducted in Chennai on Distance Education Students of Symbiosis, GNIIT, and IGNOU Students for whom Online Component is Mandatory. Majority of the course materials used by these students are online or web based. As the questionnaires were send to the mailboxes of the respondents we were able to get only 17 participants.

The samples were also selected from some of the Regular College students who were pursuing their higher studies in college for whom the necessity of using online resource is more for their study. This is also done by sending the questionnaires online. Of this we were able to get 18 participants of the expected 83.

The variables used in this study were gender, age and mode of study. Data from the spread sheet were analyzed using Microsoft excel. The Table I shows the participants breakdown of the sample. We had 35 respondents of the total sample of 100. Of the 35 respondent 17 students were students for whom the online study component is mandatory.

Learning Environment: The usual assumption with distance education students is that they learn at home with material provided with their educational institution. In this study 90% of the respondents indicated that they often or always study at home. Students have also indicated that they do study at their place of work, in the library, or in computer Lab.

Online Communication: The main components of online communication are text based, E-mail, bulletin boards and Chat rooms. This table shows the usage of online communication by students as percentage.

The results shows that most of the students use E-mail often for their study, most of them hardly prefer chat, sizeable proportions are using bulletin board. 50% of the students have never used chat rooms for their study.

Use of paper based resources by Online Distance education students Most of the online distance education provide following course materials for the study of the students, Textbooks, Printed Study Guide, Handout provided by lecturer and study resources. This table shows the frequency of use of paper-based materials by online students.

The results of survey indicate that more than 90% of the respondents preferred Text books always. Majority of respondents were not interested in the Handouts provided by the lecturers.

Usage of ICT resources by students: The results indicate that all respondents at some stages of their learning have used online grade checking, at some stages of their learning. When using online course materials over 90% have indicated that they often and always use online search tools. Electronic Library access is however not used as frequently with only 15.0% indicating that they always use this resource. This survey indicates that ICTs were very well used by the students.

Interactive components such as quizzes and online tests are widely used by the students. Nearly 70% of the respondents preferred using online quizzes.

Also around 75% of the respondents were using internet for submitting the assignments. Also around 65% of the students always used URL links for their study purpose. The access to electronic library is very poor as the data indicates nearly fifty percentages of the students hardly use these resources.

Preferred learning environment: The preferred learning environment of the regular students and the online students can be compared in this table

Both regular as well as distance education students prefer to study among themselves, similarly most of them prefer using tutorials.

Preferred physical learning environment are quite same for both distance learning students and regular campus based students. None of the regular students preferred to study using videoconferencing session.

Use of ICT Components-Comparison between regular and distance education students: This table shows the comparison chart of the regular and distance education students More than 50% of the students don't prefer using online chat for their studying purpose. Online search tools were often used by both regular and distance education students.

CONCLUSION

IT has been shown that the physical learning environments of distance students are not all that different from those used by regular on-campus students. Unexpected results from this study are that distances students' needs are apparently appear similar to that of the on-campus students. This is both in relation to resources and communication needs. Both distance and on-campus students in this study made a made selective use of online resources. Both group indicated that most of their study was done at home using paper based or web based materials. Students are able to use ICT's; there is need by course designer's and developers to maximize its potential for learning purpose. The results from the study suggests that more research needs to be done to more fully understand the environments students use for their study to make online course maximize student study needs and demands.

The most used part of the new ICTs in universities is the Internet as a delivery tool for academic content and for student support. Distance learning platforms have been developed by almost every higher education institution, as panacea for issues like the increasing number of students, lack of appropriate and enough study space, standardisation, quality assurance and control of the information delivered, increasing costs of higher education and so on.

As a result, there is now a need for support concerning the methodology of development good distance courses, the quality level of tuition offered, pedagogical and technical standards, development of pedagogical basis, operative legislative regulations, a frame for distance programmes evaluation etc.

35

Ict Pedagogy Integration in Teacher Education

INTRODUCTION

ICT has great potential for enhancing teaching and learning outcomes. The realization of this potential depends much on how the teacher uses the technology. This would in turn depend, among other things, on the kind of training that the teacher has undergone. Information and communication technologies (ICTs) have the potential to enhance access, quality, and effectiveness in education in general and to enable the development of more and better teachers in particular. As computer hardware becomes available to an increasing number of schools, more attention needs to be given to the capacity building of the key transformers in this process, namely, teachers. ICTs are one of the major contemporary factors shaping the global economy and producing rapid changes in society. They have fundamentally changed the way people learn, communicate, and do business. They can transform the nature of education – where and how learning takes place and the roles of students and teachers in the learning process.

ICT - ORIGIN & DEFINITION

Information and communications technology, usually called ICT, is often used as a synonym for information technology (IT) but is usually a more general term that stresses the role of communications (telephone lines and wireless signals) in modern information technology. ICT consists of all technical means used to handle information and aid communication, including computer and network hardware as well as necessary software. In other words, ICT consists of IT as well as telephony, broadcast media, and all types of audio and video processing and transmission. The expression was first used in 1997 in a report by Dennis Stevenson to the UK government and promoted by the new National Curriculum documents for the UK in 2000.

ICT is often used in the context of "ICT roadmap" to indicate the path that an organization will take with their ICT needs. The term ICT is now also used to refer to the merging (convergence) of telephone networks with computer networks through a single cabling or link system. There are large economic incentives (huge cost savings due to elimination of the telephone network) to merge the telephone network with the computer network system.

IMPORTANCE OF 'ICT' IN TEACHER EDUCATION

The development of any nation depends mainly on the standards of its educational institutions. Teacher has a pivotal role in the process of development. According to Dr. Sarvepalli Radhakrishnan, Mahatma Gandhi and Vivekananda teacher has a prominent role in character building, quality education, value oriented education and health promotion through their teaching. In the 21st century, education in general and quality education in particular has a dominant role in the process of development. Today's trainee teachers are tomorrow's real teachers. It is important and necessary to take care about present teacher education system. In the scientific and technological world ICT has a crucial role in the process of teaching and learning.

Globalization and technological changes have accelerated during the last fifteen years and have created a new global economy. Education is one of the main keys to economic development and improvements in human welfare. Teaching is becoming one of the most challenging professions in our society where knowledge is expanding rapidly and much of it is available to students as well as teachers at the same time. In today's world teachers need to be equipped not only with subject-specific expertise and effective teaching methodologies, but with the capacity to assist students to meet the demands of the emerging knowledge-based society. Teachers therefore require familiarity with new forms of information and communication technology (ICT) and need to have the ability to use that technology to enhance the quality of teaching and learning. Many countries including India have realized the need for providing teachers with training in ICT and have launched various professional development initiatives. However, many of the training activities to date have been one-off, crash courses which focus on computer literacy and do not enable teachers to integrate ICT in their day-to-day teaching activities and master the use of ICT as an effective tool to improve teaching and learning. The EFA Global Monitoring Report also confirms the central role of teachers in any education system, emphasizing that the quality of education is directly linked to how well teachers are prepared for teaching.

The given below table gives full information about learning and memory. ICT is a multi-dimensional tool. The impact of ICT is very much when compare to any other. More learning and memory takes place through ICT.

TABLE-1

Process of Learning and Memory

LEARNING THROUGH	WE REMEMBER
Taste 1.0%	20% of what hear
Touch 1.5%	30% of what we see
Hearing 11.0%	50% of what we see and hear
Smell 3.5%	80% of what we say
Sight 83.0%	90% of what we say and do

Thus, the very basis of learning is sense experience, and the very psychology of teaching aids is as follows:

I hear – I forget

I see – I remember

I do – I learn/understand

Information and communication technologies (ICTs) which include radio and television, as well as newer digital technologies such as computers and the Internet have been touted as potentially powerful enabling tools for educational change and reform.

'ICT' PEDAGOGY INTEGRATION IN TEACHER EDUCATION

One of the essential aims of teacher education is to enable student teachers to develop their knowledge and understanding of subject matter, children, teaching strategies, and the school curriculum, and to help them draw upon this knowledge in the shaping of their classroom practice. Typically, through lectures and seminars on teaching methods, child psychology, classroom processes, and subject matter, through classroom observation and teaching experience, through discussions with tutors and teachers about classroom practice, and through the encouragement to reflect upon and analyze their own teaching, it is expected that student teachers will build a coherent, enlightened, integrated body of knowledge that will inform, and in turn be informed by, classroom practice.

The picture depicted by Calderhead and Robson describes how teachers' professional journeys start and continue throughout their teacher preparation. One of the key features of the profession of teaching is that teacher learning does not stop with teacher preparation in teacher education institutions. Classroom practice continues to inform teachers' classroom instruction. Teachers' classroom instruction has been studied for decades. Numerous studies have analyzed teaching and how and why teachers act and teach in particular ways. In studying what teachers do in classrooms, social science research has also focused on teachers' thought processes and what they believe about their work.

Teachers think about a variety of issues during the planning and the implementation of teaching; they constantly make decisions. In reviewing the teacher thinking research, Clark and Peterson explain that teachers have theories and belief systems that influence their perceptions, plans, and actions. Teachers' teaching and the thought that precedes and follows it produce teaching preferences. A teacher's preferred way of teaching is based on the teacher's values or ideal teaching style and on the teacher's abilities and skills.

In the scientific, technological, modern and globalized world Information and Communication Technologies (ICTs) have pivotal role in the process of teaching and learning. ICT helps the students and the teachers to learn effectively with in the period. It affects the multi-senses of the individuals. It is necessary to integrate ICT methodology in Teacher Education curriculum for the best learning of the trainee-teachers.

Components of ICT in Teacher Education

Actual components of ICT in Teacher Education:

- Deployment
- Curriculum Development
- Content Availability
- Training and Usage Support
- Educational Management
- Maintenance and Technical Support

Teacher Training Approaches

Research indicates that ICT can change the way teachers teach and that it is especially useful in supporting more student-centered approaches to instruction and in developing the higher order skills and promoting collaborative activities (Haddad, 2003). Recognizing the importance of ICT in teaching and learning, a majority of the countries in the world including India have provided ICT teacher training in a variety of forms and degrees. Even though many teachers report that they have not had adequate training to prepare themselves to use technology effectively in teaching and learning, there seem to be several efforts around the world in which countries are effectively using technology to train teachers, and/or are training teachers to use technology as tools for enhancing teaching and learning.

ICT teacher training can take many forms. Teachers can be trained to learn how to use ICT or teachers can be trained via ICT. ICT can be used as a core or a complementary means to the teacher training process (Collis & Jung, 2003).

ICT Use as Part of Teaching Methods

This approach integrates ICT into teacher training to facilitate some aspects of training. Two cases below show how a variety of ICT are adopted as part of effective training methods. In these cases, teachers are provided with examples of ICT-pedagogy integration in their training process.

Captured Wisdom is a resource developed by the federally-funded (USA) North Central Technology in Education Consortium for K-12 teachers, school administrators and extended to adult literacy educators. It uses videotape and CD-ROM to help US teachers to see how technology can be integrated into their work. The Captured Wisdom (tm) CD-ROM Library is made up of stories about teachers who are making meaningful and creative uses of technology in their instruction. These CD-ROMs contain video descriptions and demonstrations of how technology is used in teachers' classrooms. They provide "examples of real educators and learners using successful practices of technology to support instruction and learning in their classrooms. Video sequences are viewed by teachers' focus groups who then discuss the strategies and techniques of classroom management, assessment, etc. In this specific case, teachers learn how to use ICT in their classrooms by actually being engaged in the process of ICT-integrated training.

Another example of this approach can be found in the School Administrators' Technology Integration Resource project. It is a bilingual Canadian initiative which provides tools and resources to help school administrators successfully integrate ICT into curriculum in their school. It includes the National Center for Technology Planning clearinghouse of school district ICT plans, advice on how to provide technology, successful practices in introducing ICT, perspectives on staff development, a beginners' guide to the Internet, etc. The focus of this project is not on the basic skill development but on the development of ICT pedagogy integration skills of educators by sharing successful cases and practical ideas.

UNICEF's Teachers talking about learning also illustrates the application of this approach to ICT teacher training. It is designed for international collaboration between teachers in developing countries using the Internet and television. It provides access to teacher training materials and useful links and promotes discussions among teachers.

All the cases discussed above use ICT as part of training methods and promote teachers' ICT-pedagogy integration in the classroom by demonstrating examples and allowing discussions among teachers throughout the whole training process. Participants of the training are asked to actually use ICT to learn about ICT skills and develop ICT-integrated pedagogies. These training strategies seem to be supported by other research that argues that teachers are likely to benefit by actively experiencing ICT skills as a learner (Jung, 2003).

ICT pedagogy approach

Emphasis is on integrating ICT skills in a respective subject. Drawing on the principles of constructivism, pre-service teachers design lessons and activities that center on the use of ICT tools that will foster the attainment of learning outcomes. This approach is useful to the extent that the skills enhance ICT literacy skills and the underlying pedagogy allows students to further develop and maintain these skills in the context of designing classroom- based resources.

UNESCO planning guide for ICT in teacher-education cites three key principles for effective ICT development in Teacher Education that were put forward by the *Society for Information Technology and Teacher Education.*

1) That technology should be infused into the entire teacher education programme, implying that ICT should not be restricted to a single course but needs to permeate in all courses in the programmes.
2) That Technology should be introduced in context. Accordingly, ICT application like word-processing, databases, spread-sheet and telecommunications should not be taught as separate topics rather encountered as the need arises in all courses of Teacher-Education programmes.
3) That students should experience innovative technology supported learning environment in Teacher-Education programmes. This requires that students should see their lecturers engaging in technology to present their subjects utilizing power point or simulations in lectures and demonstrations. Students should also have the opportunity to use such applications in practical classes, seminars and assignments.

The application of these three principles will be a mile stone towards effectively integrating ICT in Teacher-Education.

TEACHER AND TECHNOLOGY

Teacher has a prominent role in the process of teaching and learning. First of all it is necessary to give training for teachers for effective use of technology.

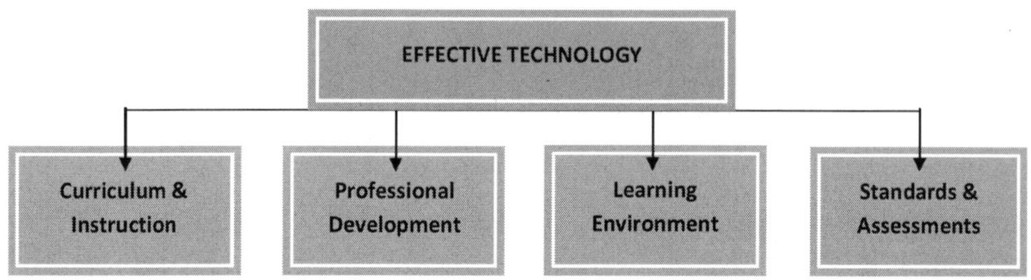

Fig-2: *Teacher and Technology*

Changing Role of Teacher

Under the changing scenario, there is a need to redefine the role of a teacher-educator. The National Council of Teacher Education, Jaipur (NCTE), based on a thorough job analysis, has come out with three areas in which a teacher-educator needs to acquire mastery. These are i) five performance areas; ii) ten competency areas; and iii) five commitment areas (NCTE, 1998). For the successful integration of ICT in teacher education, the teacher in addition to taking up the role responsibilities mentioned in these areas, must shoulder the additional, rather survival responsibilities outlined below :-

- Act as a role model for pre-service trainees and in-service teachers, demonstrating the use of technology across the curriculum.
- Encourage technology integration among the trainees, colleagues, teachers and parents.
- Be involved in planning and implementing ICT professional development training.
- Be up-to-date with the latest technological developments and advise the institutions concerning technology advancements and upgradation.

- Interact through e-mail/forum/communities/blogging with trainees, participating schools and parents.
- Aid in the implementation of technology plans of the institutions.
- Plan, design and demonstrate the use of multimedia applications for instructional use through multimedia projects.
- Examine a variety of evaluation and assessment tools including electronic portfolio assessment.
- Become active, competent online users of telecommunication services and act as model in the use of internet as an instructional tool.
- Direct trainees and teachers to digital resources that will be able to answer their questions.
- Address issues related to acceptable user policies, student safety, ethics, security, copyright, etc.
- Be involved in marketing the best practices of technology integration.
- Manage the available resources more productively to face the ever increasing financial crunch.
- Use information literacy to access, evaluate, and use information from a variety of sources.
- Have the competencies in software evaluations and advise the institutions in making the right choices.

21st Century Skills for Teacher

Globalization and advancements in technology are driving changes in the social, technological, economical, environmental and political landscapes at such a pace and magnitude that is too great, and too multiple to ignore. As society changes, the skills that students need to be successful in life also change.

Teacher has a prominent role to teach all type of skills to the students. It is the duty of institute of teacher education to develop all the skills in the trainee teachers. Teacher has a multiple role in the process of teaching and learning. All of you know about the value of teacher in our Indian tradition. He acts as a guide, philosopher, friend and parent. Among these roles a role model and effective teacher has the above mentioned skills i.e., 21st century skills. ICT helps the teacher to teach and learn these skills effectively.

CONCLUSION

Several paradoxes could be recognized in the research literature considering the use of Information and Communication Technologies (ICT) at school as well as in teacher education. Students have rich experiences of use of technology outside of school, but do not use technology for learning at school. Teachers are skilled technology users, but they are unable to take advantage of their competence and to apply it to the way they teach in school. Today's trainee teachers are tomorrow's real teacher. It is necessary and important to take care about trainee teachers. Integration of ICT in pedagogy of teacher education is important. ICT helps both in teaching and learning process. The impact of ICT is very much on the student community. It is the time to change the attitude of teachers and students towards use of ICT in teaching and learning process.

REFERENCES

1. Amareswaran, N., & Sheela Reddy, C. (2009): "*Importance of 'ICT' in Distance Education*", Published by Acharya Nagarjuna University, Guntur, Andhra Pradesh.
2. Anjali Khirwadkar. "*Integration of ICT in Education: Pedagogical Issues*".
3. Jung, I. (2005): "*ICT-Pedagogy Integration in Teacher Training: Application Cases Worldwide. Educational Technology & Society*", International Forum of Educational Technology & Society (IFETS).
4. Mike Aston, et.al (2002): "*Elementary ICT Curriculum for Teacher Training*", UNESCO Institute for Information Technologies in Education (IITE), Moscow.
5. Priscilla G. Cabanatan. "*ICT Trends in Teacher Curricula: An Asia-Pacific Perspective*".
6. Ramachandra Reddy, B. (1995): "*Educational Technology*", S.V. University Press, Sri Venkateswara University, Tirupati, Andhra Pradesh.
7. Veijo Meisalo., et. Al (2010): "*New Millennium Learners- ICT in Initial Teacher Training: Country Report Finland*", School of Applied Education and Teacher Education, University of Eastern Finland.
8. Victoria L. Tinio. "*ICT in Education*", United Nations Development Programme, Bureau for Development Policy, New York.
9. Amareswaran, N. & Ramachandra Reddy, B. "Educational *Technology for Teachers in the 21st Century*", unpublished book.

Index

D

E

F

G

H

I

K

L

M

N

O

P

Q

R